The Anti-Politics Machine

"Development," Depoliticization, and
Bureaucratic Power in Lesotho

James Ferguson

 University of Minnesota Press
Minneapolis
London

Published by the University of Minnesota Press
2037 University Avenue Southeast, Minneapolis, MN 55455-3092
Printed in the United States of America on acid-free paper

Library of Congress Cataloging-in-Publication Data

Ferguson, James, 1959-
  The anti-politics machine : "development," depoliticization, and bureaucratic power in Lesotho / James Ferguson.
    p.   cm.
  Originally published: Cambridge ; New York : Cambridge University Press, 1990.
  Includes bibliographical references and index.
  ISBN 0-8166-2437-2
  1. Rural development projects—Lesotho—Case studies. 2. Thaba Tseka Rural Development Program. 3. Lesotho—Economic conditions—1966- 4. Lesotho—Politics and government—1966- 5. Bureaucracy—Lesotho. 6. Decentralization in government—Lesotho.   I. Title.
HD2132.Z8F47   1994
338.1'86885—dc20   93-5913
                                                           CIP

The University of Minnesota is an
equal-opportunity educator and employer.

Contents

v

Figures

Tables

vii

Acknowledgments

This book is a revision of the dissertation "Discourse, Knowledge, and Structural Production in the 'Development' Industry: An Anthropological Study of a Rural Development Project in Lesotho," my Ph.D. thesis for the Department of Anthropology, Harvard University (1985). The material presented is based primarily on field research carried out in the Thaba-Tseka District of Lesotho from September 1982 to December 1983, mostly in the town of Thaba-Tseka and the village of Mashai. This research was made possible by fellowships granted by the Social Science Research Council and the American Council of Learned Societies and by the Fulbright program of the U.S. International Communication Agency. The conclusions, opinions, and other statements in this book, however, are those of the author and not necessarily those of the above organizations.

I am also grateful to the National University of Lesotho for granting me the status of research fellow in the Department of Sociology and Social Anthropology, and for extending me the use of University housing facilities at Thaba-Tseka. The Head of the Department, Mr. T. Thoahlane, was particularly helpful and supportive throughout. I am thankful to have had the opportunity to spend the summer of 1982 studying under Professor Daniel Kunene, who gave me the best possible introduction to the difficulties and delights of the Sesotho language.

In Thaba-Tseka, the District Coordinator, Mr. S. Matete granted permission for me to do research in the District, and gave my project his warm cooperation. The officers and staff of the Thaba-Tseka Project and of the Government of Lesotho endured endless questioning with friendliness and good humor, and assisted the research in ways too numerous to mention. I am particularly grateful for the cooperation and hospitality I received from the Project Coordinator, Mr. Karl Loeffler. The representative of the National University in Thaba-Tseka, Mr. Machepa, was very helpful in providing housing for me.

In Mashai, I owe thanks to far too many people to list here. Here I will only mention a very special few, and register my profound thanks to all the people who helped with the research and made me feel welcome so far from home. The local chiefs, Morena Tebalo Makoko and Mofumahali 'Mathibathere Makhaola, extended all possible cooperation and hospitality. Felix Ramone was an early and valued friend. Alina Seele rented me a house, and also proved an invaluable guide to the local ways of doing things. Interview tapes were tirelessly transcribed by Mrs. Seele, as well as by Mrs. 'Malisebo Mahloane and Mrs. Selestinah Ramone.

An earlier visit to Lesotho in August of 1981 was made possible by a Summer Research Grant from the Department of Anthropology at Harvard University. Much assistance in preparing this trip was provided by my thesis advisor of the time, Richard Huntington, who first suggested Lesotho as a research site. During the 1981 visit, I was well received by the Programme Director of the Thaba-Tseka Project, Mr. August Johnson, who gave valuable cooperation and encouragement. In Maseru, fellow anthropologist Judy Gay and her husband John offered help and hospitality both in 1981 and in 1982–3. Lesotho scholars Colin Murray and Andrew Spiegel also gave valued encouragement at an early stage. Although he may by now no longer even remember our brief encounter, I would like to note, too, that a brief visit with Charles van Onselen at this time gave moral support and profound understanding at a time when it was sorely needed.

David Brokensha first encouraged my interest in anthropology, and it was under his guidance that I first became interested in Africa and "development." Alan Zeoli provided perspective and much-needed companionship during the early months of the research. The "Bacardi School" at the Harvard Department of Anthropology provided an intellectual community within which many of the theoretical ideas offered here were first encountered and discussed. In this respect, George Bisharat and Roberto Kant de Lima have been friends, colleagues, and often teachers, and much of what follows bears the stamp of our association over the years.

I am grateful, too, to my thesis committee members, Jane Guyer, Nur Yalman, and David Maybury-Lewis, for support and advice throughout the years. Sections of the manuscript have been read and discussed at various times by the following people as well, whose valuable comments have been appreciated: Pauline Peters, John Comaroff, Pnina Motzafi, John Lepele, Parker Shipton, and Jean Comaroff. The entire manuscript was read with careful and critical eyes at a late stage by Colin Murray, Jean Lave, and Gavin Williams. Their thoughtful and perceptive comments have helped me to sharpen my argument and to avoid countless errors and misunderstandings. Most of the ideas in the book have been discussed at some length with Liisa Malkki, and these discussions have contributed greatly to the formulation of many of the ideas presented here.

Finally, Sally Falk Moore, my thesis advisor, provided guidance, encouragement, and inspiration throughout the writing of the thesis. Through her acute and sympathetic understanding of my project, and through her unwavering moral and intellectual support for it, she has over the years played an invaluable part in both the production of this book and in the development and working out of my own ideas. My debts to her, intellectual and personal, are enormous.

A note on orthography and usage

This book contains a number of quotations in Sesotho, the national language of Lesotho, which is also known by linguists as "Southern Sotho." I use the official orthography of Lesotho throughout, although many linguists prefer the revised orthography officially approved in South Africa. The Lesotho orthography has the following peculiarities which should be noted: (1) "l" is sounded as an English "d" when it appears before a "u" or an "i"; thus *"limpho"* is pronounced "dimpho"; (2) the semi-vowels represented in most Bantu orthographies as "w" and "y" are always represented as "o" and "e"; thus *"oa"* and *"ea,"* not "wa" and "ya"; (3) "th" refers to an aspirated "t" sound, somewhat like the "t" in the English "time," and not to either of the English "th" sounds; thus "Thaba-Tseka" begins with a hard "t." "Ch," however, is sounded as in English. "Tš," as in *"ho tšepa,"* indicates an aspirated "ts" sound. (4) Sesotho "o" is often sounded like an English "u" sound, or, more precisely, as the "oo" in "rook"; thus "Lesotho" is pronounced "le-soo-too," not "le-soh-toh" or "le-soh-thoh". I have everywhere written "Thaba-Tseka," the place name, with a hyphen, in keeping with the official orthography, although the hyphen is very widely dropped in practice, even in official documents. I have used the word "Basotho" to refer to the people who are citizens of Lesotho (not, as in some usages, to the "Sotho" ethnic group). The singular is "Mosotho." "Sesotho" refers to the language and culture of the Basotho. These are all properly nouns, and confusion arises when one attempts to use them as English adjectives; I therefore use simply "Sotho" unless the reference is specifically to the people or the language, on the understanding that it describes that which pertains to the Southern Sotho of Lesotho and not to other groups which might be called "Sotho".

On the English side, I have placed "development" in quotation marks throughout, in the hope that this will not prove tiresome, but will rather serve as a reminder to the reader that the book aims to problematize this concept.

Abbreviations and symbols

M	Maloti, the official currency of Lesotho. M1 equals, by definition, R1.
R	Rands, the official currency of South Africa. R1 was worth in the neighborhood of US$0.85 to $0.90 during the research period, September 1982 to December 1983.
BCP	Basotholand Congress Party
BNP	Basotho National Party
CIDA	Canadian International Development Agency
DA	District Administrator
DC	District Commissioner
DDA	District Development Authority
DDC	District Development Committee
FAO	Food and Agriculture Organization of the U.N.
FAO/WB	Food and Agriculture Organization/World Bank Cooperative Programme
FSSP	Foodgrain Self-sufficiency Programme
GDP	Gross Domestic Product
GNP	Gross National Product
GOL	Government of Lesotho
ILO	International Labour Office
LASA	Lesotho Agri-Cultural Sector Analysis Project
LLA	Lesotho Liberation Army
LMC	Livestock Marketing Corporation
LPMS	Livestock Products Marketing Services
ODM	Overseas Development Ministry (U.K.)
PMU	Para-military Unit (formerly Police Mobile Unit)
TEBA	The Employment Bureau of Africa
TTCC	Thaba-Tseka Coordinating Committee
TTDP	Thaba-Tseka Development Project
TTRDP	Thaba-Tseka Rural Development Programme
USAID	U.S. Agency for International Development
VDC	Village Development Committee
VDP	Village Distribution Point

Preface

What is "development"? It is perhaps worth remembering just how recent a question this is. This question, which today is apt to strike us as so natural, so self-evidently necessary, would have made no sense even a century ago. It is a peculiarity of our historical era that the idea of "development" is central to so much of our thinking about so much of the world. It seems to us today almost non-sensical to deny that there is such a thing as "development," or to dismiss it as a meaningless concept, just as it must have been virtually impossible to reject the concept "civilization" in the nineteenth century, or the concept "God" in the twelfth. Such central organizing concepts are not readily discarded or rejected, for they form the very framework within which argumentation takes place. One argues about God's corporeality, or about the role of legitimate commerce in the civilizing process – not about whether a theistic philosophy is justifiable, or whether Euro-centrism is to be rejected. Each of these central organizing concepts presupposes a central, unquestioned value, with respect to which the different legitimate positions may be arrayed, and in terms of which different world views can be articulated. "Development" in our time is such a central value. Wars are fought and coups are launched in its name. Entire systems of government and philosophy are evaluated according to their ability to promote it. Indeed, it seems increasingly difficult to find any way to talk about large parts of the world except in these terms.

Like "civilization" in the nineteenth century, "development" is the name not only for a value, but also for a dominant problematic or interpretive grid through which the impoverished regions of the world are known to us. Within this interpretive grid, a host of everyday observations are rendered intelligible and meaningful. Poor countries are by definition "less developed," and the poverty and powerlessness of the people who live in such countries are only the external signs of this underlying condition. The images of the ragged poor of Asia thus become legible as markers of a stage of development, while the bloated bellies of African children are the signs of social as well as nutritional deficiency. Within this problematic, it appears self-evident that debtor Third World nation-states and starving peasants share a common "problem," that both lack a single "thing": "development."

To say that "development" is a dominant problematic is, of course, not to suggest that everyone holds the same beliefs about it. Different people mean different things by "development," and it is entirely possible to have an oppositional or radical view of "development" – just as it was possible for Reformation protestants to defy the Church in the name of God, or for nineteenth-century humanitarians to attack colonial exploitation out of sympathy with the "savages." But the dominant problematic does not seem to be thus endangered. A problematic, after all, imposes questions, not answers. If "development" is today from time to time challenged, it is still almost always challenged in the name of *"real* development." Like "goodness" itself, "development" in our time is a value so firmly entrenched that it seems almost impossible to question it, or to refer it to any standard beyond its own.

How and why this central value came to exist is one question that is raised by the dominance of the "development" problematic. This is a question I hope to be able to answer in future work through a detailed historical analysis of the origins and transformations of the modern figure "development," a "genealogy" of "development." But a second and perhaps equally important set of questions is raised at the same time: how does this dominant problematic work in practice, and what are its effects? If, as I intend to demonstrate in the pages that follow, all this talking and thinking about "development" is not merely ideological icing, then what are its specific effects? What happens differently due to the "development" problematic that would not or could not happen without it? The two sets of questions are closely related, but I find it convenient to treat them separately, and to attempt to make a contribution toward answering the second question before taking on the first. It is perhaps preferable to try to get a better idea of what "development" does before hazarding an explanation for how and why it came about. I will approach these questions here through a case study of the way in which ideas about "development" are generated and put to use in one specific context: Lesotho in the period 1975–84.

The argument, in brief, is the following: "development" institutions generate their own form of discourse, and this discourse simultaneously constructs Lesotho as a particular kind of object of knowledge, and creates a structure of knowledge around that object. Interventions are then organized on the basis of this structure of knowledge, which, while "failing" on their own terms, nonetheless have regular effects, which include the expansion and entrenchment of bureaucratic state power, side by side with the projection of a representation of economic and social life which denies "politics" and, to the extent that it is successful, suspends its effects. The short answer to the question of what the "development" apparatus in Lesotho does, then, is found in the book's title: it is an "anti-politics machine," depoliticizing everything it touches, everywhere whisking political realities out of sight, all the while performing, almost unnoticed, its own pre-eminently political operation of expanding bureaucratic state power.

There will doubtless be for some a temptation to read this argument as a critique of "development" ideology, an attempt to refute the "development" picture of Lesotho by showing that it is false. Such an interpretation is understandable, but it would be a serious misreading of the argument. It is true that many of the ideas about Lesotho generated by the "development" problematic are indeed false, and it will be necessary from time to time in the discussion to point this out; but the main thrust of this study is not to show that the "development" problematic is wrong, but to show that the institutionalized production of certain kinds of ideas about Lesotho has important effects, and that the production of such ideas plays an important role in the production of certain sorts of structural change.

To say this is not, of course, to appeal to some non-existent "value-free" social science. The fact that this study does not aim to rectify or to correct "development" thinking is not a sign of some sort of improbable indifference or neutrality; it simply reflects my view that in tracing the political intelligibility of the "development" problematic, the question of the truth or falsity of "development" ideology is not the central one. If one begins, as I do, from the premise that thinking is as "real" an activity as any other, and that ideas and discourses have important and very real social consequences, then in analyzing systems of ideas one cannot be content with interrogating them for their truth value. For a social scientist, there is always another question: what do these ideas *do*, what real social effects do they have? At this point the analysis more closely resembles vivisection than critique. For the question is not "how closely do these ideas approximate the truth," but "what effects do these ideas (which may or may not happen to be true) bring about? How are they connected with and implicated in larger social processes?" This is why I speak, following Foucault, of a conceptual "apparatus" – in order to suggest that what we are concerned with is not an abstract set of philosophical or scientific propositions, but an elaborate contraption that *does* something. To say what such an apparatus does is not a critique, still less a refutation. Would we say that the vivisection of a frog constitutes a critique? Or that it aims to "refute" the frog's organs? When performing such cold-blooded operations, neither correction nor judgment is called for. One can aim only to be, in Nietzsche's terms, a good physiologist.

This book marks the beginning of an inquiry, not the end. Most of the grander and more global questions about the origin and meaning of the modern figure of "development" are bracketed and laid to one side here in order to begin to answer a circumscribed, preliminary question about the way specific ideas about "development" are generated and deployed within the context of "development" agencies in Lesotho. Future work, I hope, may have something to say about the history, or "genealogy," of "development"; this book offers only a vivisection of a conceptual apparatus: an investigation of how specific ideas about "development" are generated in practice, and how they are put to use; and a demonstration of what they end up doing, of what effects they end up producing. This leaves unanswered many questions about the "development" value and its origin, but it may perhaps give an indication of why it is necessary to question such a value in the first place.

Part I
Introduction

1 Introduction

The "development" industry in Lesotho

Lesotho is a small, land-locked country in Southern Africa, completely surrounded by South Africa (see Figure 1.1). The former British protectorate of Basutoland, Lesotho became independent in 1966. It has a population of about 1.3 million, an area of about 30,000 square kilometers, and few economically significant natural resources. In 1981/2 the Gross National Product was about $586 million. The country is extremely mountainous, and only some 10 percent of the land is arable; the rest is suitable only for grazing of livestock. Some 95 percent of the population is rural, and most of that is concentrated in the "lowlands," a narrow crescent of land lying along the western perimeter of the country, conventionally contrasted with the much larger "mountain" zone to the east (see Figure 1.2).[1] Fields are cropped chiefly in maize, wheat, and sorghum; livestock include cattle, sheep, and goats. The most important source of income for most households, however, is wage labor in South Africa, where perhaps as many as 200,000 Basotho are employed as migrant laborers (GOL 1983, World Bank 1981).

In the period 1975–84, this tiny country was receiving "development assistance" from the following bilateral sources:[2]

Australia	Israel
Austria	Korea
Canada	Libya
Cyprus	The Netherlands
Denmark	Norway
Democratic Republic of Germany	Saskatchewan (Canada)
Federal Republic of Germany	Saudi Arabia
Finland	South Africa
Ghana	Sweden
Korea	Switzerland
Kuwait	Taiwan (R.O.C.)
India	United Kingdom
Iran	United States
Ireland	

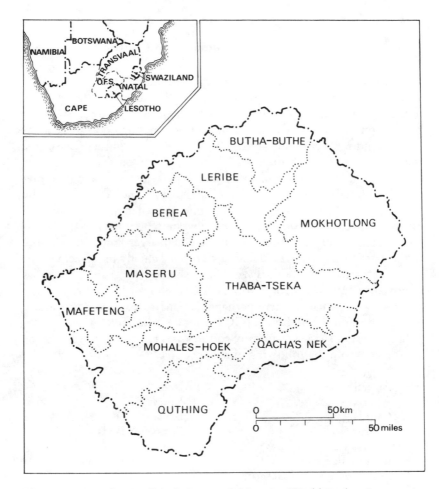

Figure 1.1. Lesotho – political. *Source*: GOL 1983, World Bank 1981.

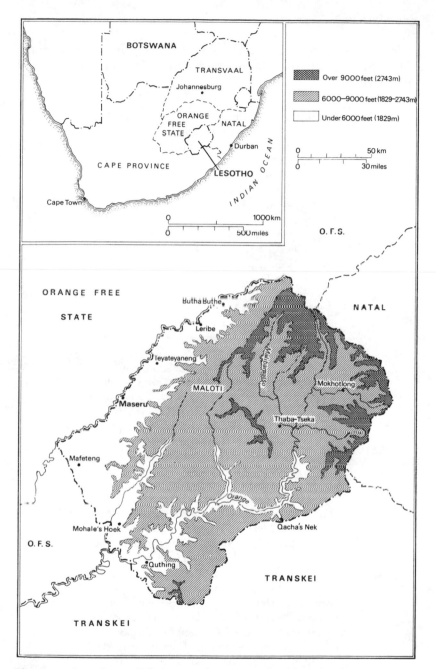

Figure 1.2. Lesotho – relief. *Source*: GOL 1983, World Bank 1981.

In the same period, Lesotho was also receiving assistance from the following international agencies and non- and quasi-governmental organizations:[2]

AFL-CIO African-American Labor Center
Abu Dhabi Fund
Africa Inter-Mennonite Mission
African Development Bank
African Development Fund
African Graduate Training (U.S.)
Afro-American Institute
Agency for Personnel Service Overseas (Ireland)
Anglo-American/De Beers
Anglo-Collieries Recruiting Organization of Lesotho
Arab Bank for Economic Development in Africa
Australian Development Assistance Agency
British Council
British Leprosy Mission
Brothers of the Sacred Heart
CARE
Catholic Relief Service
Christian Aid
Commonwealth Development Corporation
Commonwealth Fund for Technical Cooperation
Credit Union National Association (U.S.)
Danish Church Aid
Danish Volunteer Service
Dental Health International
Economic Commission for Africa
European Development Fund
European Economic Community
Food and Agricultural Organization of the U.N.
Ford Foundation
Fund for Research and Investment for the Development of Africa
German Volunteer Service
Goldfields (R.S.A.)
IMAP International (U.S.)
Institute for Development Management (Canada)
International Bank for Reconstruction and Development
International Civil Aviation Organization
International Cooperative Housing Development Association
International Development Association
International Extension College

International Labour Organization
International Monetary Fund
International Potato Production Centre
International Telecommunications Union
International Trade Centre
International Volunteer Service
Meals for Millions Foundation (U.S.)
Mennonite Central Committee
Mine Labour Organization
Near East Foundation
Netherlands Organization for International Relations
OPEC
Overseas Development Institute (U.K.)
Oxford Committee for Famine Relief (U.K.)
Save the Children Fund
Seventh-Day Adventist World Service
Sisters of the Holy Names of Jesus and Mary
South African Mohair Board
South African Wool Board
United Nations Capital Development Fund
United Nations Fund for Population Activities
United Nations Human Habitat and Settlement Fund
U.S. Peace Corps
Unitarian Service Committee of Canada
United Methodist Committee on Relief
United Nations Children's Emergency Fund
United Nations Development Programme
United Nations Volunteers
Volunteer Development Corporation
World Food Programme
World Health Organization
World Rehabilitation Fund
World University Service

Reading a list like this, or even walking down the streets of Lesotho's capital city of Maseru amidst the cosmopolitan swarm of expatriate "experts," one can hardly help posing the question: what is this all about? What is this massive internationalist intervention, aimed at a country that surely does not appear to be of especially great economic or strategic importance? From the mid 1970s on, Lesotho has received "a disproportionate volume of aid," according to one source (Wellings 1983: 496), "most of which was disbursed on astonishingly generous

7

terms." In 1979, Lesotho received some $64 million in "official de-velopment assistance," according to the World Bank (1981: 164–5), or about $49 for every man, woman, and child in the country – more, that is, (on a per capita basis) than Somalia, Ethiopia, or the Sudan, and more than Chad and Mali put together. The purpose of this aid is ostensibly to alleviate poverty, to increase economic output, and to reduce "depen-dence" on South Africa. Its dispersal has given rise to a substantial "development" industry in Lesotho, employing expatriate consultants and "experts" by the hundreds, and churning out plans, programs, and, most of all, paper, at an astonishing rate.[3]

"Development assistance" has been used for many things, of course; but a large amount of it has gone into "projects," especially "rural development projects." A 1977 official report (FAO 1977) listed over 200 rural development schemes in Lesotho; nine of these were large, expensive "area-based" projects focusing on agricultural development. Yet, if all observers of Lesotho's "development" agree on one thing, it is that "the history of development projects in Lesotho is one of almost unremitting failure to achieve their objectives" (Murray 1981: 19). Again and again development projects in Lesotho are launched, and again and again they fail; but no matter how many times this happens there always seems to be someone ready to try again with yet another project. For the "development" industry in Lesotho, "failure" appears to be the norm.

There is reason to believe that this situation may not be unique to Lesotho. It is true that Lesotho has a high concentration of "de-velopment assistance," but many other, equally unlikely looking Afri-can countries have concentrations as high or higher than Lesotho's. Through Africa – indeed, through the Third World – one seems to find closely analogous or even identical "development" institutions, and along with them often a common discourse and the same way of defining "problems," a common pool of "experts," and a common stock of expertise. The "development industry" is apparently a global phenomenon, and there is no reason to think that the "development" intervention in Lesotho, even if an extreme case, is entirely different in kind from similar interventions elsewhere in the world. Even the par-ticular "development" initiatives promoted in Lesotho may only be specific examples of a more general model. "Rural development" pro-jects are to be found scattered liberally across the African continent and beyond; and, in nearly every case, these projects seem on inspection to be planned, implemented, and justified in very nearly the same way as they are in Lesotho. What is more, these projects seem to "fail" with almost the same astonishing regularity that they do in Lesotho. As Williams (1981: 16–17) notes, "rural development does not usually achieve its objectives"; "By any criteria, successful projects have been the exception rather than the rule."

This book will attempt to make a contribution to the understanding of the "development" industry in Lesotho by exploring in detail the conceptualization, planning, and implementation of one "rural development project," the Thaba-Tseka Project, funded chiefly by the World Bank and the Canadian International Development Agency (CIDA). To the extent that this single project may be seen as part of a larger – indeed, global – apparatus, the study may have some wider relevance in an understanding of what this "development" apparatus is all about, and in providing a concrete demonstration of what is does, how it does it, and why.

The literature

But, before moving on to present the research findings, it is helpful to make explicit some theoretical points of departure. In doing this, it is useful to begin by considering the scholarly literature on "development" and "development" agencies, and explaining how this study relates to it. The question of how societies change – or, if one prefers, "develop" – is not really the issue here, and I do not propose to address the enormous literature relating to social and historical transformation; the question here concerns "development" as a social entity in its own right: the set of "development" institutions, agencies, and ideologies peculiar to our own age. The discussion that follows thus leaves to one side the enormous literature concerned with understanding social transformations, and concentrates on the relatively sparse scholarly literature that aims to understand, explain, analyze, or make sense of the "development" industry itself.

The literature on this point is divided, along sharply ideological lines, into two main camps. On the one hand are those who, either as insiders or as sympathetic outsiders, see "development" planning and "development" agencies as part of a great collective effort to fight poverty, raise standards of living, and promote one or another version of progress. For these writers, of whom a figure like Gunnar Myrdal is perhaps a paradigmatic example, the "development" apparatus is to be understood as a tool at the disposal of a planner, who will need good advice on how to make best use of it. It goes without saying for these writers that a "development" agency is at least potentially a force for beneficial change; the reason for analyzing such an entity is to enable it to perform better, to avoid failures and to maximize its success. From broad, reflective works like Hirschman's *Development Projects Observed* to detailed, empirical studies such as Morss *et al.* (1976), the focus remains technical and managerial. In this literature, the "development" apparatus is scrutinized at all levels, but always with an eye to locating what goes "wrong," why, and how it can be fixed. Even the broader and more speculative discussions in this vein remain a brand of policy science, locating problems and arriving at recommendations addressed to planners within "development" institutions.[4]

Most anthropologists who have explicitly made development agencies or projects the focus of their research fall into this camp. An early example is Reining's analysis (1966) of the Gezira cotton scheme. For Lesotho, there is Wallman's important study (1969) in a similar vein. Several writers on "development anthropology" have urged that many problems encountered by "development" agencies can only be solved by taking an anthropological view of the "development" institutions themselves (Brokensha *et. al.* 1980, Cochrane 1971). More recently Chambers (1980) has written on "experts" in rural Africa, while Hoben (1980) has published a policy-oriented anthropological analysis on the functioning of the USAID bureaucracy.

The most ambitious attempt to date at an anthropological analysis of "development" as an international institution is Robertson's *People and the State: An Anthropology of Planned Development* (1984). Although more sensitive than many to the politically loaded contexts in which "development" planning may be embedded, Robertson, too, ends up falling comfortably within the tradition of seeing the "development" apparatus as a practical tool for the solution of universal problems. "Development" planning, for Robertson, is to be understood as "mankind's most ambitious collective enterprise" (1984: 1), the activity of nation-states attempting to bring into being "ideal worlds." "Development" agencies, in this view, are left with the task of trying to implement these often unrealistic plans. The role of the scholar in this apparatus is to try to see to it that the "ideal worlds" pursued by states are consistent with what we know about how real societies actually work, so that "development" planning can set itself objectives capable of being realized. "Development" projects are thus to be interpreted as lamentably inexpert attempts by society to remake itself; while, for social science, utopian theorizing is apparently the order of the day.

The second approach to conceptualizing "development" institutions is the radical critique associated with neo-Marxism and dependency theory.[5] Authors representing this tradition do not generally spend much time discussing the international "development" establishment, and have little regard for those "Fabians" like Myrdal who put themselves at its service. The issue is generally treated in the context of a political denunciation along the following lines: If (and this is the first postulate of neo-Marxism) capitalism is not a progressive force but a reactionary one in the Third World – not the cause of development but the obstacle to it, not the cure for poverty but the cause of it – then a capitalist-run development project is a fundamentally contradictory endeavor. If it is meant to promote imperial capitalism (and why else would capitalist institutions like the World Bank, USAID, etc. do it?) then it cannot at the same time be an instrument for development, at least not for "real" development. The purpose of a development project is to aid capitalist exploitation in a given country, these writers argue, either by incorporating new territories into the world system, or working against radical social change, or bribing national elites, or mystifying the *real* international relationships, or any number of other mechanisms which seem to be called up as needed on an *ad hoc* basis. The implication is that any concrete aid program, be it an early 1960s "big dam" project, late 1970s "basic needs," or whatever, is explained, almost by definition, by the "logic of capital."[6]

A related argument has been advanced by Lappe and Collins (1979, Lappe *et al.* 1980), who reason that: (1) poverty is not a *sui generis* fact or a consequence of global scarcity but only a symptom of powerlessness; (2) international aid projects by their very nature, whoever they claim to "target," do not make the radical changes in political and economic structures that could alone empower the poor; therefore (3) aid projects cannot be expected to help to eradicate poverty since they only reinforce the system which in the first place causes the poverty. Lappe and Collins offer a powerful and well-documented political argument, but it does not help us to understand the different forms of intervention that have over the years been practiced under the name of "development" since it gives only a negative characterization of what an aid project (or, by implication, *any* national or international maneuver that falls short of posing a fundamental challenge to the entrenched system of exploitation) does: it does *not* help the hungry as it is supposed to, it only strengthens the powerful. The argument is still organized around the politically naive question: "Do aid programs really help poor people?" Thus attention is paid to what aid projects do, but once again only to show that they "fail," i.e. that they do not reduce hunger, or to claim that they are "showcase projects," which "distract our attention" from the "overriding functions" of development aid, functions specified only as strategic and imperialistic (Lappe *et al.* 1980: 122).

We have, then, an important body of recent literature, and two fundamentally opposed notions of how to interpret the "development" apparatus. Which position will the present study take?

This question can perhaps be illuminated by making a comparison with Paul Willis's important book *Learning to Labour: How Working Class Kids Get Working Class Jobs*. Willis's book encounters an enormous body of literature, the "education" literature, and finds that literature divisible into two camps based on the authors' attitudes toward the fundamental nature or purpose of the institution "the school." The liberal, from the eighteenth century onward, regards the public school as an instrument for creating an enlightened, egalitarian society, a society with equal opportunity for all. Thus the question in recent times has been how to use and reform schools so that they can help to eradicate the economic, social, and political gaps which separate whites and blacks, workers and middle-class, men and women.[7] Against this view has arisen a Marxist critique which argues that, contrary to the claim that schools are either actually or potentially forces for democratic ends, these institutions were established from the very beginning to achieve the opposite. Schools, the Marxists argue, were established by the capitalist state in order to reproduce labor power for an industrial order whose jobs were organized hierarchically. They are not tools for engineering social equality – they are by nature mechanisms for reproducing labor power for a class society. This is known as the "reproduction" thesis.[8]

Willis, for his part, rejects the Liberal argument as politically naive and takes it as a fact that class relations are reproduced under capitalism (working-class kids *do* get working-class jobs) and that the schools play an important part in this. But he moves beyond "reproduction theory" by refusing to be satisfied with this. Yes, reproduction occurs through (in part) the school, but "for all we are told of how this actually happens, schools may as well be 'black boxes'." This, he observes, is neither theoretically nor politically adequate. Instead, Willis offers a detailed ethnography of what actually happens when the apparatus of schooling is brought to bear on a group of working-class kids. He finds that there is no mechanistic imprinting of the characteristics required by the capitalist state on its passive victims, as the reproduction theory might suggest, but rather an ongoing battle between school power on the one hand, and resistance based in working-class culture on the other. And it is, ironically, *through* this resistance that the task of "reproduction" is eventually accomplished. The resistance provoked by schooling is thus an essential part of the explanation for how labor power is reproduced. The school indeed accomplishes the task assigned to it in reproduction theory, but in an unexpected and startling way, a way which underlines the ambiguities of resistance and the scope for choice and political action in a world that is always structured but never determined.

Similarly, when one reads much of the literature on the "development" industry, one finds oneself doubly dissatisfied – with the liberals, whose only concern seems to be with directing or reforming an institution whose fundamental beneficence they take as given – and with the neo-Marxists, who seem satisfied to establish that the institutions of "development" are part of a fundamentally imperialistic relation between center and periphery and take the matter to be thus settled.

But the matter is not settled, any more than the issue of the school is settled by showing that the schools are part of a system of reproduction of labor power. For if, as the neo-Marxists argue, an international development project is to be understood not as a humanitarian attempt to overcome poverty but as an important instrument of imperial and class-based control, then one ought to be interested enough to look and see *how* this control is effected. One cannot, as Willis rightly notes, expect things to simply snap into place through mysterious "black box" mechanisms simply because Capital "needs" for them to do so. A structure always reproduces itself through a process, and through a struggle; and the sense of a structure, Willis shows, can only be grasped through that sometimes surprising and ironic process, and never by merely labeling the structure with the name of those whose interests it serves.

A few recent studies of "rural development" make an important start toward such an understanding of the "development" apparatus by looking at the interventions of "development" agencies not for what they don't do or might do, but for what they do. The edited collection by Heyer, Roberts, and Williams (1981), for instance, is not much interested in the polemics over whether or not "rural development" is *really* a matter of "helping the poor," or as one formula (Chambers

1983) has it, "putting the last first." They quickly dismiss this liberal view, noting that empirically there "appears to be little foundation for the assumption that the activities of rural development programmes lead to the improvement of the welfare of the rural population, let alone the rural poor" (Heyer *et al.* 1981: 10). But this is seen as neither surprising nor especially illuminating; after all, as Keith Griffin remarks in his refreshing preface to the volume, "More often than not, the government has represented interests other than those of the rural poor and it is hardly surprising, therefore, that public intervention has in practice been harmful to the majority of the rural people rather than beneficial" (Heyer *et al.* 1981: vii). For Heyer *et al.*, this is not the main issue; the task is not to denounce the "rural development" establishment for what it is not, but to analyze it – not in terms of its own proclamations, but as a social institution in its own right, supported and maintained not by "capitalism" in the abstract, but by historically specific political and economic interests in each case. This attempt to see "rural development" interventions as real historical events, susceptible of the same sort of political-economic explanation as any others, is found in several recent works in addition to the volume by Heyer, Roberts, and Williams (1981), including Williams (1976, 1985a, 1986), Beckman (1977), Bernstein (1977, 1979) and the articles in Galli (1981).

It is an important advance to have moved the discussion on the "development" industry beyond the widespread ideological preoccupation with the question of whether it is to be considered a "good thing" or a "bad thing," a benevolent force to be reformed or an exploitative maneuver to be denounced. Insofar as works in the political economy tradition like Heyer *et al.* (1981) and Galli (1981) insist that "rural development" is the name for a complex set of institutions and initiatives encompassing "multiple, and often contradictory, interests" (Heyer *et al.* 1981: 12), they are in full agreement with the aims of the present work. However, the way in which most of these authors have gone about analyzing the complex reality they have identified as "rural development" is significantly different from the approach that will be taken here.

First of all, the political economists are often too quick to impute an economic function to "development" projects, and to accept the premise that a "development" project is primarily a device for bringing about a particular sort of economic transformation – a transformation variously glossed as "capitalist penetration," "commoditization," "capitalist development," "the expansion of the capitalist mode of production," etc. In this vein, for instance, Beckman (1977: 3) claims that rural "development" projects "serve to subject peasants to the imperative of producing for an external market under monopolistic relations of exchange," while Bernstein (1977: 65) declares as if self-evident that rural "development" projects "operate objectively to incorporate the peasantry further into commodity relations."

It is clear in reading scholarly literature on "development" that the word "development" is used to refer to at least two quite separate things. On the one hand, "development" is used to mean the process of transition or transformation toward a modern, capitalist, industrial economy – "modernization," "capitalist development," "the development of the forces of production," etc. The second meaning, much in vogue from the mid 1970s onward, defines itself in terms of "quality of life" and "standard of living," and refers to the reduction or amelioration of poverty and material want. The directionality implied in the word "development" is in this usage no longer historical, but moral. "Development" is no longer a movement in history, but an activity, a social program, a war on poverty on a global scale. Liberals and "development" bureaucrats regularly conflate these two meanings, implicitly equating "modernization" with the elimination or alleviation of poverty. Against this view, the critics insist that the two are different, that capitalist development in Africa is very often the *cause* of poverty and not its cure, and that it is usually not in the interests of the rural poor at all. For the liberal, a rural development project brings "development," in one or both of the above senses, and that is all to the good. For the critics discussed above, a rural development project is part of "the expansion of the capitalist mode of production" – "capitalist development" – which is often not so good at all for the poor "peasants." Class formation, growing inequality and landlessness, decreased self-sufficiency, and increased poverty are commonly cited results. But the point to be emphasized here is that both the "development" establishment *and* many of its most articulate critics accept that a rural development project does in fact – for better or worse – bring about some sort of "development," some sort of economic transformation toward a well-defined end point.[9]

The second major point to be emphasized in the political economy type of approach of the writers under discussion is the extremely important place occupied in their analyses by "interests." The existence and structure of the "development" industry, and what happens when it is deployed in various different settings, are analyzed by identifying the

Introduction

various interests that are involved. A "development" project is taken to be explained when all the different interests behind it have been sorted out and made specific. The interested agents may be classes, national governments, or individuals, but whoever the actors are taken to be, explanation takes the form of attributing an event or a structure to a particular constellation of "interests."

With regard to both of these points, the approach taken here will be rather different, for both empirical and theoretical reasons. Empirically, "development" projects in Lesotho do not generally bring about any significant reduction in poverty, but neither do they characteristically introduce any new relations of production (capitalist or otherwise), or bring about significant economic transformations. They do not bring about "development" in either of the two senses identified above, nor are they set up in such a way that they ever could, as will be seen in the chapters that follow. For this reason, it seems a mistake to interpret them as "part of the historical expansion of capitalism" (Galli 1981: x) or as elements in a global strategy for controlling or capitalizing peasant production, a solution to "the peasant problem" (Williams 1981).

At the same time – again, empirically – there is no easy congruence between the "objective interests" of the various parties and the stream of events which emerges. Unquestionably, there are a number of different interested parties whose interests can be identified and made explicit. The interests of the World Bank in promoting "development" projects have been well analyzed by Williams (1981), Payer (1983) and others; the economic stake of a country like Canada in "development" interventions in Africa has been made clear by Freeman (1984). But while it is certainly relevant to know, for instance, that the World Bank has an interest in boosting production and export of cash crops for the external market, and that industrialized states without historic links to an area may sponsor "development" projects as a way of breaking into otherwise inaccessible markets, it remains impossible to simply read off actual events from these known interests as if the one were a simple effect of the other. One may know, for instance, that Canada sponsored a rural development project in Thaba-Tseka, and one may know as well that the Canadian government has an interest in promoting rural development programs because it helps Canadian corporations to find export markets for farm machinery (among other things), but this pairing of facts does not constitute an acceptable level of explanation, and in fact leaves many of the empirical details of the Canadian role absolutely mysterious.

Theoretically, as well, the approach reviewed above is inadequate to

16

the task this study sets itself. The most important theoretical differences will be brought out in the following section.

Some theoretical points of departure

The first issue to be raised, perhaps, is that the present study is an anthropological one. Unlike many anthropological works on "development," this one takes as its primary object not the people to be "developed," but the apparatus that is to do the "developing." This is not principally a book about the Basotho people, or even about Lesotho; it is principally a book about the operation of the international "development" apparatus in a particular setting.

To take on the task of looking at the "development" apparatus anthropologically is to insist on a particular sort of approach to the material. As an anthropologist, one cannot assume, for instance, as many political economists do, that a structure simply and rationally "represents" or "expresses" a set of "objective interests"; one knows that structures are multi-layered, polyvalent, and often contradictory, and that economic functions and "objective interests" are always located within other, encompassing structures that may be invisible even to those who inhabit them. The interests may be clear, and the intentions as well; but the anthropologist cannot take "planning" at its word. Instead of ascribing events and institutions to the projects of various actors, an anthropological approach must demote the plans and intentions of even the most powerful interests to the status of an interesting problem, one level among many others, for the anthropologist knows well how easily structures can take on lives of their own that soon enough overtake intentional practices. Whatever interests may be at work, and whatever they may think they are doing, they can only operate through a complex set of social and cultural structures so deeply embedded and so ill-perceived that the outcome may be only a baroque and unrecognizable transformation of the original intention. The approach adopted here treats such an outcome as neither an inexplicable mistake, nor the trace of a yet-undiscovered intention, but as a riddle, a problem to be solved, an anthropological puzzle.

It is at this point that the issue of discourse becomes important. For writers such as Heyer *et al.* (1981) and Galli (1981), official discourse on "development" either expresses "true intentions" or, more often, provides an ideological screen for other, concealed intentions: "mere rhetoric." The bulk of "development" discourse, with all its professions of concern for the rural poor and so on, is for these writers simply a misrepresentation of what the "development" apparatus is "really" up to. The World Bank may talk a lot about helping poor farmers, for instance, but in fact their funds continue to be targeted at the large, highly capitalized farmers, at the expense of the poor. The much publicized "new strategy," then, is "largely rhetoric," serving only a mystifying function (Williams 1981).

In the anthropological approach adopted below, the discourse of the "development" establishment is considered much more important than this. It may be that much of this discourse is untrue, but that is no excuse for dismissing it. As Foucault (1971, 1973) has shown, discourse is a practice, it is structured, and it has real effects which are much more profound than simply "mystification." The thoughts and actions of "development" bureaucrats are powerfully shaped by the world of acceptable statements and utterances within which they live; and what they do and do not do is a product not only of the interests of various nations, classes, or international agencies, but also, and at the same time, of a working out of this complex structure of knowledge. Instead of ignoring the orderly field of statements produced by the "development" apparatus on the grounds that the statements are ideological, the study below takes this field as its point of departure for an exploration of the way in which "development" initiatives are produced and put into practice.

It should be clear from the above that the approach to be taken to the problem of the "development" industry in Lesotho will be, in keeping with the anthropological approach, "decentered" – that is, it will locate the intelligibility of a series of events and transformations not in the intentions guiding the actions of one or more animating subjects, but in the systematic nature of the social reality which results from those actions. Seeing a "development" project as the simple projection of the "interest" of a subject (the World Bank, Canada, Capital, Imperialism) ignores the non- and counter-intentionality of structural production, and is in this way profoundly non-anthropological. As in the case of Willis's treatment of the schooling apparatus (1981), one must entertain the possibility that the "development" apparatus in Lesotho may do what it does, not at the bidding of some knowing and powerful subject who is making it all happen, but behind the backs of or against the wills of even the most powerful actors. But this is not to say that such institutions do not represent an exercise of power; only that power is not to be embodied in the person of a "powerful" subject. A "development" project may very well serve power, but in a different way than any of the "powerful" actors imagined; it may only wind up, in the end, "turning out" to serve power.

At this point, the theoretical approach of the present work links up with another important body of literature, closely associated with the work of Foucault (1979, 1980a, 1980b). Using a decentered conception of power, a number of recent studies (e.g. Foucault 1979, 1980a, Donzelot 1979, Pasquino 1978, Procacci 1978, Jones and Williamson 1979) have shown how the outcomes of planned social interventions can end up coming together into powerful constellations of control that were never intended and in some cases never even recognized, but are all the more effective for being "subjectless." This theoretical innovation makes possible a different way of connecting outcomes with power, one that avoids giving a central place to any actor or entity conceived as a "powerful" subject.

Perhaps the best example of this kind of analysis is Foucault's "genealogy" of the prison (1979). The prison, Foucault shows, was created as a "correctional" institution. It was intended to imprint on the inmates the qualities of good citizenship: to make criminals into honest, hard working, law abiding individuals, who could return to a "normal" place in society. This idea of "rehabilitation" was behind the establishment of modern prisons throughout the world, and it continues to be offered as the chief justification for maintaining them and, from time to time, reforming them. But it is obvious upon inspection, according to Foucault, that prisons do not in fact "reform" criminals; that, on the contrary, they make nearly impossible that return to "normality" that they have always claimed to produce, and that, instead of eliminating criminality, they seem rather to produce and intensify it within a well-defined strata of "delinquents." While such a result must be conceived as a "failure" from the point of view of the planners' intentions, the result has quite a different character when apprehended as part of a different "strategy." For the constitution of a class of "delinquents," Foucault argues, turned out to be very useful in taming "popular illegalities" and transforming the political fact of illegality into the quasi-medical one of pathological "delinquency." By differentiating illegalities, and by turning one uniquely well-supervised and controlled class of violators against the others, the prison did end up serving as part of a system of social control, but in a very different way than its planners had envisioned. "If this is the case," Foucault writes:

19

the prison, apparently "failing", does not miss its target; on the contrary, it reaches it, in so far as it gives rise to one particular form of illegality in the midst of others, which it is able to isolate, to place in full light and to organize as a relatively enclosed, but penetrable, milieu . . .
For the observation that prison fails to eliminate crime, one should perhaps substitute the hypothesis that prison has succeeded extremely well in producing delinquency, a specific type, a politically or economically less dangerous – and, on occasion, usable – form of illegality; in producing delinquents, in an apparently marginal, but in fact centrally supervised milieu; in producing the delinquent as a pathologized subject . . . So successful has the prison been that, after a century and a half of 'failures', the prison still exists, producing the same results, and there is the greatest reluctance to dispense with it.
(Foucault 1979: 276–7)

The point to be taken from the above argument is only that planned interventions may produce unintended outcomes that end up, all the same, incorporated into anonymous constellations of control – authorless "strategies," in Foucault's sense (1979, 1980b) – that turn out in the end to have a kind of political intelligibility. This is only another way of approaching the problem noted by Willis (1981) in his discussion of the school cited above: the most important political effects of a planned intervention may occur unconsciously, behind the backs or against the wills of the "planners" who may seem to be running the show.

This will turn out to be one of the key problems raised by the operation of the "development" apparatus in Lesotho, and the approach that is adopted owes much to the literature so briefly discussed above. The complex relation between the intentionality of planning and the strategic intelligibility of outcomes is perhaps the single most important theme winding through the pages that follow. As this theme appears and reappears in the chapters below, one cardinal principle will be illustrated again and again: intentional plans are always important, but never in quite the way the planners imagined. In the pages that follow, I will try to show how, in the case of a development project in Lesotho, intentional plans interacted with unacknowledged structures and chance events to produce unintended outcomes which turn out to be intelligible not only as the unforeseen effects of an intended intervention, but also as the unlikely instruments of an unplotted strategy. Specifically, the remaining chapters will show how outcomes that at first appear as mere "side effects" of an unsuccessful attempt to engineer an economic transformation become legible in another perspective as unintended yet instrumental elements in a resultant constellation that has the effect of expanding the exercise of a particular sort of state power while simultaneously exerting a powerful depoliticizing effect. It is this unauthored resultant constellation that I call "the anti-politics machine," for reasons that I hope will in the end become clear. The remaining chapters aim to explore how such an unlikely "machine" works, and to understand better what it does.

Part II
The "development" apparatus

2 Conceptual apparatus: the constitution of the object of "development" — Lesotho as "less developed country"

Few developing countries faced such bleak economic prospects and were so ill-prepared as Lesotho when it gained independence in October 1966. In few countries of the world was economic independence more remote from political independence than in Lesotho. In spite of the fact that Lesotho is an enclave within highly industrialized South Africa and belongs with that country, Botswana, and Swaziland to the rand monetary area and the Southern African Customs Union, it was then virtually untouched by modern economic development. It was and still is, basically, a traditional subsistence peasant society. But rapid population growth resulting in extreme pressure on the land, deteriorating soil, and declining agricultural yields led to a situation in which the country was no longer able to produce enough food for its people. Many able-bodied men were forced from the land in search of means to support their families, but the only employment opportunities were in neighboring South Africa. At present, an estimated 60 percent of the male labor force is away as migrant workers in South Africa.
World Bank Country Report on Lesotho (1975), page 1, paragraph 1.

Have you ever read any criminological texts? They are staggering. And I say this out of astonishment, not aggressiveness, because I fail to comprehend how the discourse of criminology has been able to go on at this level. One has the impression that it is of such utility, is needed so urgently and rendered so vital for the working of the system, that it does not even need to seek a theoretical justification for itself, or even simply a coherent framework. It is entirely utilitarian. I think one needs to investigate why such a "learned" discourse became so indispensable to the functioning of the nineteenth century penal system.
Michel Foucault, "Prison Talk" (1980b)

From the point of view of an academic scholar of Lesotho, the first paragraph of the World Bank Report will no doubt seem bizarre. The assertion that Lesotho in 1966 was "a traditional subsistence peasant society," "virtually untouched by modern economic development," along with the apparent implication that the migrant labor system originated only in recent years, will seem not only incorrect but out-landish. The scholar will feel compelled to point out that Lesotho has served as a labor reserve supplying migrant wage labor to South African mines, farms, and industry for more than a century; and will perhaps draw up in his or her mind a short list of some of the "modern economic developments" which had "touched" Lesotho prior to 1966: the introduction of a money economy and the establishment of Lesotho as a market for Western commodities; the introduction of plough agriculture and a host of new cash and subsistence crops; the introduction of merino sheep and angora goats, and the cash cropping of wool; the establishment and growth of a modern colonial/state administration; the development of a national elite; the growth of a capital town; the construction of airports, roads, schools, churches, and hospitals; and last, but not least, the establishment of the migrant labor system and the transformation of Lesotho into a labor reserve for the South African industrial economy. These "modern economic developments" had all been introduced long before 1966. Consider the following excerpt from the article on "Basutoland" in the *Encylopaedia Britannica* of 1910 (eleventh edition):

Basutoland is one of the greatest grain-growing countries of South Africa. The richest tract of land is that between the Maluti mountains and the Caledon river. In summer the country appears as one waving field of wheat, millet and mealies; whilst on the mountain slopes and on their flat tops are large flocks of sheep, cattle and goats, and troops of ponies ... The chief exports are wheat, mealies, Kaffir corn [*sic*], wool, mohair, horses and cattle. The great bulk of the imports are textiles ... The average annual value of trade for the five years ending the 30th of June 1905 was: Exports ₤215,668, imports ₤203,026. Trade is almost entirely with the Orange River Colony and Cape Colony. The Territory is a member of the South African Customs Union. Some 60,000 Basuto (annual average) find employment outside the Territory, more than half of whom seek farm and domestic service. A small proportion go to the Johannesburg gold mines, and others obtain employment on the railways.

Communication over the greater part of the Territory is by road; none of the rivers is navigable. A state-owned railway, 16½ miles long, starting from Maseru crosses the Caledon river and joins the line connecting Bloemfontein and Ladysmith. The railway follows, N.E. of Maseru, the right bank of the Caledon, and affords a ready means of transport for the cereals raised on the left or Basuto side of the river. Highroads, maintained by the government, traverse every

26

part of the country, and bridges have been built across the Caledon
... There is a complete postal and telegraphic service and a telephone
line connects all government stations ...

Education is given in schools founded by missionary societies, of
which the chief is the Société des Missions Evangéliques de Paris. A
large proportion of the people can read and write Sesuto (as the
Basuto language is called) and English, and speak Dutch, whilst a
considerable number also receive higher education. Many Basuto at
the public examinations take higher honours than competitors of
European descent. There are over 200 schools, with an average
attendance exceeding 10,000. A government industrial school (opened
in 1906) is maintained at Maseru, and the Paris Society has an
industrial school at Leloaleng. The social condition of the people is
higher than that of the majority of South African natives.

The fact is, then, that Lesotho entered the twentieth century, not as a
"subsistence" economy, but as a producer of cash crops for the South
African market; not as a "traditional peasant society," but as a reservoir
exporting wage laborers in about the same quantities, proportionate to
total population, as it does today. Lesotho was not "untouched by
modern economic development" but radically and completely transformed by it, and this not in 1966 or 1975 but in 1910.

Academic scholars of Lesotho, of all stripes, acknowledge this transformation. I will give details in later sections; suffice it to say that it is
almost inconceivable that a serious scholar of Lesotho's history could
say that Lesotho in 1966 was "a traditional peasant, subsistence society," "virtually untouched by modern economic development," or
maintain that labor migration and the cash economy is something new in
Lesotho's history.

One would be mistaken, however, to suppose that the paragraph cited
from the World Bank Report is simply an error, the sign of gross
ignorance or incompetent scholarship. It is true that this paragraph (like
the remainder of the Report, and like the documents of other "development" agencies in Lesotho) does not meet the accepted norms of
academic discourse; such a statement would not likely be found in an
academic dissertation on Lesotho. But the authors of this statement, the
authors of the World Bank Country Report on Lesotho, cannot simply
be dismissed as second-rate academics. It must be recognized that what
is being done here is not some sort of staggeringly bad scholarship, but
something else entirely, just as Foucault recognized that criminology is
not simply a backward social science but a special sort of discourse with

27

a special job to do. What is needed is not so much a correction or setting straight of the discourse of the "development" industry in Lesotho (though such a critique is of course possible) as a way of accounting for it, and of showing what it does. The analysis therefore begins by noting the discontinuity between the World Bank Report and academic norms – "out of astonishment, not aggressiveness" – and sets itself the task of understanding the discursive framework and the institutional conditions within which statements such as the ones I have cited are no longer bizarre and unacceptable, but comprehensible, and even necessary.

The argument will proceed in the following manner. First, it will be necessary to demonstrate with care what has as yet been only asserted – that "development" discourse on Lesotho is distinguishable from academic discourse, and that the difference between the two types of discourse is due to two different sets of rules of formation for discourse, or two different problematics, and not to any necessary difference in intellectual quality or individual authors' abilities. Secondly, in order to make sense of the domain of discourse that will have been thus picked out, it will be necessary to show what the "development" discourse in Lesotho *does* – what theoretical tasks it accomplishes, and to what effect. Finally, it will remain to show how and why this discourse maintains its own distinctive qualities, its closure. There are questions, then, of fact, function, and mechanism.

The first question will be addressed through a close textual analysis of the World Bank Country Report on Lesotho ("Lesotho: A Development Challenge," 1975). Here will be examined in detail the peculiar emphases, interpretations, construals, and fabrications which combine to produce a unique "development" perspective on Lesotho, a perspective which must inevitably appear badly distorted from the point of view of the scholar.

In answering the second question, it will be necessary to demonstrate that what appeared, in the first section, as simple distortions of reality can be shown to be essential steps in the necessary theoretical task of constituting the complex reality of Lesotho as a "Less Developed Country," an "LDC"; and this in order to set up a target for a particular sort of intervention: the technical, apolitical, "development" intervention. The characteristics of this theoretical construct, the LDC, will be described in some detail, as will the techniques used in the theoretical work of translation of certain unmanageable sorts of facts into a more acceptable register.

28

In the third section, the task will be to show why it is necessary for "development" discourse to take the form it does; we must uncover the institutional and ideological constraints and imperatives that structure the formation of the "development" discourse.

Two cautionary notes may be appropriate before going further. First, the discourse with which I am concerned here is the discourse of "development" agencies working in Lesotho in the middle and late 1970s. The entity I am describing is thus bounded in time and space. Similarities no doubt can be demonstrated with "development" discourse elsewhere and at other times, but it is not my purpose to explore these similarities here.

Second, my concern here is with "development" discourse on Lesotho, not with what I am calling "academic discourse." Academic discourse on Lesotho has of course its own rules of formation and responds to its own ideological and institutional constraints, which could well be·the subject of another analysis. Like "development" discourse, academic discourse deals not simply with "the facts" but with a constructed version of the object. This does not imply, of course, that the two versions are somehow equally true or equally adequate to any given purpose.[1] Indeed, the reader will see in the analysis to follow that I write from within academic discourse, and that I unreservedly accept the academic judgment that much of "development" discourse on Lesotho is wildly inaccurate. *But that judgment is not itself the point of the analysis.* Rather, I take the incompatibility of "development" discourse and academic norms as a point of departure for an exploration of the distinctly different way that "development" discourse is structured. The point of introducing the idea of "academic discourse," then, is neither to rectify "development" discourse, nor to arrive at generalizations about discourse produced in academic settings, nor to imply a sharp or absolute schism which does not in fact exist. The point is only to reveal something about the discourse produced by "development" institutions in Lesotho by showing that the "development" literature is full of statements which would be unacceptable in most academic settings, while at the same time many observations and lines of thought commonplace in scholarly literature on Lesotho are effectively excluded from the discourse of "development."

The World Bank Country Report

As an example of the normativity governing "development" literature on Lesotho, I will take the World Bank Country Report on Lesotho, entitled "Lesotho: A Development Challenge." This Report was published in 1975, just as the Thaba-Tseka Project was beginning with World Bank funding. The World Bank Report was drawn up during the same period as the plans for Phase One of the project. The "development" problematic that will be examined here, then, is the very one which presided over the design of the Thaba-Tseka Project. The 1975 Report reveals the larger conception within which the concrete initiatives of the Thaba-Tseka Project made sense.

By restricting the inquiry for the moment to a single, comprehensive, bounded text such as this one, I hope to avoid the charge that the examples to be treated are improperly selected, unrepresentative, or merely accidents. The Report presents a single, integrated portrait of Lesotho as the "development" problematic sees it, and it does so in the space of sixty-nine pages, plus appendices. It will thus be possible to treat each section of the Report with some care, and to gauge the relative emphases placed on different issues and aspects within the whole of the Report.

It is also important, for the purposes of this study, to discuss a text of good intellectual and professional quality. The World Bank is perhaps the most prestigious of "development" organizations. They pay high salaries and attract top talent. Their reports are considered authoritative in the "development" field. One can be sure that, if the World Bank Country Report looks different from anything a good academic might produce, it is not because it is second-rate work produced by second-rate talent; on the contrary, such a text must be presumed to be a product of first-rate talent. If the document fails to meet prevailing academic norms, I shall argue, it is not because it is "second-rate work," but precisely because it was produced under a different system for "rating" work, a different discursive normativity.

Each section of the Report will be discussed in turn, giving a brief summary and highlighting some of the significant points which will need to be analyzed more systematically in the next section of the chapter.

The Preamble: "Lesotho's challenge"

Let us quote the first three paragraphs of this section in full:

Few developing countries faced such bleak economic prospects and were so ill-prepared as Lesotho when it gained independence in October 1966. In few countries of the world was economic independence more remote from political independence than in Lesotho. In spite of the fact that Lesotho is an enclave within highly industrialized South Africa and belongs with that country, Botswana, and Swaziland to the rand monetary area and the Southern African Customs Union, it was then virtually untouched by modern economic development. It was and still is, basically, a traditional subsistence peasant society. But rapid population growth resulting in extreme pressure on the land, deteriorating soil, and declining agricultural yields led to a situation in which the country was no longer able to produce enough food for its people. Many able-bodied men were forced from the land in search of means to support their families, but the only employment opportunities were in neighboring South Africa. At present, an estimated 60 percent of the male labor force is away as migrant workers in South Africa.

At independence there was no economic infrastructure to speak of. Industries were virtually non-existent. Whatever commerce there was, was largely in the hands of South African traders. The few commerical banks catered mainly for the small expatriate community. Education was dominated by foreign religious missions which had been quite active, giving Lesotho one of the highest literacy rates in Africa; but school curricula bore little relation to local conditions and to the development needs of the country. Former colonial rule was geared to administering the country and was not development oriented. At independence many colonial civil servants left. At the same time, the new government had to assume numerous new tasks for which few qualified Basotho were available. Government revenue was very low – so low, in fact, that half of the recurrent budget and all of the capital budget had to be financed from foreign assistance, leaving the government little freedom in determining level and direction of expenditures.

There are several reasons why Lesotho has remained at such a low stage of social and economic development. One reason is that, until about 1950, the British government did not really attempt to introduce any development, expecting that the country would eventually be incorporated into South Africa and assuming that it would be more or less automatically developed as an indirect result of the strong expansionary forces in South Africa. But even when

thoughts of incorporation were abandoned after the rise of the apartheid policies in South Africa, the British administration seems to have remained resigned to a low-level stagnation of Lesotho's rural economy. Apart from its eroding soil, Lesotho had few other known natural resources that could be developed; and the prevailing system of land tenure was seen to stand in the way of agricultural and industrial progress. In the five years before independence, capital expenditure was, on the average, less than R1 million a year, much of it for building up a local administration.
(World Bank 1975)

The remaining two pages of the Preamble describe the official development plans proposed for Lesotho since 1965.

There are a number of points here that need to be underlined. First is the idea, introduced in the first paragraph and brought up time and again throughout the report, that Lesotho represents an aboriginal economy, that it is a "traditional" society somehow untouched by the modern world. Lesotho in 1966, we are told, was "a traditional subsistence peasant society," which was "virtually untouched by modern economic development." Through government inaction, Lesotho was left by the wayside, outside of the stream of "modern economic development." This is an extremely important claim, on which much that follows depends: Lesotho is not merely poor; it is poor because it has "remained at ... a low stage of social and economic development." True, "an estimated 60 percent of the male labor force is away as migrant workers in South Africa," but this is treated as a recent response to population pressure on the part of an isolated "traditional subsistence peasant society." Note, too, that the relationship with South Africa appears here as one of accidental geographical juxtaposition: "Many able-bodied men were forced from the land in search of means to support their families, but the only employment opportunities available were in neighboring South Africa." There will be more to say about this later.

This picture of Lesotho's history is truly fantastical. Let us consider labor migration and the claim that it is a recent response of a pristine, "traditional" economy to population pressure. Ashton, the principal ethnographer of the Basotho, reported in 1952 that:

Labour migration is not new to the Basuto, and is, in fact, nearly as old as their contact with Europeans. During the famines and the troublous times of the Free State wars (intermittently from 1851 to 1868), numbers of men sought employment with the Europeans in

Natal and the Cape for money to buy food. After the political settlement of 1868, work abroad became more regular, and considerable scope for employment was offered only 180 miles away by the opening of the Kimberley diamond mines. Thither men flocked in their thousands to work for money for guns, clothes and agricultural implements and for the ten shilling tax imposed in 1869. By 1875, out of a total population of 127,325, of which the number of able-bodied men was estimated at 20,000, 15,000 men were getting passes to work outside the territory for long or short periods, and by 1884 this number had doubled itself. By 1908, 78,000 men out of a population of 350,000 "went abroad at intervals for work."
(Ashton 1967: 162)

The Report's picture of primordial isolation and underdevelopment is also challenged by basic and well-known facts about the history of agriculture in Lesotho. The 1910 Encyclopaedia article's account of Lesotho's booming production of agricultural goods for export has already been cited. The *Oxford History of South Africa*, for its part, reports that:

In 1837 the Sotho of Basutoland (which then stretched west of the Caledon) [i.e. beyond its modern boundaries] had grain stored for four to eight years: in 1844 white farmers "flocked" to them to buy grain. During 1872 (*after* the loss of their most fertile land west of the Caledon) the Sotho exported 100,000 muids [i.e. 185 lb. bags] of grain (wheat, mealies, and kaffir-corn [*sic*]), and in 1877 when the demand for grain on the diamond fields had fallen "large quantities" were held by producers and shopkeepers in Basutoland.
(Wilson and Thompson 1969)

The *Oxford History* also notes that Basotho had begun working on the diamond fields in 1870 (realizing that "guns, as well as horses and blankets, might be earned by working there") and that production had began to drop by the beginning of this century. A close parallel is noted between the agricultural histories of Lesotho and the Transkei in South Africa and it is observed that Lesotho, like the Transkei, has had its economy shaped by the growth of industry and markets in South Africa, and has seen a gradual decline from booming agricultural production in the nineteenth century to overwhelming dependence on migrant wage labor in recent times (Wilson and Thompson 1972: 55–103).
But the World Bank Report's claim that Lesotho in 1966 was a

"traditional subsistence peasant society," "virtually untouched by modern economic development" is not merely unusual or controversial; it is unknown in the scholarly literature. According to one academic economist who reviewed the report, the claim "seems to be almost the exact reverse of the truth, unless the meanings of words are stretched in extraordinary and mystifying ways" (Cobbe 1978: 136). It is not only the well-known recent writers influenced by neo-Marxist and dependency theory, like Murray (1981) and Palmer and Parsons (1977), who reject the view of Lesotho as an aboriginal economy; that view is rejected just as surely by the old liberal orthodoxy against which the radical challenge originally arose, as the earlier citation of the *Oxford History* shows. Compare Leonard Thompson's assessment of Lesotho at independence with that of the World Bank:

By 1966 most people had forgotten that Moshoeshoe's subjects had once been a self-sufficient peasantry, producing a surplus of grain for sale to Whites in exchange for manufactured goods. The population had increased to nearly a million and Basutoland had become a net importer of food, in spite of the fact that people were making heroic efforts to grow wheat and pasture livestock high in the Maluti as well as in the lowlands. Land shortage and soil erosion were grave problems and all the political parties declared that the conquered territories beyond the Caledon River should be returned ... In the regional context, colonial Basutoland became a dormitory for migrant workers, who commuted between their rural homes and white South Africa's farms, mines, and factories, where they encountered such rigid colour bars in employment and wage levels that they could not acquire sufficient skills nor earn enough money to generate economic growth at home.

In 1962 a report of the World Health Organization estimated that two-thirds of the BaSotho were seriously under-nourished. At the time of independence about half of the men of working age were employed in the Republic and about 80 percent of the population were dependent on the wages they earned there.
(Thompson 1975: 326–7)

Other examples here include Ashton, whom I have cited above, and Wallman (1969: 5), who found that Lesotho in 1966 was less an untouched "traditional subsistence" economy than a place that "might be described as a dormitory suburb of peasants who commute back and forth across the border."

Even the most conservative accounts of Lesotho have no need to deny

Lesotho's early incorporation into a regional industrial economy. Leistner, writing for the Africa Institute of Pretoria, declares that "any meaningful analysis of the territory's economy and prospects must be based on a thorough appreciation of its position as an enclave in the Republic's economy," and speaks of the need to develop an account of the "structural changes in the territory's economy during the past century," including its "transformation into a money economy" and "the integration of its economy into the world economy" (Leistner 1966: 2, 28). The World Bank Report, in sharp contrast to all of the above, seems to deny that these transformations lie in the past at all, and imagines that they will be introduced at some time in the future.

Another point to be underlined in the Preamble is the introduction of an essential vision of what Lesotho is and what it means to be "less developed." We are told, for instance, that 60 percent of the male labor force are working as wage laborers in South Africa, and yet Lesotho "still is, basically" a "traditional subsistence peasant society" – this last presumably a well-known entity. What does it mean to say that a population of proletarians is "basically" a subsistence peasant society? Why would one say such a thing? These are questions to be explored in the later sections of this chapter.

Another interesting feature of the Preamble is the way it treats the question of infrastructure. We are told in the second paragraph that: "At independence there was no economic infrastructure to speak of. Industries were virtually non-existent." This statement is clearly complementary to the notion that Lesotho is an isolated, aboriginal economy, and it is made possible only by a highly circumscribed *geographical conception* of infrastructure and industry. Industry, in this conception, only exists if it lies within national boundaries. So we are told that "Industries were virtually non-existent" and, at the same time, that most of the men were working in industries! Where another observer might say: "By 1966 Lesotho was completely incorporated into an industrial regional economy – sixty percent of the male labor force found employment there," the World Bank Report says: "At independence industries were virtually non-existent." Likewise, for the World Bank, the fact that the railroad was on the far side of the river makes it non-existent, while the 1910 Encyclopaedia article notes that the railroad took Lesotho's grain to market, thus feeding the mining communities and making Lesotho the "granary of the Orange Free State" (see Murray 1981).

The same type of imposed limitation obscures the extent of pene-

35

tration by commercial enterprise. "Whatever commerce there was," we are told dismissively, "was largely in the hands of South African traders" – and that is an end to the discussion of commerce. The implication seems to be that commerce in the hands of foreigners somehow doesn't count; but from very early on virtually all parts of the country were penetrated by South African retailers and traders, whose economic impact was enormous. The same maneuver removes banks from the field of view. The one bank which cannot be discounted due to its association with foreigners, the Post Office Savings Bank, is simply ignored.

The last point to be noted in the Preamble, and perhaps the most obvious, is what we may call the "governmentalist" assumption: the assumption that whatever economic changes have or have not happened in Lesotho are to be explained by reference to Lesotho or Colonial government policy. In this Preamble, and again and again in the Report as a whole, the question of "stage of social and economic development" is reduced to the question of (Lesotho) government policy. The economy appears as a simple reflex of state or colonial policy – when in Lesotho nearly all the determinants of economic life lie outside of the national boundaries. (There is, interestingly enough, hardly any reference to *South African* state policy, which has had far more effect on the economic life of the Basotho than has that of Lesotho.) "There are several reasons why Lesotho has remained at such a low stage of social and economic development," we are told. But only one reason is discussed: "that, until about 1950, the British government did not really attempt to introduce any development."

In fact, the course of Lesotho's economic development was controlled by forces far more powerful than the British colonial administration. But, even accepting the Report's somewhat obsessive focus on government policy as the ultimate causal variable, it is clear that the colonial past was not the featureless void the Report attempts to make of it. We have seen that the early colonial period saw booming agricultural production, as well as the construction of such basic infrastructure as roads, post offices, telephone lines, schools, courts, police stations, and hospitals. But the colonial government was also active in the areas of agriculture and soil conservation in the period prior to 1950. Palmer and Parsons, for instance, no admirers of colonialism, report that:

Famine, erosion, and falling agricultural production prompted government reaction from 1935 onwards. Between 1935 and 1952,

nearly 140,000 hectares of lowland were terraced and 165,000 hectares of mountain were protected from erosion with buffer grass strips, while in 1942 52,379 small dams were built and 18 million trees planted – though most of the trees failed to take root because of drought. Colonial and royal coercion combined finally to "purify" the nation's sheep to merino standard, by eliminating inferior stock from breeding, while 12,000 vegetable plots were established with state encouragement.
(Palmer and Parsons 1977: 25)

These are precisely the sorts of interventions the World Bank and others have promoted in Lesotho in recent years; if Lesotho is poor it is not because no one has ever tried such "development" before. But the World Bank Report, like all "development" discourse on Lesotho, tends toward a picture in which the colonial past is a blank, economic stagnation is due to government inaction, and "development" results from "development" projects. The reasons for this peculiar privileging of government policy in explaining economic processes will be discussed in a later section.

"The Setting"

The first sub-section under this heading, called *"The Country,"* gives a brief geographical summary of the country. This includes an account of Lesotho's severe soil erosion problems, along with the cheery claim that "the technical answers to solve them are there." The section concludes with an inventory of non-agricultural "resources": water, diamonds, and tourism.

"Human resources"

This sub-section offers a brief account of the demographic and health situation, with some statistics on population and population growth. The only point which needs to be underlined here is the Report's dismay over population growth and the pressure it puts on "limited land resources," and its suggestions for a "population policy" which would promote "family planning" and provide "guidance and assistance" to those seeking to migrate out of Lesotho. It is not clear what is meant by this last point, since South Africa permits no permanent settlement of foreign workers, and accepts migrant laborers only on its own terms and in fixed numbers. If the suggestion is, as it appears, that the government should seek to boost the number of temporary workers migrating to South Africa (and how else could the proposed action be part of a "population policy" to ease the pressure on the land?), it is a strange one, since the number of legal migrants is effectively set by the South African authorities.

"Land tenure: an insurmountable obstacle?"

This sub-section contains a discussion of the importance of the traditional land tenure system – in which land is allocated for use, but never bought or sold – as an obstacle to "transforming Lesotho's subsistence society into an agricultural cash economy along Western lines" (World Bank 1975: 9). It is interesting to note that what is assumed in this proposed transformation – apart from the odd idea that a society can be transformed into an economy – is that we are concerned not only with land rights, or even only with agricultural production, but with the introduction of a "cash economy" – something that was done more than a century before the Report was written. The traditional system, we are told, "was adequate for a traditional agricultural society where there were few additional needs to be satisfied beyond pure subsistence and where land was relatively abundant. Since this was the type of society that people had known for a long time, little need for changing the system was felt." Now, with the introduction of a modern, cash economy, the system will have to move by a "slow evolution" toward private ownership. But the picture of the "traditional society" against which these changes are to take place is again fanciful. Land has not been abundant in Lesotho since the 1860s, when so much of it was lost to the Dutch settlers, and "agricultural" Lesotho has had to import maize since the 1920s, although it exported large amounts in the nineteenth century. But in the World Bank scheme, the past is characterized by subsistence, traditional land tenure, and stagnation; in the future lies the cash economy, a "slow evolution of tenurial concepts," and agricultural exports. The Report thus places land tenure in the context of an imaginary transformation from a non-market, subsistence, aboriginal economy to a modern, Western cash economy, when the real twentieth-century transformation is instead from an agricultural export cash economy to a labor export cash economy. Lesotho has not been a "non-market," "subsistence" economy since before the middle 1800s at least.

In the World Bank scheme of things, the reason Lesotho's archaic tenure system has not yet been reformed is because the aboriginal economy itself has not yet been transformed, and this in turn can be traced to a lack of development projects. We are told: "in the absence of agricultural development schemes, it was never demonstrated to the people that anything worthwhile could be achieved on their land; therefore, people saw no need for changes." Once development projects have shown the way, the old tenure system will gradually give way: "[B]y involving chiefs and people from the very outset and showing them that agricultural productivity can, indeed, be increased dramatically on their land, people are prepared to speed up the slow evolution of tenurial concepts, once they are convinced that changes are to their benefit."

"Economic ties with South Africa"

This is one of the most striking sub-sections of the report. The first eight paragraphs of the section deal at some length with the currency and customs union arrangements with South Africa. Then, at the end, one paragraph is added on concerning "other ties," which is worth quoting in full:

Lesotho's economic ties to South Africa go far beyond the monetary and customs area arrangements. South Africa is the main outlet for Lesotho's exports. Only a few of the merchandise exports are consumed in South Africa; three of the four most important export commodities – wool, mohair, and diamonds – are re-exported overseas. Trade statistics do not provide a country-by-country breakdown of merchandise exports, but imports from outside South Africa are probably small. For its outward communications, Lesotho depends on South African rail, air, and telecommunications services. Most of the electricity used in Lesotho is generated in South Africa. Most industries have been developed through South African investment. Lesotho's young tourist industry depends nearly entirely on the South African market. Also, most of the service industries in Lesotho are South African owned. South African companies and individuals dominate insurance, foreign trade, and the domestic wholesale and retail business. Traditionally, South Africa has provided employment to a large portion of Lesotho's labor force. At present, about 60 percent of the male labor force and about 10

percent of the female labor force are working in South Africa. There is no doubt that Lesotho derives significant benefits from its rich neighbor. But on the other hand, it is equally clear that the maneuverability of the government in its economic policies is de facto severely hampered by the country's close ties to South Africa. The government, therefore, is anxious to diversify Lesotho's international relations. It is increasingly seeking more financial and technical assistance from other countries and multi-lateral agencies; it is attempting to attract more private investment from overseas; and it is presently negotiating some form of association with the European Economic community.
(World Bank 1975)

One should note here the two rather staggering sentences about labor, buried as they are in the middle of the last paragraph of the sub-section, and the rapid segue into the pluses and minuses of the exchange relations with the "rich neighbor." This is a characteristic maneuver in "development" discourse on Lesotho: first dividing up a historically structured unity into two separate national entities, then reducing their structural relation to a few "ties" between "neighbors." There will be more to say about this later. The main point for now is that, from the "development" point of view, the currency and customs arrangements seem to be far more important "ties" than anything in the last paragraph. It remains to be explored why this should be so.

"Trends in the economy as a whole"
"Summary"

This sub-section begins with a disclaimer and an assertion:

Economic indicators for Lesotho are scarce and unreliable. The government's own budget statistics are the only reliable information available. Production statistics are virtually non-existent. Whatever indicators there are, however, all point to poverty and stagnation over a long period of time, reflecting the country's poor natural resources and lack of development in the past.
(World Bank 1975)

This passage is worthy of note for its frank description of the quality of the statistics which are used to generate the very precise-looking figures given in the rest of the Report, and especially in the Appendices. We are explicitly told here, for instance, that all the figures on production are based on "virtually non-existent" statistics and "unreliable" information. At the same time, it is interesting to observe that these "virtually non-existent" indicators are used to support the suggestion of "poverty and stagnation over a long period of time, reflecting the country's poor natural resources and lack of development in the past."

"National accounts"

This sub-section opens with a warning that the national account data which follow should be taken "merely as a rough illustration of the economic framework and should be viewed with great caution." The estimates presented are based on recent Bureau of Statistics figures; but we are told that "because of some obvious inconsistencies and omissions, they do not yet provide a basis for serious analysis."

Such cautions notwithstanding, an analysis follows. We are given the table on the following page (Table 2.1) on the industrial origin of the Gross Domestic Product, which is quite remarkable when we recall that we were told only in the last paragraph that "production statistics are virtually non-existent."

For most of the entries on this chart, there is no serious basis for even a rough estimate in any of the available statistical or documentary sources, as the Report has itself noted. What is interesting here is that we are told there is no basis on which production figures can be compiled, and then given a whole page of precise-looking production figures. We will find the same throughout the Report. In "development" discourse, the fact that there are no statistics available is no excuse for not presenting statistics, and even made-up numbers are better than none at all. Later sections will explore why this should be so.

The next point discussed is the difference between GDP and GNP in Lesotho, which requires confronting the subject of remittances from migrant laborers. It is noted, with some surprise, that earnings of migrant workers in South Africa may have totaled R60 million in 1970 ("more than Lesotho's own GDP!"). To figure Gross National Product, it is assumed that 25 percent of those earnings are sent to Lesotho "in one way or another." There appears to be no basis for such an estimate, and it can be nothing more than a wild guess. What information there is on this crucial point indicates that the proportion is a

Table 2.1. *Industrial origin of GDP at factor cost, 1966–1967 and
1970–1971*

	1966/7		1970/1	
	Million rand	Percent of total	Million rand	Percent of total
Rural sector	*25.1*	*63.9*	*25.6*	*60.2*
Agriculture	18.9	48.1	19.1	44.8
Home industries	0.5	1.2	0.5	1.2
Construction	0.5	1.4	0.6	1.4
Ownership of dwellings	4.8	12.3	5.2	12.1
Other services	0.4	0.9	0.3	0.7
Other sectors	*14.1*	*36.1*	*16.9*	*39.8*
Productive sectors	*1.4*	*3.6*	*2.3*	*5.4*
Mining, quarrying	0.7	1.8	0.7	1.7
Manufacturing	0.3	0.8	0.7	1.7
Water, electricity	0.1	0.3	0.3	0.6
Construction	0.3	0.7	0.6	1.3
Service sectors	*12.7*	*32.5*	*14.6*	*34.4*
Commerce, catering, transport, communications	5.5	14.0	5.8	13.6
Financial and professional services	0.4	1.1	0.5	2.8
Ownership of dwellings	1.0	2.6	1.2	2.8
Community services, including government administration	5.4	13.8	6.8	16.0
Other services	0.4	0.9	0.3	0.8
Total	39.2	100.0	42.5	100.0

Source: World Bank 1975.

great deal higher. McDowall (1973) found, on the basis of a sample
survey of 170 returning miners in 1973, that approximately two-thirds
of total cash earnings returned to Lesotho either as cash or goods. Van
der Wiel (1977: 70) estimated on the basis of a 1975 survey that the figure
was 72 percent. Similar figures have been used by the Ministry of
Finance in its official estimates. But the World Bank Report, as we have
seen earlier, systematically minimizes the importance of migrant labor

in the economy of Lesotho. The estimates on remittance reflect this tendency.

The sub-section concludes with a discussion of investment, again giving precise-looking figures for items that are simply not kept track of in any meaningful way (see also World Bank 1975: Appendix Table 2.2).

"Employment"

This sub-section gives statistics on Lesotho's workforce, and describes an increasing trend in the number of men migrating to work in South Africa. What must be noted in this sub-section is, first, that these statistics contain a number of errors and internal contradictions; and secondly, that these mistakes systematically exaggerate the suddenness of the increase in the incidence of migrant labor in such a way as to create an impression of a recent "crisis." The errors and internal contradictions are documented in a footnote.[2] Here it need only be noted that the numbers are not simply off; they are skewed in such a way as to suggest what was claimed in the Preamble: that a "subsistence" economy is breaking down and people are only recently for the first time leaving the land to seek wage labor.

This sub-section also contains a brief reference to the then current wage increases in the mines, along with a proposal to increase cash incomes from farming to the point where they will compete with incomes from mining. This last proposal is worth underlining, for it appears to be wildly unrealistic on the face of it. Farm cash incomes, we are told, in order to keep pace with wages in South Africa, will have to be increased to some R300 a year, from the current average level of "no more than about R20 a year." But in fact, in 1975, when the World Bank Report was published, the average annual wage for black workers in the South African gold mines was R947 and rising fast. In order to keep pace with these wages, cash incomes from farming would have to be increased by nearly 50-fold, and the increase in mine wages would have to be stopped in its tracks. The Report notes, hopefully, that in the tiny Leribe Pilot Project cash incomes from farms were doubled (from R20 to R40), but not only does this fall pathetically short of mine wage levels, it is not even a fair measure of potential agricultural improvement. The increases in income were made possible only by heavily subsidized inputs which could never be replicated on a larger scale. The cost of the project per farm family was about US$290 per year; the actual jump in average family income was about $22 annually (Morss *et al.* 1976: V2: E–23).

"Wages"

This sub-section discusses wage levels in Lesotho. Wages in South Africa are discussed only insofar as they affect wage levels in Lesotho, in spite of the fact that according to the Report's own figures (World Bank 1975: p. 18) more than ten times as many Basotho are in wage employment in South Africa as in Lesotho. There is no discussion of the dramatic wage increases for migrant workers in South Africa which were in progress while the Report was being written, nor even of the effects of these increases on wage levels within Lesotho. The reasons for the Report's ignoring of wage increases in South Africa both as a phenomenon in itself and as a determinant of wages paid in Lesotho are discussed below.

"Income distribution"

This is one of the strangest sub-sections of the entire Report. At the time the Report was written, there existed almost no information on income distribution, at least for the rural areas. Yet we are presented with the following statistics on rural income distribution (see Table 2.2).

The only source given for these figures is the *1970 Census of Agricul-*

Table 2.2. *Distribution of income Rural population*

Percent earned by	Farm income	Total income
Lowest 5%	2	4
Lowest 20%	9	16
Lowest 40%	22	33
Highest 40%	58	47
Highest 20%	33	26
Highest 5%	11	8

Source: World Bank 1975.

Table 2.3. *Distribution of wealth*
Rural population

Percent owned, respectively held by	Cattle	Arable land
Lowest 5%	3	2
Lowest 20%	14	8
Lowest 40%	31	21
Highest 40%	48	61
Highest 20%	26	37
Highest 5%	9	11

Source: World Bank 1975.

ture Report, but the 1970 Agriculture Census (itself riddled with in-accuracies) contained no information about incomes. How did the Report arrive at its figures? First it looked at the distribution of "pro-ductive assets," and found that the distribution is remarkably equal (see Table 2.3). But these statistics look nothing like the ones in the 1970 Census report. Over half of all rural households in Lesotho own no cattle at all according to that report, while the World Bank Report claims that the lowest 40 percent own 31 percent of the cattle. The land figures are similarly garbled. Once the distribution of production assets is arrived at, it is assumed, without any supporting evidence, that households which are poor in terms of the above "productive assets" are those whose members tend to migrate to work in South Africa, and that migrant labor thus equalizes the differences in distribution of "produc-tive assets." Numbers are then invented for the amount of income which the poor families are presumed to receive from this migrant labor, and everything is thus shown to work out to a "remarkably even distri-bution of incomes." But of course since the income from migrant labor is in fact by far the largest source of household income, this equality was assumed from the start, and it could hardly have worked out otherwise (see Turner 1978, ILO 1979 for a discussion).

Thus in place of an income distribution sharply stratified by the question of access to wage labor and remittances, the World Bank Report manages, with some difficulty, to construct a picture of an egalitarian agricultural society with almost no economic differentiation, a society in which migrant labor appears only as a reluctant alternative to farming on the part of those who lack "productive assets." The reasons for such a violent reconstruction will have to be explored in later sections.

"External trade"

This sub-section begins with a stronger than usual disclaimer on the quality of the statistics. Prior to 1970, all data was collected by questionnaires sent to traders, it is stated, and all figures are therefore likely to be underestimated. The available figures are presented, in the form of a table (see Table 2.4). In the second paragraph, however, we are told that

Table 2.4. *Estimated value of imports and exports of goods, 1966–1972 (in million rand)*

	1966	1967	1968	1969	1970	1971	1972
Imports							
Foodstuffs, beverages, tobacco	7.1	5.4	5.5	6.7	7.2	6.9	11.7
Crude materials	0.4	0.4	0.4	0.3	0.3	0.6	0.5
Mineral fuels, etc.	1.0	1.6	1.2	1.4	1.5	1.7	2.4
Animal and vegetable oils	0.2	0.2	0.1	0.1	0.2	0.3	0.4
Chemicals	1.3	1.7	1.7	1.5	1.3	1.8	2.2
Manufactured goods	9.8	10.7	11.3	9.9	8.8	11.9	20.7
Machinery and transport equipment	2.0	2.5	2.6	2.8	3.1	4.1	5.0
Other imports	1.2	1.2	1.2	1.1	0.6	0.7	–
Total	22.9	23.8	23.9	23.9	22.9	28.0	43.0
Exports							
Live animals	0.5	1.2	1.2	0.6	0.8	0.7	0.9
Foodstuffs	0.2	0.5	0.4	0.7	1.1	0.3	0.7
Wool	a/	1.5	1.5	1.4	0.9	0.8	2.0
Mohair	a/	0.5	0.6	0.7	0.6	0.5	1.1
Diamonds	0.7	1.0	0.4	1.2	0.7	0.2	0.2
Other exports	0.2	0.2	0.1	0.2	0.2	0.4	1.1
Total	a/	4.9	4.2	4.9	4.2	3.0	6.1
Trade deficit	a/	18.9	19.7	19.0	18.7	25.0	36.9

a/ No comparable figures available.
Source: World Bank Report 1975: Appendix Table 3.1.

these figures are not credible. They must be rejected, it is argued, for two reasons:

1 It is impossible to reconcile the apparent trade deficit with "known and estimated inflows of remittances, transfers, and capital ... Whatever is known of these flows ... suggests that actual exports must have been at least three times as much as recorded exports." But the figures are inconsistent only because the report has already discounted, for its own reasons, the role of remittances from South Africa (World Bank 1975: 16–17) in its estimates (see discussion above in "National Accounts" on the percentage of wages sent home). Without the report's low estimate of remittances, the size of the trade deficit and its increase over time are both entirely consistent with migrant earnings in RSA. The report has already stated that migrant earnings in RSA were "about R60 million in 1970" (World Bank 1975: 16); if even a third of that amount found its way back to Lesotho, the reported trade deficit for 1970 (R18.7 million) could be accounted for without inventing new export figures. By 1972, the deficit figure had risen sharply to R36.9 million, but this corresponds to a sharp rise in wages for mine workers and a jump in the number of workers recruited in that year.

2 The second argument is based on a perceived contradiction between large numbers of livestock and very low export figures, leading to the claim that it is "almost inconceivable" that exports are not higher than recorded. In moving from the size of the national herd to conclusions about what the export figures must be, it is assumed that the animals are being raised for export, which, as a later chapter will show, they are not.

The sub-section ends up concluding that instead of a huge trade deficit financed by wages earned abroad, as the figures would seem to indicate, there are in fact hidden, unrecorded agricultural exports – making actual exports "at least three times as much as recorded exports" – which make up the apparent trade imbalance. But this assertion is based only upon the unsupported and improbable estimate of remittances discussed above, along with the judgment that a large livestock herd must produce large export returns.

Let there be no misunderstanding: the Report is no doubt right to mistrust the trade figures; they, like most statistics available for Lesotho, should be handled with tongs, if at all. The point of the discussion here is not to defend the GOL statistics but to explore the techniques of theoretical construction which lead the Report to accept *some* funny figures (however unlikely they may appear) while rejecting others in favor of unsupported "estimates." The trade figures contradict the agricultural picture of Lesotho the Report has been straining from the first paragraph to draw, and so they are rejected; meanwhile the estimates on remittances – for which there exists no evidence – are taken as facts which can be used to rebut the offending trade statistics. The picture of Lesotho as a country that exports agricultural products (rather than wage labor) to balance its imports is constructed here not on the basis of flimsy numbers, as in earlier sections, but in contradiction to them.

"Government operations"

This is the longest section so far, which is perhaps the most significant thing about it for our purposes. It is appropriate to say only a few words about this section here, in order to be able to move on to more interesting sections which follow. It is noteworthy, however, that this whole section on "government operations" is in fact almost entirely a discussion of government finances. A major concern is Lesotho's lack of "absorptive capacity" – that is, its inability to raise its level of expenditure fast enough to take advantage of the funds being offered by various donors. There is no reference in the "Government Operations" section to the notorious inefficiency and top-heavyness of the Maseru bureaucracy, and no mention of the well-known corruption in government, although these are clearly recognized in other forms of discourse as important aspects of "government operations" in Lesotho (see, for instance, Wellings 1983).

"The sectors"

There will not be space to explore all of these "sectors" in detail, but it is helpful at least to have a look at what the "sectors" are taken to be. They are: Agriculture, Mining, Water Resources, Manufacturing Industries, Tourism, Transportation, Public Services, Education, and Banking. At first glance, it appears that these "sectors" are not even the same kinds of things. In what way is "Banking" the same class of thing as "Water Resources"? What are they all "sectors" *of*? The economy? But is "transportation" really a sector of Lesotho's economy? Is "water resources"? Where is commerce? What about service industries? As a description of the classes of economic activity in which people in Lesotho are engaged, this classification is inadequate on the face of it. The fact is that these "sectors" have no unity, and in fact make no sense, unless we see them not as a description of an economy, but as a list of things which might potentially be "developed" – possible points of insertion for a "development" agency. I will comment in detail only on agriculture, as it is of special importance to what will follow.

"Agriculture: characteristics of the sector"

In this sub-section, basic facts of geography and cropping patterns are presented, and agricultural practices and trends are described. Crop farming, we are told, "is generally primitive and yields are low." Stock farming, too, provides little return, in spite of a large livestock population, because farmers are not commercially oriented. Cattle are used for ploughing, social obligations, and prestige rather than generating income, while sheep and goats are used for domestic slaughter and, it is stated, "everyday currency," and are often used to pay for "school fees, clothes, government taxes, and so forth." This last claim, that sheep and goats are used as "everyday currency," is fantastical, and hence particularly interesting; it will be discussed in a later section.

The Report goes on to present information on "trends and developments in the agricultural sector," taken from the agricultural censuses of 1950, 1960, and 1970, which "provide a fairly reliable broad picture of overall development and characteristics of the industry" (see Table 2.5).

Table 2.5. *Production and yields of major crops*

Production (thousand metric tons)	1950	1960	1970
Maize	114	111	67
Sorghum	49	54	57
Wheat	50	58	58
Peas	8	12	5
Beans	1	1	4
Crop yields (200-pound bag per acre)			
Maize	5.3	3.7	2.3
Sorghum	4.0	3.8	3.1
Wheat	4.5	3.8	2.4
Peas	4.5	3.3	1.8
Beans	1.5	1.6	1.0

Source: World Bank 1975.

With respect to crops,

> the picture is most alarming. The dramatic decrease in crop yields
> over the two decades is very striking. The total area of arable land has
> remained the same – some 900,000 acres; but the area of land fallow
> decreased from 207,000 acres in 1950 to 95,000 acres in 1970, which
> suggests that (because of the population pressure) land is not properly
> rested at present. The reasons for the sharp decline in yields of all
> crops are progressing soil erosion and bad husbandry practices, which
> have led to depletion of the soil.
> (World Bank 1975)

But the statistics on which this picture of precipitous decline is based
fall apart under even a little scrutiny. The dramatic decline in maize
production shown by the figures – from 214,000 tons (1950) to 121,000
(1960), to 67,000 (1970) – seems to be entirely due to sampling error (see
Figure 2.1).[3]

The figure for maize production from the 1949/50 agricultural census
is clearly very unusual, being approximately twice the highest total for
any of the preceding years. The census report itself acknowledged that
"these estimates are considerably higher than any given in previous
years and are likely to arouse some controversy" (Douglas and Tennant
1952: 81). This is especially so since, as later examination has shown, the
trade figures for 1950 show neither dramatic increases in maize exports
nor diminution of imports, as one might expect if the figures were
accurate (Turner 1978). Even if the census results are accepted, however,
it is clear at a minimum that the 1949/50 season was, as the census report
itself emphasized, "far from typical" (Douglas and Tennant 1952: 29).
All this must cast suspicion not only upon the 1949/50 census, but also
(and especially) on the procedure of drawing sweeping conclusions
from the three sample years 1950, 1960, and 1970. Yet this is one of those
statistics that persists in "development" discourse as if it had a life of its
own. However often the error is exposed (e.g., Turner 1978, ILO1979,
LASA 1978), these same numbers continue to be cited over and over
again, in order to suggest an urgent need to create "development"
programs to respond to the "crisis" in agriculture.

The section on livestock is also based on the agricultural censuses,
although it is acknowledged that "the information on livestock in the
agricultural censuses is thought to be less reliable than the data on
crops." This is a polite way of putting it; in fact, the livestock figures

from the 1970 Census are riddled with the most obvious and gross sorts of internal contradictions. These figures, however, are used to describe not only overall numbers and regional trends, but also to arrive at figures for annual income per household from livestock (1976: 40 [Table 5.3]). This is surprising since the 1970 Census contains no information on incomes. The estimates of annual household income from livestock given in the table cannot be anything but the wildest guesses, though they are given to the penny.

The section concludes with a summary of "the main constraints to development of the small farming units": "lack of knowledge of modern farming practices; lack of credit and marketing facilities; and a shortage of male labor, as well as of draft animals at the time of field preparation and planting" (p. 41). The last two items lead into a short discussion of share-cropping, which is linked not only to lack of male labor and traction, but to lack of credit facilities.

"Government policies and programs"

This sub-section begins with a summary of the agricultural portion of the First Five Year Plan, and ends with a review of the major agricultural "development" projects in Lesotho at the time of the Report. The review of the Five Year Plan is quite straight-forward, but some of the claims made for the "development" projects should be noted.

The Leribe Pilot Project, discussed here in glowing terms, has already been discussed above (see "Employment" pp. 43–4). More important is the large, World Bank funded Thaba Bosiu Rural Development Project. The Report describes the US$12 million project, and gives projections of five-fold increases of household income to come from the improved farming promoted by the project. The yield projection on which such predictions were based, however, have later proved to have been wildly inaccurate. Estimated yields of 1,600 lbs/acre for maize, for instance, were confronted with actual yields for participating farmers of only 358 lbs/acre. At the end of the project period, total yields were actually less than at its start (World Bank 1979 [Project Performance Audit Report]). Given available information indicating marginal returns accruing to investment in agriculture in Lesotho, the audit considers "it is surprising that the whole viability of the project was not seriously questioned during the appraisal review process."

There are also brief references to the Senqu River Project, and a yet to be formulated "major livestock project" to involve the World Bank and CIDA, which will turn out to be the Thaba-Tseka Project.

"Constraints on development"

This is a one-paragraph summary of obstacles to agricultural development. "As in most developing countries, the major constraints on improving agricultural production are tenurial and institutional." Tenure is not at present a major constraint on the improvement of crop production, we are told, but "the future development of the livestock industry in the mountain areas is wholly dependent on tenurial changes ... Speedy enactment and enforcement of the drafted regulations which will make fencing of mountain pastures and rotational grazing possible (see page 11) are absolutely essential to future livestock development" (World Bank 1975: 45).

"Government institutions and services"

This sub-section discusses the need for planning, extension, marketing facilities, and, especially, credit. The Report regards it as obvious that there is a "conspicuous lack of credit for the purchase of farm inputs," and declares that "credit will play a critical role in all future major agricultural projects."

"Outlook for development"

The introduction to this section describes the outlook for funding and implementing government "development" programs, discussing problems of training and "absorptive capacity."

"Financial resources"

This short sub-section is exclusively concerned with internal revenue, foreign assistance, and public debt. Foreign assistance is seen to be plentiful and public debt is low.

"Growth of the economy"

In this sub-section, the prospective "growth of the economy" is seen as a remarkably simple function of the success or failure of the above-mentioned government programs. The Report projects a rate of growth in GDP of 5 percent per annum for the period 1971–9. We are told that this is based on the following assumptions:

1 "[A]gricultural projects lead to a doubling of production in the project area over a gestation period of, say, seven years, which amounts to an annual rate of increase of 10 percent. Agricultural projects presently in execution or being started extend over some 10 percent of the country's farmland. If the government manages to extend the coverage to some 50 percent by the 1979–80 period, the growth of total agricultural output may then accelerate to 5 percent a year."
2 "In mining, the mission assumes the establishment of a medium-size diamond mine as well as rehabilitation and encouragement of small-scale diamond production by local diggers."
3 In manufacturing, a 15 percent growth rate is assumed, which is "an extrapolation of what might have been the growth rate in manufacturing in the last three years."
4 "The services sector," it is estimated, "could grow at a rate of 5 to 6 percent a year, mainly as a result of tourism development and of an expansion of government administration and services."

In retrospect, what is surprising in these estimates, apart from the wildly overoptimistic projections for the ability of agricultural development projects to boost production (no development project in Lesotho has ever come anywhere close to doubling the total production of a region),[4] is the failure to take any account of the role of wages for migrant workers in South Africa in stimulating economic growth. The Report was written at a time when wages were being dramatically increased (see Table 4.2 in Chapter 4), and the actual growth being registered in GDP in the middle seventies was directly attributable to those increases. It was not agriculture or mining that led to expanding GDP – both were stagnant over the period, or even lost ground – but a boom in retail trade, construction, and service industries reflecting the influx of cash earned in South Africa. The Government's Third Five Year Plan, reviewing the period, noted: "The principal expansionary factors in the economy remained expenditure by migrant workers, foreign aid, and customs revenue inflows, all of which induced secondary economic activity in building and construction, the service sector, and central Government . . . The unforeseen growth of the construction sector, commerce, catering, and Government services accounts for most of the increase in GDP" (GOL 1980: 7, 31). Yet the World Bank Report's forecast of economic growth in the economy pays no attention

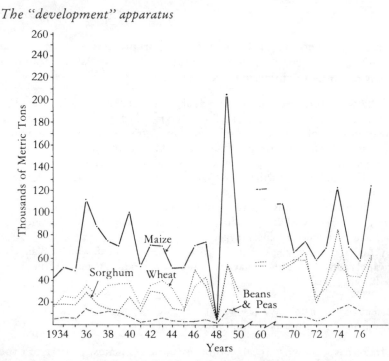

Figure 2.1. Crop production in Lesotho – 1934–1976. *Source*: LASA 1978: VI–4.

to the impact of wages in South Africa, even when discussing possible growth in the service sector, whose modest projected growth rate is seen "mainly as a result of tourism development and of an expansion of government administration and services."

It is only in the second part of the concluding sub-section that migrant labor makes its first appearance, in the discussion on employment. The Report remarks on "how vulnerable the stability of Lesotho's economy and society is to conditions in South Africa over which Lesotho's government has no control," and observes that under any circumstances "a substantial number of Basotho will continue to work in South Africa." Since this is so, it is suggested that in addition to attempting to create employment opportunities in agriculture, the government should consider training its workers for more skilled, high-paying jobs in the South African economy. This is something that the three technical schools in Lesotho have in fact been doing for many years now, albeit unintentionally. But as such training is likely to encourage rather than discourage out-migration, to encourage rather than discourage the neglect of agriculture, this final recommendation seems peculiarly out of touch with the rest of the Report.

The "less developed country"

The peculiar representation of Lesotho which emerges from the World Bank Report must not be understood as simply the product of mistakes or errors. There are, indeed, mistakes and errors in the Report just reviewed, and there are nearly as many in most other such reports. But these mistakes and errors are always of a particular kind, and they almost invariably tend in predictable directions. The statistics are wrong, but always wrong in the same way; the conceptions are fanciful, but it is always the same fantasy. This section will describe the version toward which all "development" discourse on Lesotho seems to tend, the picture of Lesotho as a species of a well-known genus, the genus "Less Developed Country," or LDC.

The idea that Lesotho is "less developed" brings together and confuses the two possible usages of the word "development" which were discussed in Chapter 1. In the first sense, one speaks of "development" as a progression toward a known end point, usually modern industrial capitalism. Thus people speak of the development of the forces of production, the development of "modern society," the development of capitalism, and so on. In the second sense, so much in vogue in the late 1970s, "development" is taken to mean improvement in quality of life or standard of living, and the elimination or alleviation of poverty. It should be clear upon inspection that the development of capitalism and the elimination of poverty are, if not positively antithetic (as many neo-Marxists argue), at any rate not identical. But it seems to be a theoretical necessity in "development" discourse (for reasons to be explored shortly) for the two notions of "development" to be co-present and even conflated. This is nowhere more apparent than in the definition of countries full of poor people as "less developed countries."

The implicit argument is of the sort known to logicians as a fallacy of equivocation, of the form: (1) all banks have money; (2) every river has two banks; therefore, (3) all rivers have money. The fallacy, of course, consists in changing the meaning of one of the terms of the syllogism in the middle of the implication. The "development" version goes as follows: (1) poor countries are (by definition) "less developed"; (2) less developed countries are (by another definition) those which have not yet been fully brought into the modern economy; therefore, (3) poor countries are those which have not yet been fully brought into the modern economy.

In the process of theoretically constituting Lesotho as an LDC, there is a strong tendency for the characteristics outlined below to be attributed to the country by "development" discourse. The attribution of these characteristics has already been shown in the analysis of the World Bank Report. They are here presented more systematically, with additional illustrations taken from other authoritative texts of the "development" establishment, under four headings, summarizing the essential features of the "development" representation of Lesotho as LDC.

The aboriginal economy

In "development" discourse, Lesotho appears as an aboriginal economy, "virtually untouched," as the World Bank Report claimed, "by modern economic development." The claim is not always so extreme, but there is always a tendency to explain the poverty of the Basotho by positing a backward, primordial, unpenetrated economy, which is "less developed" because it has not yet been brought into the modern world economy. The economy is "subsistence" – although almost nobody is in fact able to "subsist" on what they grow – and is contrasted to a "modern, cash economy." It is imagined that the country has remained somehow cut off from the cash economy, and it is sometimes even suggested, as in the World Bank Report, that livestock constitute "everyday currency" – as if Lesotho were some sort of pre-monetary economy and livestock a kind of primitive money. Indeed, I was actually told by a "development" expert working for the EEC that the reason Basotho were so reluctant to sell their cattle was that they did not yet understand or trust paper money. In the "development" version of things, "less developed" means historically retarded, and poverty appears as a result of not yet having been introduced to the modern world. This is, of course, only the specific application to Lesotho of a much more general "development" dogma – that, as a World Bank policy paper put it (World Bank 1975: 3), rural "development" is "concerned with the modernization and monetization of rural society and with its transition from traditional isolation to integration with the national economy."

In this perspective, one great problem is isolation. If Lesotho is undeveloped because it has been an unpenetrated backwater, "virtually untouched by modern economic development," then developing it requires connecting it with the rest of the world and establishing the modern prerequisites to progress. This means, first of all, roads and communications. It is astonishing how much importance "development" accounts seem to place on roads. It is imagined, for instance, that "farm to market roads" will make possible a transition from "subsistence farming" to commercial production for export, and thus almost by themselves transform "traditional" agriculture (see, for instance, USAID 1978: 68; also material to be presented later from the Thaba-Tseka Project). The problem, of course, is that in the "farm to market" scheme, Lesotho is the market, not the farm. "Agricultural" Lesotho is in fact a heavy *importer* of food, livestock, and just about everything else, and building roads most often simply lowers the price of imported South African food, making it harder than ever for local farmers to grow crops profitably (cf. Chapter 8 below).

In the emphasis on roads, one can see not only an assumption that farmers in Lesotho are potential exporters, but also the assumption that the failure to produce saleable surpluses up to now is due to the absence of opportunities for selling agricultural goods – hence the importance of markets. One sometimes gets the impression reading "development" reports on Lesotho that markets are some sort of remarkable new invention which are being introduced to Lesotho for the first time. In fact, as I have shown, Basotho have been marketing crops and livestock, often in very great quantities, since the 1840s, and those with surpluses to sell have always known how to go about selling them. That Lesotho is no longer able to produce such surpluses today is very sad, but it can hardly be blamed on a failure to "introduce markets," or on a lack of contact with the wider market economy. Yet it is regularly assumed in the "development" literature that the reason people are not selling crops or livestock is simply that they have never had the opportunity to do so: the introduction of markets to Lesotho-as-LDC will stimulate production of crops and livestock, and will even bring about de-stocking, as people have for the first time the opportunity to dispose of their worthless animals (see USAID 1978; also FAO/World Bank 1975 and other planning documents of the Thaba-Tseka Project).

A similar emphasis is placed on the provision of credit. In an LDC, where the cash economy is on such a precarious basis, there must be "a conspicuous lack of credit for the purchase of farm inputs," and it is obvious that "credit will play a critical role in all future major agricultural projects" (World Bank 1975: 45–6). It is never explained exactly why the need for credit is so critical. It is true that most Basotho invest very little in agriculture – probably due to their intelligent appreciation of the low potential and high risks of capital intensive farming in Lesotho – but this is usually not a matter of being unable to obtain the cash to make such an investment. Most families have access to wage-earnings or remittances, and this money most commonly comes in large lumps which could easily be used for agricultural inputs, but for the most part is not. Yet in the "development" picture, the need for credit is almost an axiom. Needing credit is part of what it means to be an LDC.

One final feature of the "aboriginal" portrait drawn by "development" discourse is that the less developed society is "traditional." People's attitudes and values are not yet in harmony with modern economic life. Whether they take the form of backward land tenure laws or reluctance to sell livestock, "social/traditional constraints" stand in the way of change. "The traditional Basotho value structure is conservative" (USAID 1978: 3, 53). Achieving "development" is thus largely a matter of changing values and attitudes, of winning over individual Sotho hearts and minds. In its extreme forms, "development" discourse sometimes even speaks as if the problem of poverty is all in the head – as if impoverished villagers could escape their condition by a simple change of attitude or intellectual conversion (cf. Chapter 3, p. 86, Chapter 8, pp. 234–235). The religious imagery suggested by the common self-description of teams of "development" experts as "missions" is thus well sustained in their search for "converts."

The peasant society

The premise of all "development" analysis of Lesotho is that it is a stagnated agricultural peasant economy which requires only the correct technical inputs to become "developed." It has been shown that the World Bank Report systematically exaggerates the importance of agriculture and ignores the role of Lesotho as a labor reserve. But this is not unusual; "development" reports regularly twist their words, and often their numbers as well, to make Lesotho fit the picture of the "peasant society." This means not only that the importance of wage labor is understated, but that a particular image of "peasant agriculture" is systematically promoted.

We have seen how the World Bank Report conjured up statistics to support a picture of an egalitarian society of small farmers with almost no economic differentiation, in which migrant labor appears only as a reluctant alternative to farming on the part of those who lack "productive assets." Migrant labor, in this view, tends to be seen as a recent and alarming manifestation of a "crisis" in subsistence agriculture. The World Bank Report uses bad statistics, we have seen, to try to show an extremely sudden and precipitous drop in agricultural production in recent years (see "*Characteristics of the Sector*" in the "Agriculture" section); at the same time numbers are twisted to exaggerate the suddenness and extent of the recent increases in migrant labor (see "*Employment*" in "Trends in the Economy as a Whole"). The drift is always toward a picture in which migrant labor is a recent response to a crisis in agriculture, an inessential feature somehow added on after the fact to an existing peasant economy.

This picture is encountered again and again in "development" reports. "Agriculture is the backbone of the economy" we are told. "Agriculture supports 85 percent of the population." These statements occur again and again, no matter how many times they are shown to be fallacious, for there is something almost necessary in these overstated claims for agriculture, something which allows even the most obvious exaggerations to pass without notice. Thus one joint FAO/World Bank report, giving background for a proposed livestock project, solemnly states that "about 70 percent of the GNP comes from the sale of pastoral products, mainly wool and mohair" (FAO/World Bank 1975: Annex 1, p. 7), when a more conventional figure would be 2 or 3 percent. Elsewhere (FAO/World Bank 1975: Annex 5, p. 9), the report claims, more soberly, that all of agriculture accounts for 70 percent of GDP, but even this contrasts with the usual estimates of about 40 percent. (The latest, corrected official statistics [GOL 1987: 19] give the figure for 1975 as just 32.5 percent.)

In "development" discourse, Basotho are, by decree, "farmers." Even people with no land and no animals are "farmers." The World Bank Report declares (World Bank 1975: 39): "There are about 187,500 farm households in Lesotho. Of those, some 185,000 have land for crop cultivation. The majority of the landless farm households own some livestock which is grazed on communal land." In what respect are the remainder, who have no land and no livestock, "farm households"? Another report (Thaba-Tseka 1981b) remarks: "Of the total of 34 farmers surveyed it was found that 29 were farmers (main income from farming) ..." There are no unemployed in Lesotho, according to the table on employment in the USAID Country Strategy Statement (USAID 1978: Table 10), since anyone without a job is defined as a subsistence farmer. When people fail to act like farmers, this reflects ignorance and "traditional" attitudes. Hence the almost magical potential powers ascribed to agricultural extension in the "development" literature.

This need to construct a picture of an agricultural country accounts for the otherwise inexplicable hostility of "development" discourse to improvements in wages and living standards for Lesotho's workers. The wage increases on the mines of the middle 1970s are nearly always interpreted as a threat to agriculture and hence as an obstacle to "development." Several "development" experts told me that Lesotho would be better off if employment at the mines were closed to Basotho, as this would redirect manpower into agriculture and force "farmers" to take "development" more seriously. This is an incredible thing to hear when one knows that only something like 6 percent of average household income derives from crop farming, and it is certain such a measure would lead to mass starvation, but it is intelligible within the mythology of the "development" discourse. See Figure 2.2, an extremely revealing chart by an FAO economist (in Senqu 1978) which claims to illustrate, among other things, how the fact that the population is "relatively well fed, well sheltered, and well clothed" is an obstacle to "agricultural development." (One should also note that the six starting points for the explanation of "how, economically, Lesotho became what she is today" effectively exclude from the field of view all historical, structural, and political causes in favor of technical, "traditional," and geographic ones.)

The national economy

The "development" paradigm insists on taking the country as the basic unit of analysis. It is always "Lesotho's problems," "Lesotho's options," "Lesotho's dependence on South Africa," and "Lesotho's economy." A national economy is a necessary attribute of an LDC, and it is this national economy that is either rich or poor, developed or undeveloped.

"What should they do?" an earnest "development" expert in Maseru once asked me as we discussed my experience in rural Lesotho. "What should who do?" I wanted to know. "Lesotho," he replied. "Do you mean the government?" I asked. The man looked confused for an instant, then said, more emphatically, as if I had not heard him the first time, "Lesotho."

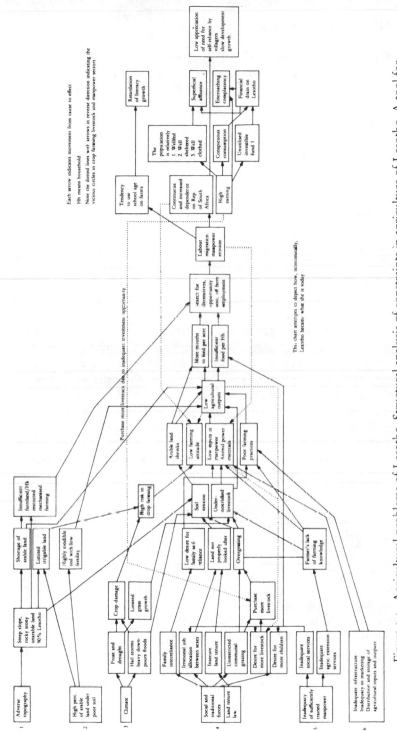

Figure 2.2. Agricultural problems of Lesotho. Structural analysis of constraints in agriculture of Lesotho. A tool for agricultural development planning. *Source*: Tesfa Guma, FAO Farm Management Economist, Senqu River Agricultural Development Project, January 1977.

"What should Lesotho do?" This is always the question in "development" talk, but consider the range of different questions which lie unexplored beneath: "What should the elite clique that rules Lesotho do?", or "What should the mineworkers do?", or "What should the political opposition do?", or "What should the aid agencies do?", or "What should the unemployed do?", or any number of other questions. By posing all problems and issues that might come up as problems of "national development" – in a country like Lesotho, literally everything is treated as an "aspect" of "development" – the problematic avoids the formulation of any issue, problem, or program for action based on entities other than the state, effectively excluding from the field of view both conflicts within the nation and forces which transcend it.[5] One sees the same type of thing in the United States and elsewhere, with talk of "the nation's problems," what is "good for the economy," and so on, of course. But in Lesotho there is hardly any other basis for official discourse than this nation-fetishized "development" talk.

But it is not only that the country is conceived as a quasi-individual; it is also conceived as an economy. Lesotho, as an LDC, is taken to constitute a natural economic unit, responsive to national economic planning, and entering into relations with South Africa only as one economy with another. A national economy, in this scheme, is rich or poor according to the natural resources that lie within its boundaries (together, of course, with the extent to which they have been "developed"). Thus poverty in an LDC is a matter of some combination of geography and "lack of development," and in Lesotho geography has been inexplicably unkind (see Figure 2.2). "Poverty in Lesotho is primarily resource related," the AID report tells us (USAID 1978: 45). As a poor country with a small resource base and an over-large population, Lesotho must enter into dependent relations with its richer "neighbor," hence Lesotho's "dependence" on South Africa.

Geography may seem a strange way to go about explaining why one group of people is poor while its neighbors are rich. After all, we would not seek to explain why the people in the South Bronx are poor by noting that the South Bronx lacks natural resources and contains more people than its land base can support. The South Bronx is a slum, and that is a social fact, not a geographical one. But for "development," an LDC must be looked at as a national economy, and Lesotho is thus not an impoverished labor reserve, but a "dependent" national economy. This generates some peculiar sorts of explanations.

In the oddly geographical, "national economy" conception of things, for instance, it is rarely asked *why* Lesotho is resource-poor (the answer of course is that most of the good Sotho land was taken by "neighboring South Africa") or *why* it has the peculiar national boundaries it does (the answer being that it was created as a "native reserve" and labor pool for the South African economy). History as well as politics is swept aside, and the relationship between the two "national economies" of Lesotho and South Africa is seen as one of accidental geographic juxtaposition, not structural integration or political subordination. Remember the "Preamble" to the World Bank Report (cited on page 31ff. above), which described migration as a recent consequence of population growth and stagnation, with the destination of that migration ("neighboring South Africa") appearing as a simple accident of geography. The boundaries of Lesotho are taken to define a "society" with a corresponding "economy," and the only relevant relation with South Africa is one of "dependence" of one national economy upon another, as a secondary and derivative fact.

In reality, of course, the "country" of Lesotho only came into existence and took its current boundaries in the course of the formation of a particular form of regional economic organization, into which it was forced as a labor reserve (see Murray 1981). The delimitation of Lesotho's current boundaries was an integral part of the process of creating an African working class (with its distinctive characteristic of being tied to a rural base). In the "development" version, the resultant and secondary fact of political boundaries is taken as the starting point for understanding "labor migration" as a kind of exchange between two "countries" or two "national economies," when in fact the form of regional economic organization was the central issue in a historical struggle which started before there was such a thing as a "country" of Lesotho and ultimately created the modern state of Lesotho as, from the very start, a labor reserve. The fact of economic subjugation is primary, the political boundaries incidental to that. This is clear if we consider what would happen if Lesotho were incorporated (or had been long ago) into South Africa as a Bantustan. At a stroke, there would be no more "ties" with South Africa, no more "national dependence," no more labor leaving "the country." But economically, very little indeed would be changed.

The procedure implicitly employed by "development" discourse on this point is the following: take a geographically defined part of the regional economy, treat it as a self-contained "national economy," note that it functions imperfectly as such due to its "dependence" on the whole, and blame that dependence on the geographical definition with which one began. But one could perform precisely the same exercise for the South African Bantustan of Basotho Qwa-qwa, for instance, and conclude, as the World Bank did for Lesotho (World Bank 1975: 13), that "there is no doubt that Qwa-qwa derives significant benefits from its rich neighbor." As long as the question is "Why is Qwa-qwa (as a national economy) poor?" then one must point to lack of resources, overpopulation, and "dependence." If one asks instead why the people who live in Qwa-qwa are poor (and why they live in Qwa-qwa!), one generates a rather different sort of answer, of course: a long sad tale of conquest, land loss, forced removals, influx control, repression, denial of political rights, depressed wages, and enforced "redundancy." But there is little room for these kinds of questions and answers in "development" discourse, for reasons yet to be explored.

Governmentality

In "development" discourse, Lesotho, as an LDC, tends to be presented as the possessor of an economy which is not only defined in national terms, but is also almost perfectly responsive to national government policy. The "development" of a national economy tends to be seen as something which comes about as a result of "development" planning and "development" projects, while a lack of "development" can only be the result of government neglect. In the Preamble to the World Bank Report, the only reason given for "why Lesotho has remained at such a low stage of social and economic development" is that, "until about 1950, the British government did not really attempt to introduce any development." "Development" discourse does not usually assume that government has absolute and total control, of course, but it does systematically tend to produce analyses which suggest that that which is under state control is determinant, while that which lies beyond its control is secondary.

In its economic projections, for instance, the World Bank Report considers that whether the GNP goes up or down is a simple function of whether or not the current five-year "development" plan is well implemented, and has nothing to do with whether or not the mineworkers get a raise this year. Among the "ties" with South Africa, the most important by far seem to be the Customs Union and the currency arrangements – the "ties," that is, which are most subject to control by Lesotho government policy. Agricultural production in Lesotho is low, according to the World Bank Report, because, "in the absence of agricultural development schemes, it was never demonstrated to the people that anything worthwhile could be achieved on their land; therefore, people saw no need for changes" (World Bank 1975: 9). The key variable, in the governmentalist construct, is the presence or absence of agricultural development schemes. (One might observe, of course, that in the booming agricultural export economy of the nineteenth century, when prices and land availability were favorable and Lesotho was known as the "granary of the Orange Free State", "the people" somehow managed to understand "what could be achieved on their land" even without the miraculous agricultural development schemes.) In the most extreme versions, the entire economy of Lesotho appears as a reflex of state policy – a representation, of course, which reserves an extraordinarily important place for policy and "development" planning.

The state itself, meanwhile, tends to appear as a machine for implementing "development" programs, an apolitical tool for delivering social services and agricultural inputs and engineering economic growth. Military metaphors – successful "operations," well-executed "attacks" and "assaults" on "targets," etc. – abound, and the image is of a single, unitary, righteous army doing battle against a universal enemy. Issues involving the political character of the state and its class basis, the uses of official position and state power by the bureaucratic elite, the functions of bureaucratic "inefficiency" and corruption – matters which are central to academic understandings of modern African states – are nowhere to be found in the "development" version of Lesotho. The state represents "the people," and mention of the undemocratic nature of the ruling government, or of the political opposition, is studiously avoided. "Parliament," the USAID report of 1978 tells us, "representing the people of the country, has a key role in policy formulation through its authority for approval of development plans and annual budget estimates" (USAID 1978: 4). The World Bank report, for its part, makes literally no mention of politics. In the extreme "development" representation, the state has no interests except "development," and Jonathan's authoritarian government is even seen as attempting to empower the poor through programs of "popular participation." Where "bureaucracy" is seen as a problem, it is not a political matter, but the unfortunate result of poor organization or lack of training. Organizational reform and education are remedies. In Lesotho as LDC, the bureaucratic apparatus, like the economy, responds unambiguously to the directives of planners, and the state machinery has policies, but no politics.

Even outside of the state, politics is conspicuous by its absence. "The people" tend to appear as an undifferentiated mass, a collection of "individual farmers" and "decision makers." The impression of an egalitarian "peasant society" is actively promoted, as for instance in the World Bank's discussion on income distribution, and "the farmers" are distinguished from one another only by their relative receptiveness to "new ideas" and "development" (hence "lead farmers," "progressive farmers," etc.). Political parties almost never appear, and the explicitly political role played by "development" institutions such as the Village Development Committees is ignored or concealed (World Bank 1975: 10; cf. Chapter 8 page 247, below).

At the end of this involved process of theoretical construction, Lesotho can be represented in "development" discourse as a nation of farmers, not wage laborers; a country with a geography, but no history; with people, but no classes; values, but no structures; administrators, but no rulers; bureaucracy, but no politics. Political and structural causes of poverty in Lesotho are systematically erased and replaced with technical ones, and the "modern," capitalist, industrialized nature of the society is systematically understated or concealed. One arrives at a picture of a basically agricultural economy which, although potentially prosperous, is now producing under primitive, ancient conditions lacking basic infrastructure and modern techniques, and so has been unable to accommodate recent population growth.

Impediments to "development" of the "national economy" are thus located in lack of roads and markets, lack of training and education, lack of agricultural inputs, unfamiliarity with a money economy, lack of credit, etc. Problems which loom largest in other, non-"development" accounts, such as structural unemployment, influx control, low wages, political subjugation by South Africa, parasitic bureaucratic elites, and so on, simply disappear. In the course of being run through the theoretical machine of "development," an impoverished labor reserve becomes a "traditional, subsistence, peasant society"; wage laborers become farmers; the determinations of South African state and capital over the economic life of the Basotho disappear; and a government of entrenched elites becomes an instrument for empowering the poor.

It should be clear at this point that this particular theoretical construction continues to be produced and reproduced, in the face of massive and well-known contradictory evidence, for good and necessary reasons. I shall explore these reasons in the following section.

"Development" as discursive regime: mechanisms of closure

If it is true that "development" discourse on Lesotho characteristically constructs a unique and – to the academic – strange and distorted picture of the country, one must inquire as to why that should be so. One needs to know not only why statements are acceptable in "development" discourse that would be considered absurd in academic settings, but also why many acceptable statements from the realm of academic discourse – or even from that of common observation – fail to find their way into the discursive regime of "development."

Is it the case that we have a closed system of knowledge, an *episteme*, in Foucault's sense? Clearly not. We can see that "development" discourse does operate within a familiar broad contemporary configuration of Western knowledge (though it is of course not possible to analyze that contemporary *episteme* here). And it is easy to trace the lineage of many of its characteristic lines of thought – from modernization theory, for instance, or neo-classical economics. But tracing the origins of particular elements of "development" thought does not explain the observed difference. "Development" is not a different intellectual tradition, insulated from a second, discrete "academic tradition," and "development" experts are not incapable of thinking the thoughts that academics think. They are trained in the same way as academics, and many report-writing "development" consultants are themselves academics; most surely know how to think and write as academics. As different as they are, "development" discourse and academic discourse draw on a common stock of ideas and traditions. They do not exist in two different epistemological worlds.

But, if the two discourses operate within virtually identical epistemic constraints, how is it that "development" discourse comes to have its distinctive regularities? Where, if not from the *episteme*, do the "rules" come from? As long as one treats discursive practices as autonomous (Foucault 1976), the answer to this question must remain mysterious. As Dreyfuss and Rabinow (1983: 79–85) have argued, discursive regularities or "rules of formation" cannot be elevated to causal principles. What is needed instead is a way of connecting observed discursive regularities to non-discursive practices and institutions (as Foucault did in later work). This suggests at least the beginnings of an answer to our question. What changes when we move from academic discourse to "development" is not the library of available thoughts, but the institutional context into which both discourse and thought are inserted.

A very simple example will illustrate what this means. "Development" discourse in the period under review made no reference to local politics in Lesotho, or to the fact that the ruling government was unpopular and unelected. This was not something which is unknown to the "development" writers; it was however something that was necessarily left unspoken in a World Bank Report. In a more subtle way, there are a host of statements and lines of thought which are, if not actually forbidden, at any rate profoundly unhelpful in the discourse of a "development" agency. Writers who produce such discourse would not necessarily be censored or suppressed, as would the unfortunate who mentioned local politics, but they would find their analyses quickly dismissed and discarded as useless, as indeed they would be.

Colin Murray, perhaps the most respected academic social scientist to have written on Lesotho, concludes his monograph with the following words:

The Basotho have a justifiable pride in their long tradition of national resistance. But they are faced with larger and very difficult questions in the years to come. Can they develop a full historical consciousness of the structural processes which gave rise to the labour reserves? Can they transcend the social and political divisions which are explicit in the strategy of ethnic nationalism and implicit in the "constellation of Southern African states" envisaged by South African prime minister P. W. Botha? In so doing, can they help to give political expression to the interests of southern Africa's rural proletariat as a whole? The answers to these questions will depend, in the first place, upon the evolving character of the post-colonial state. Subordinate as it is to the interests of foreign capital, and preoccupied as it is with repressing or co-opting internal opposition, the strategic possibilities for change, conceived within the confines of Lesotho's national autonomy, are very narrow. In the second place, therefore, the answers to the larger questions will depend upon the developing struggle within South Africa itself.
(Murray 1981: 177)

Such a conclusion is well supported by everything we know about Lesotho, but the fact is that the guide to action that it suggests for those who are concerned to help bring about progressive change in Lesotho is of absolutely no use to an institution such as the World Bank. An academic analysis is of no use to a "development" agency unless it provides a place for the agency to plug itself in, unless it provides a charter for the sort of intervention that the agency is set up to do. An analysis which suggests that the causes of poverty in Lesotho are political and structural (not technical and geographical), that the national government is part of the problem (not a neutral instrument for its solution), and that meaningful change can only come through revolutionary social transformation in South Africa has no place in "development" discourse simply because "development" agencies are not in the business of promoting political realignments or supporting revolutionary struggles.

Even academic authors whose conclusions are not so political as Murray's fail to provide the charter or justification for "development" interventions that "development" institutions require from an analysis. Consider the conclusion to a recent social science textbook on Lesotho:

> Finally, let us step back from these speculations about possible futures and reiterate what we see as the most likely future. It is, regrettably, grim for the bulk of the Basotho. Lesotho will continue to be governed by autocratic and sporadically repressive regimes, with domestic politics characterized by sharp dissension and occasional violence. The country will remain heavily dependent economically on South Africa, with migrant earnings the mainstay of the economy. Inequalities of income and wealth will become more severe, and the poor – especially those without access to migrant earnings or local cash wage jobs – will become more impoverished. Industrial development will be slow and halting, and tourism stagnant and discouraged by political instability and the symptoms of growing urban poverty. This is a bleak prognosis, and we hope the Basotho will find a way to avoid it. It is difficult, however, to see what that way might be.
> (Bardill and Cobbe 1985: 200–1)

Once one sees why "unhelpful" analyses like these are banished, it is easy to see why certain other sorts flourish under the "development" regime. For an analysis to meet the needs of "development" institutions, it must do what academic discourse inevitably fails to do; it must make Lesotho out to be an enormously promising candidate for the only sort of intervention a "development" agency is capable of launching: the apolitical, technical "development" intervention. The "development" intervention is a highly standardized operation. The forms of rural intervention available to "development" agencies (irrigation schemes, crop authorities, credit programs, integrated rural development programs, etc.) come, as Williams (1986: 12) has noted, as "large standardized packages," "exported from one country to another and from one continent to another." "Development" agencies are in the business of trying to "sell" these packages, trying to locate and justify potential applications for them. As Tendler has shown, a prime institutional need of the agencies and the bureaucrats is to "move money" (Tendler 1975: 88–90), to spend the money they have been charged with spending, and to put their resources into action. Their problem is to find the right kind of problem; the kind of "problem" that requires the "solution" they are there to provide. This is the institutional context within which "development" discourse is located.

move money

The analysis that is most helpful to a "development" agency, then – and the one that will naturally rise to the top of authoritative "development" discourse – is the one that "moves the money," the one that presents Lesotho as a likely target for the standard "development" intervention, and serves as a charter to justify and legitimate the sort of programs that the bureaucratic establishment is there to execute. Other representations may of course occur in "development" discourse, but they will be less useful, and hence less used. Through a kind of conceptual "natural selection," the theoretical apparatus of "development" thus always tends toward the representation of Lesotho as an entity, the LDC, which may be defined as the ideal country that, in order to become prosperous and solve all its problems, requires precisely those things which "development" agencies are set up to provide. The discursive regime of "development" thus inevitably ends up reconstructing Lesotho, sometimes almost unrecognizably, as a generic "LDC" – a country with all the right deficiencies, the sort that "development" institutions can easily and productively latch on to.

The homogenizing results of such representations can be almost comical – many reports on Lesotho look as though they would work nearly as well with the word "Nepal" systematically substituted for "Lesotho." But the complexity of the work of recasting – the difficulty of fitting the troublingly particular details into the pre-given, generic grid – should not be minimized. Given the complexity of the task, and the refractory quality of the empirical object, the process of construction of the "LDC" is bound to differ from place to place. I have shown some of the characteristic maneuvers used in this construction in the Lesotho context, but, in different countries, different theoretical maneuvers are no doubt required to produce a usable representation of the object. Indeed, even in Lesotho, the techniques used in the World Bank Report do not represent the only possible solution to the puzzle of how to represent Lesotho in such a way as to maximize the potential role of "development" agencies. They are, however, in fact characteristic of the methods most commonly used in "development" discourse on Lesotho in the period under review.

To sum up: the most important theoretical premises in the construction of the "development" representation of Lesotho, together with their institutional rationales, are the following:

First, it must be *aboriginal*, not yet incorporated into the modern world, so that it can be transformed by roads and infrastructure, education, the introduction and strengthening of the cash economy (as against the "traditional subsistence sector"), and so on. A representation which failed to mask the extent of Lesotho's penetration by the "modern" capitalist regional economy of Southern Africa would be unable to provide a convincing justification for the "introduction" of roads, markets, and credit, as it would provide no grounds for believing that such innovations could bring about the "great transformation" to a "developed," "modern" economy. Indeed, such a representation would tend to suggest that such measures for "opening up" the country and exposing it to "the cash economy" would have little impact at all, since isolation from the world economy has never been Lesotho's problem.

Secondly, it must be *agricultural*, so that it can be "developed" through agricultural improvements, rural development projects, extension, and technical inputs. A representation in which Lesotho appeared as a labor reserve for South African mining and industry, and in which migrant wage labor was recognized as the basis of Basotho livelihood would leave the "development" agencies with almost no role to play. The World Bank mission to Lesotho is in no position to formulate programs for changing or controlling the South African mining industry, and it has no disposition to involve itself in the political challenges to the South African system of labor control known as *apartheid*. It is in an excellent position, however, to devise agricultural improvement projects, for the agricultural resources of Lesotho lie neatly within its jurisdiction and always present themselves as waiting to be "developed." For this reason, they tend to move to center stage in "development" accounts, and Lesotho thus becomes a nation of farmers.

71

Thirdly, it must constitute a *national economy*, in order to support the idea of national economic planning and nation- and sector-based economic programs. In a representation in which this notion of national economy is absent, the economic center of gravity is seen as lying squarely within South Africa, and thus as inaccessible to a "development" planner in Lesotho. Without the idea that Lesotho's boundaries define a national economy, no great claims can be made for the ability of programs based in Lesotho to bring about the sort of transformation "development" agencies claim to be able to bring about. The "development" apparatus unconsciously selects for representations in which it appears possible for "development" agencies to deliver the goods they are set up to promise.

Fourthly, it must be subject to the principle of *governmentality*. That is, the main features of economy and society must be within the control of a neutral, unitary, and effective national government, and thus responsive to planners' blueprints. If a representation for any reason tends to suggest that the "problems" of a country lie beyond the reach of national government policy, then it at the same time tends to deny a role to "development" agencies in addressing those problems. Because "development" agencies operate on a national basis, and because they work through existing governments and not against them, they prize representations which exaggerate the power of national policy instruments, and have little use for representations which emphasize the role of extra-national or extra-governmental determinations. Because government is the tool for planning and implementing economic and social policy, representations which ignore the political character of the state and the bureaucracy and downplay political conflicts within the nation-state are the most useful. Representations which present the state in such a way as to bring into question its role as a neutral tool of enlightened policy must force upon the "development" agencies a political stance they are ill-equipped to take on, and for this reason must fall by the wayside.

It must be evident by now that in a country like Lesotho, where capitalism and the labor reserve economy were well established more than a century ago, where farming contributes only 6 percent of rural household income, where concepts such as national economy and governmentality are more than usually absurd, and where nearly all the major determinants of economic life lie outside of the national borders, the task of drawing up governmentalist plans for transforming a

72

"national economy" through technical, apolitical intervention requires preliminary theoretical rearrangements of a more than usually violent or imaginative kind. Lesotho is for this reason a privileged case in which the nature of this theoretical rearrangement is particularly visible, and in which the schism with academic discourse is unusually pronounced. It is to be expected that in other countries, where the economic situation is less far removed from that of the mythical generic LDC (countries possessing greater national autonomy, greater economic cohesion, and greater governmental control over the economy), the discontinuity between "development" discourse and academic discourse will be less sharp, and less easily observed, although the same processes may be at work.

Conclusion

The effects of the theoretical work done by "development" discourse on Lesotho are far-reaching. The constitution of Lesotho as a suitable theoretical object of analysis is also, and simultaneously, its constitution as a suitable target for intervention. The image of Lesotho as "LDC," once constructed, thus shapes not only the formation of reports and documents, but the construction of organizations, institutions, and programs. The next chapter will show that this is the case. The rest of the book is devoted to exploring the consequences.

3 Institutional apparatus: the Thaba-Tseka Development Project

The "development" apparatus in Lesotho does not make its effects felt only through documents and reports, but also through policies, programs, and, most characteristically, "projects" – especially "rural development projects," of which Lesotho, as noted in Chapter 1, has had more than its share. This chapter is concerned with only one of these projects, the Thaba-Tseka Development Project,[1] which began in 1975, and came to an end, of sorts, in 1984. Detailed analysis of aspects of the implementation and effects of the project will be presented in Part IV. This preliminary description is meant, first of all, to offer a brief account of how the Thaba-Tseka Development Project was conceived, funded, and organized, and what it was expected to do. It is primarily concerned to introduce some of the institutional instruments characteristically available to and put to use by the "development" apparatus in Lesotho.

In addition to providing factual background material for later sections of the book, however, this chapter must also establish some connection between the theoretical constructs of "development" discourse discussed in the last chapter and the programs and policies which a functioning "development" project actually attempts to implement. It is not impossible to imagine that the official discourse in which Lesotho is so carefully constructed as an "LDC" might operate only as a sort of polite but necessary fiction, used to obtain funding or justify projects at high levels, but playing no significant role at the more concrete level of actual institutions, programs, and day to day operations. In fact, it will be shown that this is not the case, that the "development" problematic does indeed preside over both the design and implementation of actual "development" projects. In the case of the Thaba-Tseka Project, it will be shown that the programs and actions of the "developers" are only intelligible within a frame of reference which includes the peculiar "development" representation of Lesotho as LDC. The "rural development project" thus appears not as some sort of "practical" sphere, far removed from the theoretical machinations of the last chapter, but as the site where the elaborate conceptual apparatus of "development" is first put into play, and has its most concrete and visible effects.

The Thaba-Tseka Development Project

Background

In November of 1974, a joint "mission" led by the FAO/World Bank Cooperative Programme and comprising staff members of the World Bank Regional Mission in Eastern Africa and the Canadian International Development Agency (CIDA), visited Lesotho to prepare, in cooperation with the Government of Lesotho (GOL), the first phase of a "mountain area development project" to be funded by the World Bank's International Development Agency and CIDA. This mission produced a plan for a $15 million First Phase Project centering on a 53,000 hectare area around Thaba-Tseka, high in the mountains of what was then Maseru district (see Figure 3.1). Of the $15 million, CIDA pledged $6 million, the World Bank about $5.5 million, ODM about $1.5 million, and the Government of Lesotho about $2.4 million (CIDA 1978P). Final approval of the project came with the signing of a Memorandum of Understanding between Lesotho and Canada on May 8, 1975.

The idea of "developing" the relatively sparsely settled and isolated mountain regions was in part a response to the disappointing results obtained by various "development" projects in the lowlands in earlier years. The FAO/World Bank mission reported that:

Many of the agricultural resources of Lesotho's lowlands and foothills are over-utilized, and soil erosion has become an acute problem. Government has concentrated to date nearly all its efforts for development there ... However, progress has been slow and is limited in scope. Government now realizes that the economic development of the country cannot be achieved without exploiting more fully the production potential of the mountain areas. (FAO/World Bank 1975: 3).

The mission considered the unexploited mountain areas to be rich agricultural resources, but lamented that: "Owing to poor access, Government has been unable in the past to stimulate developments in the mountains" (FAO/World Bank 1975: 3). Very little of the mountain land is arable (about 5 percent), so the project would have to concentrate on livestock and range development. Crops and other matters would be addressed as well, but the fundamental idea of "mountain development" was to open up and develop the rangeland in the interior of the country for increased commercial livestock production.

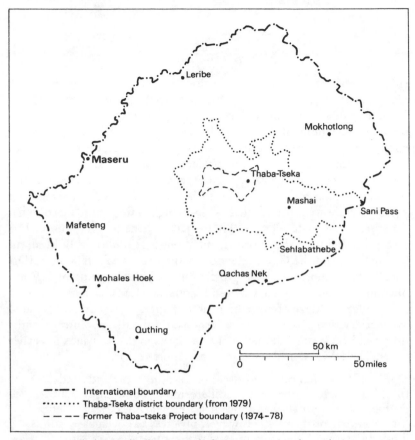

Figure 3.1. Thaba-Tseka district and phase one project boundaries.
Source: CIDA 1978P.

Phase One

The 1975 Report of the FAO/World Bank mission gave the following summary of the proposed Phase One activities:

The project's main investments would be the establishment of a Regional Centre at Thaba-Tseka and of a road link with Maseru. It would also improve feeder roads within the project area in order to facilitate the supply of inputs and the marketing of farm produce.

The project would improve crop production amongst farmers. Based on information from past and current projects in the lowlands, the project would supply the inputs necessary for improving the

76

efficiency of arable farming. Based on experience elsewhere, the project would develop low-cost techniques for improving forage production from mountain rangelands. Working within the traditional land use system, it would develop organization forms amongst livestock owners suitable for the management of improved rangelands.

Living conditions in the villages would be improved by some basic investments in water supply, sanitation and in supplying construction material and fuel.

The agricultural developments would require support through investigation, evaluation, training and extension, which the project would supply. A Phase II mountain area development project would be prepared.
(FAO/World Bank 1975: 7)

I will now examine the details of the project's proposed components one at a time, along with the justification or rationale offered for each. My concern here is to describe the concrete measures that were proposed for Phase One of the project, and to discover the lines of thought that led the planners to propose them. I am not concerned here with what actually happened when these programs were put into effect, as this will be the subject of Part IV.

The most visible and most expensive of the components of the proposed project were those concerned with roads and infrastructure. The most important of these components were: (1) the construction of an all-weather road linking Thaba-Tseka to the capital city of Maseru; and (2) the construction of a "regional centre" at Thaba-Tseka, comprising office buildings, staff housing, warehouse and workshop facilities, and a "Farmers' Training Centre," and equipped with electricity and a piped water system.

The roads and infrastructure components are seen as central elements of the plan for "mountain development." The region has remained undeveloped due to its isolation; in order to develop, it must be better linked with Maseru. This is so for two reasons. First, if "development" is to be introduced by the state, the state must have good access to the territory to be "developed." This means roads to connect with the capital as well as facilities (a "regional centre") for a strong and permanent government presence in the region. "Owing to poor access," the FAO/World Bank Report states (1975: 3), "Government has been unable in the past to stimulate development in the mountains." Government access is the first prerequisite to "development." Secondly, better roads would have a more direct effect on the economic "development" of the region by providing markets for surplus agricultural production, and thus promoting commercial farming. The road would "allow farmers to switch from mainly subsistence maize production to the production of wheat" for the market, as well as "reducing transportation costs for existing produce" (FAO/World Bank 1975: 3, 4). Both the road and the "regional centre" would thus make possible a strong government or "development" presence in the area while at the same time forging economic links to the outside world. Both these innovations are considered essential prerequisites to any sort of "development" in the mountain region.

The most important project components, after roads and infrastructure, are seen to be those concerned with livestock and range management. "The contribution which can be made by the mountains in Lesotho's economic development," the FAO/World Bank Report states, "will largely depend on livestock development." Livestock production "must play the major role in the development of the mountain areas" (FAO/World Bank 1975: Annex 1, 10, 12). Rangeland is to be developed through: (1) the testing and introduction of new techniques for increasing forage potential through seeding and fertilization of pastures, and (2) a scheme of grazing associations and controlled grazing blocks to improve range management and prevent overgrazing of the communally held pasture lands. Seeding techniques would involve the introduction of selected legumes and grasses on selected pasture lands, and appropriate fertilization to support them. The range management scheme calls for dividing the 32,800 hectares of cattle-post grazing lands[2] within the project area into eight blocks of about 4,000 hectares each, and introducing grazing associations on three of them. Each grazing association would pool individual herds into a single unit for scientific management and would be open only to farmers with improved stock and following recommended management practices. Grazing association members would have exclusive grazing rights in the three designated grazing blocks. The remaining five blocks would be left "open," but overgrazing would be controlled through the introduction of resting and rotational grazing. Livestock support services would be introduced to provide better veterinary care and access to improved stock and stud facilities. Extension agents would urge commercial production and instruct farmers on principles of scientific herd management.

The proposed "development" of crop production "would be based

78

on a switch from the current subsistence crops (maize) to cash crops (wheat and peas), for which the area's ecology is more suitable" (FAO/World Bank 1975: Annex 1, 11). The crop program is linked to the livestock and infrastructure components, too, since:

Farmers are interested in this switch as soon as they have easy access to market places. Developments would also integrate crop and animal production by introducing fodder on marginal arable lands. All these developments would require access to improved inputs and extension. (FAO/World Bank 1975: Annex 1, 11).

The main emphasis would be on better land preparation and the supply of improved inputs "along the lines successfully introduced by the IDA supported Thaba Bosiu Project" (FAO/World Bank 1975: 9).[3]

The crops program centered on two key components: the provision of new inputs through a system of project services and "Village Distribution Points" and the provision of new knowledge through a system of agricultural extension. The Village Distribution Points would be located in every second or third village in the project area and would sell fertilizer, pesticides, and improved seeds. In addition, the project would run an agricultural implement shop in Thaba-Tseka which would sell and repair ox-drawn implements, and attempt "the introduction of harrows and planters." The project would also provide a R65,000 revolving fund for agricultural credit, and undertake some supplementary mechanization with small tractors. On the extension side, farmers would be contacted by extension agents and instructed on the merits of improving cultivation, using new inputs, and switching to cash crops such as wheat, peas, seed potatoes, and fodder crops for livestock production. "Lead farmers" would be selected to help spread the word to their less enlightened peers. The combination of new techniques and new markets was supposed to bring great results: maize yields were projected to rise from some 300 kg/ha to 1,000 kg/ha by Year 3 of the Project; wheat yields were to rise from 400 kg/ha to 1,300 kg/ha (FAO/World Bank 1974: 14).

In addition to the agriculture and infrastructure components, plans for Phase One of the project called for a program of "village development" as well as a study and plan for "Phase Two" of the project. "Village Development" referred to the provision of piped drinking water to some sixteen villages, the construction of sanitation facilities for the local primary schools, and the establishment of some thirteen enclosed woodlots to help ease the shortage of fuel and building materials. "Phase Two" will be discussed next.

Phase Two

During the months of March and April of 1978, a series of discussions and meetings were held concerning the start of "Phase Two" of the Thaba-Tseka Project. Although at that time there was nearly a full year left in the "Phase One" plan, the time for Phase Two was judged to be ripe. This was because, first, the Government intended to create a new district centered at Thaba-Tseka and hoped to link this effort with a new, revitalized project, and secondly, because Phase One of the project was due to run out of money in May of 1978, almost a year ahead of schedule (TTRDP Report, January–June 1978).

At the time of these meetings, it was clear that Phase One of the project would be able to meet its commitments to road and townsite construction on schedule, but that it had made little or no headway in achieving its targets in agricultural production. The first CIDA evaluation (CIDA 1978E) reported in June of 1978 that, although construction was completed on schedule, "[a]gricultural and other rural development objectives have suffered as a result of the priority placed on townsite construction. The project has, for the most part, failed to attend to many agricultural concerns stressed in initial project documents" (1978E: 4).

With the infrastructure in place and with the Government planning to spin off a new district, CIDA planners and project personnel saw an opportunity to recast the Thaba-Tseka Project in a dramatic new way. Instead of being a regionally based livestock project, as it had originally been planned, it was now to be an "integrated rural development project," involved in a host of agricultural and non-agricultural activities and operating over the whole of the soon-to-be-created Thaba-Tseka district. This represented a sizeable increase in geographical size for the project, as well as scope. The new Thaba-Tseka district comprised an area of 4,270 square kilometers (compared to 530 square kilometers in the Phase One project area) and contained perhaps 100,000 people (against about 10,000 in the old project area). In December 1978, CIDA signed on to supply C$7.7 million over a five year period to support the new "integrated" project (CIDA 1978P: 5).

The new Phase Two of the project was supposed to continue all the on-going activities of Phase One, and get to work as well on those agricultural components which had been planned but had never quite got off the ground. But it was also intended to expand the scope of the project, and to change its nature in a fundamental way.

First of all, Phase Two simply included a great many more components than Phase One had. In part this was a reflection of an explosion in the number of individual agricultural projects (everything from fish ponds to root cellars was represented); but the growth also included new sorts of activities that the Phase One plans never envisioned. "Integration" meant bringing "development" not just to livestock or even just to agriculture but to all realms of life simultaneously. Health, education, transportation, social services, local crafts and industry, agriculture: all were to be "developed" at the same time by a single, integrated, project authority. With Phase Two, the project ceases to be a pilot project in livestock "development" and takes on a range of activities which almost suggests a mini-state. Consider the list put out by the Thaba-Tseka Project of "Projects in Operation, April 1, 1980," attached to this chapter as an appendix.

The new project plans encompassed some sixty-five component programs, divided into eight functional divisions: Administration (handling accounting, warehousing and stores, and secretarial services), Agriculture, Education, Economic Analysis and Evaluation (responsible for making studies, collecting data, and assisting the evaluation of the project), Rural Development, Mechanical (a mechanical workshop for vehicle repair), Health, and Technical (responsible for construction of roads, buildings, "rural technology" and village water supplies). Agriculture remained the largest division, but the project's agricultural activities were now supplemented by a range of different programs: a trade school teaching carpentry and construction, a rural health worker program, experimental solar ovens, and dozens more. A glance at the appendix to this chapter will give a good indication of the range of activities envisioned for the project under Phase Two.

There was more to the idea of "integration," however, than a large and diverse list of projects to be undertaken. Crucial was the idea that the project, along with a District Coordinating Committee, would play a centralized coordinating role in the administration of the new district. All the involved Ministries were to operate in Thaba-Tseka only through the medium of the Thaba-Tseka Project – or, as it began to be called, the Thaba-Tseka Rural Development Programme – so as to maximize coordination and improve the efficiency of "development" activities and government services alike. This idea and its attempted

81

implementation will be discussed at length in Chapter 7 below. For the moment it is only necessary to point out that the plans for Phase Two envisioned a complete identity (through merger) of the government apparatus with that of the "development" project. In the plans for "integration" of the different ministries under a single "development" authority, government and "development" came to be seen as the same activity.

The project and its targets

The programs and activities planned and implemented by the Thaba-Tseka Project were clearly aimed at a "target society" with the distinctive and particular characteristics we have already seen attributed to Lesotho in the more general characterizations of "development" discourse. Later chapters will discuss in detail the assumptions behind concrete project initiatives in livestock (Chapter 6), crops (Chapter 8), and integrated decentralized administration (Chapter 7); here the task is only to highlight the general perception of the object which presided over the creation and design of the project and to relate this perception to the "development" problematic described in Chapter 2.

The Thaba-Tseka Project was from the start conceived as an agriculture project aimed at the "peasant society" representation of Lesotho already encountered in "development" discourse. Project documents nearly always exaggerated the importance of agriculture and understated or ignored the role of migrant wage labor. The FAO/World Bank Report (1975) declared: "Lesotho's agriculture is subsistence in nature with maize being the principal staple crop. Farmers obtain cash through the sale of surplus animals, fibres from their sheep and goats, wheat and vegetables such as peas" (Annex 7, 1). No mention was made in this passage of migrant labor, although this was of course the most important way by far that "farmers" in Lesotho obtained cash. "Agriculture provides a livelihood for 85% of the people," the same report stated (Annex 1, 7). Livestock, the focus of the Thaba-Tseka Project, was described in the revised Phase Two Plan of Operations (CIDA 1982) as an "industry" which is "the mainstay of the mountain areas." The FAO/World Bank plan for Phase One declared that agriculture accounts for 70 percent of GDP (nearly twice the usual estimates) (1975: Annex 5, 9); elsewhere the same report made the astonishing claim that "about 70% of the GNP comes from the sale of pastoral products, mainly wool and mohair" (Annex 1, 7). (A more conventional estimate would be 2 or 3 percent.) The revised 1982 Plan of Operations (CIDA 1982) was still faithfully repeating that agriculture contributed 60 percent of GNP, at least four times the generally accepted figure (see, for instance, FAO 1983: II, 2). The report accepted and reproduced the World Bank's faulty figures showing "a remarkable equality of income in Lesotho" (see above, Chapter 2), even though the Mission's own survey data on livestock contradicted the assumptions on which the income figures were based[4] (FAO/World Bank 1975: Annex 1, 8). The inhabitants of the project area were always "farmers," and the centrality of agriculture in the local economy was the unquestioned premise of the entire project (cf. Chapter 6, Chapter 8 below).

A second and equally fundamental perception of the "target population" in the eyes of the Thaba-Tseka planners was that it was *isolated.* Overcoming isolation was seen as the key to stimulating "development" for a number of reasons. First, since the principle of governmentality decrees that lack of "development" is due to lack of government action, isolation provided a needed explanation for why such action was not undertaken – the inability of "Government" to reach the area: "Owing to poor access, Government has been unable in the past to stimulate development in the mountains" (FAO/World Bank 1975: 3). This isolation is painted in stark terms. At the start of the project, one document claims (TTRDP "Review of Accomplishments," 1981), it encountered "an isolated community which was devoid of any kind of services, Government or otherwise." Just how improbable a statement this is will be seen in succeeding chapters (see especially Chapter 6 and Chapter 8), but this belief is an extremely important one which comes up again and again in the descriptions of and justifications for the project. Planters and harrows, for instance, are to be "introduced" to the area by the project – as if these common agricultural implements had never before been available in Thaba-Tseka. The same false novelty was suggested for project proposals for livestock stud facilities and improved stock procurement, although both services were already provided in Thaba-Tseka by the government Livestock Improvement Center there. In proposing the Village Distribution Point scheme, the FAO/World Bank Report paints a picture of total isolation: "Within the core area, no improved inputs are available for farmers to purchase, nor is there a distribution system to handle them." In a footnote, however, we are told that "there are only 4 main traders plus a very small Coop Lesotho in the area." Five major sources of agricultural inputs seems not so small a number for sixteen villages, but it is not enough to break the grip the image of isolation exerts on the planner's imagination.

The isolation imagined for the region is not simply a matter of difficult transportation and hard-to-find supplies, however; it is also an economic isolation, a lack of contact with the money economy and the modern world of the market. Planning documents for Phase Two, for instance, suggested that the "introduction" of livestock marketing facilities by the project would bring about de-stocking, since farmers would suddenly be able to find a market for their surplus unproductive animals. The implication is that up to the time of the project, farmers had been stuck with unwanted animals which they kept simply because they could not find a place to sell them. This claim will be explored in detail in Chapter 6 below, but it is already apparent that it implies that Thaba-Tseka stock-keepers had not encountered the market until the project introduced it. In the projections for crop "development," a picture is painted of the project area as an isolated group of agricultural villages with little or no contact with markets or stores. It is declared that "Maize is now grown extensively as it is the staple food and cannot be bought" (FAO/World Bank 1974: 9). "Once improved access has been provided to the area and maize can be purchased easily, the extension staff would encourage farmers to grow more wheat at the expense of maize" (FAO/World Bank 1975: Annex 3, 4). The suggestion is that people are forced to grow the subsistence crop rather than the cash crop because they are so isolated they cannot buy food when they need it; once it becomes possible to buy maize, everyone will be able to switch to cash crops. In fact, the people of the project area had long been buying large amounts of maize; another section of the very report just cited reveals (FAO/World Bank 1975: Annex 7, 11) that in the previous year (1973) – before the road was built – one trader alone brought in 500 tons of maize.

Poor access, in the "development" scheme of things, not only results in isolation from government services and retail trade; it makes commercial agriculture impossible due to lack of markets. The project proposals for both livestock and crop production assume that the existence of the road will create a market which did not previously exist and thus bring about a shift to commercial production. This question will be explored in later sections (Chapter 6, Chapter 8), but it should be noted here that many of the project's activities and projections make sense only on the premise that the area had no significant access to markets prior to the arrival of the Canadians.

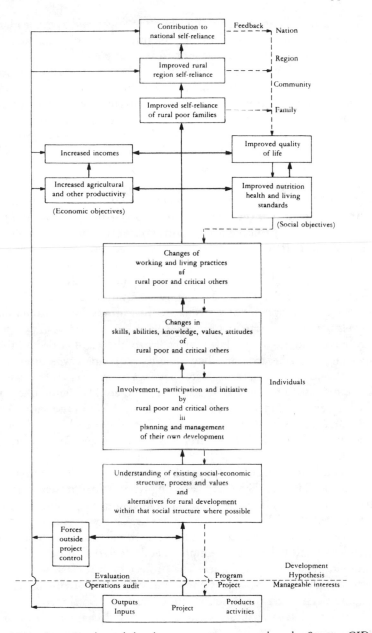

Figure 3.2. Integrated rural development: purposes and goals. *Source*: CIDA 1978F: 33.

Most of the initiatives undertaken by the project, and even the idea for the project itself, pre-supposed this picture of an isolated, backward, agricultural economy which stands to be completely transformed by some combination of technical inputs, new knowledge, and infrastructure. The programs of the Thaba-Tseka Project were conceived and designed as interventions in an isolated, aboriginal, peasant society, and the "development" proposed consisted of a package of technical innovations designed for backward farmers along with a series of measures to link up these traditional farmers with the modern market economy. The design and overall conception of the project, as well as the justifications and projections put forward to support it, are intelligible only in the context of the "development" problematic described in Chapter 2.

Another feature of the "development" problematic whose influence can be seen in the project's design is the conception of "the people" as a simple agglomeration of "individuals," a conception that, as was noted in Chapter 2, reduces political and structural causes of poverty to the level of individual "values," "attitudes," and "motivation." In this perspective, structural change is simply a matter of "educating" people, or even just convincing them to change their minds. I was often told by "development" experts in Lesotho, for instance, that, while Lesotho may have had no natural resources, with the right attitude almost anything could be accomplished. The case of Japan was often cited: Japan has no resources. If the Basotho were a bit more energetic, and had the kind of attitude the Japanese had, Lesotho could develop like Japan. The burden of "underdevelopment" is thus placed on the shoulders of each and every individual Mosotho, and "development" appears largely as a task of education, the introduction of changes in "traditional" attitudes.

This individual-centered approach was evident in the planning of the Thaba-Tseka Project. The very revealing schematic representation constructed by Thaba-Tseka's planners of the "Purposes and Goals" of "Integrated Rural Development" illustrates this well (see Figure 3.2). "The centrality and criticality of the individual's values, involvement, knowledge and behaviour is emphasized," declared an official project report in presenting this figure. The project took its task to be one of performing certain operations upon "individuals": convincing, educating, and persuading the Basotho into becoming "developed."

In the next two chapters some of the actual characteristics of the "target population" will be described in some detail and contrasted with the essential features ascribed to it by the "development" apparatus.

But, before going on to a description of the local social setting, it is necessary to point out that the design of the rural development project outlined here contained embedded within it not only a picture of the "target population," but also a conception of the project's own nature, and that of the government through which it worked. This is a point that will be explored in later chapters (especially Chapter 7); here the need is only to underline the fact that the project took no account of its own necessary embeddedness in local political struggles, and conceptualized the relationship between project and local government in a way that misrepresented both as disinterested parties with only the interests of the poor "farmers" at heart. No doubt the political analyses of many individuals on the scene were considerably more sophisticated than this, but the official thinking that presided over the creation of the project (and it is this that is at issue here) saw government and project alike as neutral instruments of "development," providing technical solutions and social services to the rural poor.

Conclusion

This chapter has given a brief sketch of the structure, history, and aims of the Thaba-Tseka Development Project. The details of the most important project initiatives, along with an analysis of what happened when they were actually implemented, will be presented in Part IV below. But it should be clear even from this brief account that the Thaba-Tseka Project was an institutional apparatus designed to operate upon precisely the sort of "less developed country" that we saw so painstakingly constructed of Lesotho by the conceptual apparatus in Chapter 2, and that the project was set up to provide technical solutions to "problems" which were not technical in nature. We have seen that the conceptual apparatus systematically translated all the ills and ailments of the country into simple, technical problems and thus constituted a suitable object for the apolitical, technical, "development" intervention which "development" agencies are in the business of making. Now, in this chapter, we have been concerned with one part of the institutional apparatus designed to execute that intervention: the "development" project. First technical problems such as isolation, lack of markets, lack of credit, unfamiliarity with a cash economy, lack of education, lack of fertilizer, lack of tractors, lack of purebred livestock, lack of farmers' associations and cooperatives, and lack of appropriate energy technology are exaggerated or invented to take the place of things like unemployment, low wages, influx control, political subjugation by South Africa, and entrenched bureaucratic elites; then an institutional apparatus is unleashed to combat these largely illusory technical problems. The Thaba-Tseka Project, as even this brief sketch suggests, and as the chapters to come will demonstrate more clearly, was a part of this institutional apparatus; it was a project which aimed to supply technical solutions to problems that had been invented or highlighted solely for the purpose of being able to propose technical solutions to them. The results of this contradictory endeavor will be the subject of Part IV of the book.

Before exploring the outcome of the "development" intervention in Thaba-Tseka, however, it will be necessary to present some material concerning the nature of the society that was the object of such theoretical and institutional manipulation by the "development" apparatus. Part III, which follows, will describe and explain some of the more important characteristics of "the target population" of Thaba-Tseka and the wider society of which it is a part.

Appendix: Thaba-Tseka Development Project, "Projects in Operation, April 1, 1980"

The following is a list of project activities (broken down by "Division") during "Phase Two" of the Thaba-Tseka Project. It is directly excerpted (with some corrections made to obvious typographical errors) from a report issued by the Thaba-Tseka Rural Development Programme, entitled "Projects in Operation, April 1, 1980."

Administration

Project/Activity	Brief Description
1. General Administration	This is a support service. Activities include General office activities, the registry, typingpool, office cleaning and the F.T.C.
2. Accounting	Another support service, activities include payroll, General Accounting and Audit.
3. Procurement and Warehouse	A support service. Services include

procurement of goods from within
Lesotho and South Africa, and
transfer of goods to destinations.
Also handles transport scheduling
in the Maseru Office.

Agriculture

Project/Activity	Brief Description
1. Village Distribution Points	This is an activity to provide farm inputs closer to the farmer. Eventually, it is hoped, all the 3 V.D.P.'s still operated by the Programme will be transferred to the People. Already one such V.D.P., at Ha Soai, has been transferred to the people. The activity also involves assisting people to set up their own V.D.P. with the technical assistance from the Co-operatives Division of the Ministry of Rural Development. Already, a co-operative V.D.P. has been set up at Ha Nkokana.
2. Extension	This is an extension arm of the Division. At the moment, the section is experiencing problems in obtaining suitable manpower for its activities, with only about 5 extension agents to cover 100,000 people or at least 20,000 households per extension agent.
3. Irrigation	This is an activity to utilize the abundant water resources of the district to increase food production.
4. Farmer Training	This is an activity to improve the productivity of farm activities through the training of Farmers on selected topics.

89

5. Crops Research	This is an activity to identify crops that would do well in the mountain environment, both nutritionally and in terms of yields. The main goal is to identify food crops that would contribute significantly to the goal of self-sufficiency in staples.
6. Soil Conservation Food Aid Gangs	This includes a number of projects in the district that employ food-for-work gangs to work on soil conservation. It is also involved with setting up village based conservation schemes.
7. F.T.C. Gardening	This is a project to research on vegetables that are suitable for the mountain environment and to act as a demonstration on the best methods of growing vegetables.
8. Piggery	This is both an experimental and a demonstration project on how to keep pigs in the mountains.
9. Dairy	This is both an experimental and a demonstration project, designed to identify the breeds that will do best in the production of milk in the mountains.
10. Poultry Layer Unit	This is both an experimental and a demonstration project, designed to identify the least costly way of raising chickens by local people.
11. F.T.C. Nutrition & Handicrafts	This is a programme aimed at improving the quality of life through women. The nutrition part is designed to improve the Health of Families, through women (the ones concerned with nutrition) and through craft production, women could earn more money for their families.

12. Commercial Gardens	This project attempts to involve small farmers in commercial vegetable production, through the provision of the technical know-how and credit.
13. Communal Gardens	This project involves the motivation of village people to set up communally owned vegetable gardens, and also advances credit for the purchase of inputs.
14. Root Cellar	The main goal of this project is to assist farmers with food storage (to retain its freshness) during the dry winter months, especially vegetables.
15. Grazing Land bank and Indigenous Seed Collection	In this project, specially made small cages covered with diamond wire mesh are placed over selected parts of the range. The cage allows the vegetation to recover undisturbed, as long as the results are required. Data collected from such an exercise are then used to evaluate the productivity of the range under optimum conditions as well as the rate of recovery of the range under proper management.
16. Stable/Horse Transport	This is a horse transport pool, and horses are available to all Divisions, on request. In the absence of roads to most villages, the horse pool has assisted officers to carry out extension work in most parts of the district.
17. Livestock Genetic Improvement	This is an activity to introduce improved breeds of sheep, goats, and cattle into the District. Its extension arm involves the purchase on behalf of farmers, improved breeds from the Republic

18. *Livestock Disease Control*

of South Africa and elsewhere in the country.
In this activity, disease eradication campaigns (e.g. scab) are carried out throughout the District, and farmers are assisted with diagnosis of disease and the sale of drugs.

19. *Livestock Grazing Associations*

This is a project to set up Graziers' Associations in which a group of farmers are assisted to fence up part of the grazing land in order to control grazing.

20. *Livestock Marketing*

Stock sales (sheep and cattle) are held every Tuesday of the last week of the month. Farmers either sell their animals directly to the Programme, which then markets them in Durban, or the Programme assists farmers by consigning cattle to Durban. These livestock sales have also attracted other buyers in the country.

21. *Range and Pasture Research*

This project involves research into ways of increasing the carrying capacity of the range. This includes introducing grass varieties that will yield higher than existing varieties.

22. *Abattoir*

This is a project to assist local butchery owners with the slaughter of animals. Besides contributing to the destocking effort of the Programme, it should also avail the urban area with meat that has been approved by Health.

23. *Fish Production*

This project is partly experimental and partly a demonstration effort on how to raise trout in the region.

24. *Basotho Pony Project*

This project is run independent of the Programme by the Irish

	Government. Its main objective is to build a National Stud Farm by breeding the best Lesotho Pony mares with the best Irish Stallions. Its main goal is to arrest the deterioration of the Lesotho Pony.
25. Woodlots and Nursery Research	This is an afforestation project in which selected areas of the district are fenced off, and planted with trees. Research is underway to identify species that may do well in the mountains.

Education

Project/Activity	Brief Description
1. C.O.S.C. Night School Apprenticeship	This project assists serving officers to upgrade their academic education to COSC level, so that they can qualify for international scholarships. This is designed to improve the productivity of the work-force within the programme, without having to hire more people.
2. Training in Lesotho and other African Countries	To upgrade the productivity of the staff in programme, officers are sent for short and medium term courses in Lesotho and other African countries.
3. Training Overseas	Since the inception of the Programme, officers have been sponsored for study overseas, mainly in Canada. In the 1980/81 financial year scholarships have been availed to the district for study in Europe, U.S.A. and Australasia, as well.
4. Video and Playback System and Publications	This is an activity to produce [an] educational video for the District as

93

an extension tool. It is also designed to catalogue progress and important moments on the district Development. It is also designed to provide low cost entertainment for the residents of Thaba-Tseka.

5. Support to Local Schools (including Katlehong)

This is a project to assist district schools to complete necessary infrastructure and the townsite Primary School to complete its building up to grade 7.

6. J.C. and C.O.S.C. Apprentices

In the 1980/81 financial year apprentices have been taken by the Health and Agriculture Divisions only. The 17 students all spend 6 months in Thaba-Tseka undertaking various projects for the Divisions concerned before writing a scholarship qualifying test. Those who pass the test will then be sponsored to the various institutions for training.

Economic Analysis and Evaluations

Project/Activity	Brief Description
1. Social and Economic Surveys	Social and Economic Surveys are conducted by the Division on behalf of other divisions in the Programme throughout the District.
2. Cost Studies	The Division also undertakes cost studies on aspects of the Programme operations at the request of the Programme.
3. Evaluation Studies	Once baseline data has been collected and projects are implemented, it is the duty of the Division to monitor the Projects'

activities and conduct end of
project evaluations.

Rural Development and Cooperatives

Project/Activity	Brief Description
1. Support to On-going Rural Development	The role of Rural Development Division in this project is to mobilize villagers, organize committees and then invite the relevant technical division to implement the activity.
2. Coordination of D.V.S. Clinic Projects	The role of the Division in this project is to coordinate the technical team from Danish Volunteer Services and the local community for the improvement of local clinics.
3. Training Courses	The main role of the Division in this activity is to select villagers for training on various rural development activities.

Mechanical Division

Project/Activity	Brief Description
1. Repairs to plant, equipment and machinery	This involves the repair of all equipment, machinery and vehicles, both private and government in the District.
2. Transport Pool	This involves the scheduling of vehicles in the transport pool, for use by all the Divisions in the District. Work also involves preparing transport charges for all Divisions.
3. Tractor Hire	Tractors are hired to all Divisions, as well as to farmers.

Health

Project/Activity	Brief Description
1. Pilot Village Health Worker Programme/Mohlanapeng	The main goal of this activity is to upgrade primary health at the village level, through the training, development & supervision of village health workers, in villages surrounding Mohlanapeng Clinic; construction and installation of a clinic, provision of piped water in villages where V.H.W. operate, and conducting a pilot study on the effectiveness of using V.H.W. using 6 pilot and 4 controlled villages.
2. Rural Health Training Centre Programme	The main goal of this activity is to provide a cadre of rural health personnel with appropriate practical field experience before they are deployed in their final postings in the T.T. District. This will be attained through field training of Nurse Clinicians, Nurse Assistants, Nurse Attendants and Health Assistants at the Mohlanapeng Rural Health Centre.
3. Townsite Health Programme	The major goal of the activity is to attend to the Public health needs of the T.T. Townsite and to execute the health function of the District centre through the provision of regular health talks, general public health talks, first aid courses, procurement of protective clothing, inspection of the F.T.C. and abattoir, post-mortems and family planning.
4. Paray/District Hospital Programme	The major goal of this programme is to provide basic health services at the primary, secondary and tertiarty levels to the largest possible number of people within

the T.T. District at a cost which is charged at GOL health facilities. This will be achieved through assisting Paray in purchasing specific medical equipment, transportation of food to clinics through Programme vehicles, purchase of expensive and hard to get drugs, supply of personnel, specialist visits to Paray, and provision of nursing staff.

5. St. James Hospital

The main goal of this project is to provide basic health services at the lowest possible cost to the largest possible number of people in the District. This will be attained through the provision of transportation, via the Programme, for Clinic food and equipment and the supply of personnel and facilities for village health worker programme.

6. Rural health Technology Research and Development

The main goal of this project is to improve certain aspects of village life which have a direct bearing on the community's health status through the introduction of more effective and relevant technology. This will include the following items: water improvement, appropriate irrigation methods for communal gardens, Hospital handicrafts for long-term illness patients, new methods of food preparation and preservation, solar stills for producing distilled water, solar autoclaves for sterilization at clinics and improved [*sic*].

7. Rural Health Centres

The main objective of this activity is to standardize the services offered through the various health facilities in the district. The

Programme includes the upgrading of clinics at key locations, the supply of drugs, and the supervision of health personnel in these institutions through the Office of the D.M.O.

Technical

Project/Activity	Brief Description
1. Draft Power Training	This project aims at training donkeys and horses to pull ploughs and carts (as draft animals). It also tests the efficiency of these animals, including oxen while undertaking various tasks. A number of people will be trained as trainers of donkeys, oxen and horses, and eventually, trained animals will be made available for hire to villagers.
2. Hides and Skins Improvement	This is a project to train villagers in proper techniques of hides and skins preparation so as to supply the local and perhaps an export market.
3. Leather Works	This is a project to assist local leather workers to improve their product and management. Attempts will also be made, in the financial year, to expand their range of products.
4. Farm Implement Testing	This project tests available farm implements for durability and efficiency. Also various agric. techniques will be tested to see if overall agricultural productivity in the mountains can be raised.
5. Block Plan, Crusher, Drilling and Blasting	The main objective of this project is to produce crushed stone and blocks to meet the building requirements of both the

government and the private sector. The crushed stone is also used on the roads.

6. *General Construction* — The main task of this project is to carry out any construction activity not undertaken by Village Construction and District maintenance, using District crews in the urban area or District.

7. *District Road Construction and Maintenance* — This project undertakes and supervises all district road construction and maintenance utilizing food for work crews (16 foremen and 600 crews).

8. *Village Water Supply* — This Project undertakes surveys and designs and installs all village water supply systems in the district.

9. *Village Construction* — This project undertakes all construction activities outside the urban area using village crews or contractors.

10. *District Maintenance* — This project undertakes all maintenance work of government facilities in the District, and is responsible for maintaining the townsite structures.

11. *Trade Center* — This project is responsible for running a 10 month training course in building and carpentry utilizing the building of health and other government centres as teaching areas.

12. *Wind Power Experimentation* — This is a project to evaluate the potential of producing electric power from wind, most of the experimentation was carried out in October 1978 to May 1979. Some

	data construction will continue during the coming financial year.
13. Solar Project	In this project, basic prototypes for solar heating, solar food drying, and solar cooking are developed. Extension work involves introducing the ideas developed to the people.
14. Micro Hydro-electric	This is an experimental project, in which a small hydro-electric plant will be installed and its efficiency tested in terms of water utilisation and use. A short term consultancy will be used to evaluate its usefulness.
15. Maintenance and Production Facility for Farm Equipment	This project is a support activity to the Agricultural Technology Unit. It is also a production facility to produce marketable prototypes, that will eventually finance all other activities.

Part III
The "target population"

4 The setting: aspects of economy and society in rural Lesotho

Formal political structure

When Lesotho attained independence on October 4, 1966, it was formally constituted as a constitutional monarchy, with a bicameral national parliament made up of an elected National Assembly and a Senate. Administration was effected through a national civil service organized into Ministries of Finance, Agriculture, Works, Interior, Justice, Health, Education, Police, Foreign Affairs, Communications, and the Prime Minister's Office. The country was divided into nine administrative districts: Maseru, Berea, Leribe, Butha-Buthe, Mokhotlong, Qacha's Nek, Quthing, Mohale's Hoek, and Mafeteng (see Figure 4.1). (The tenth district of Thaba-Tseka was created in 1980.) Elected District Councils in each district had jurisdiction over selected matters related to agriculture and livestock, maintenance of bridle paths and selected roads, fisheries, public health, public order, and the regulation of trade, commerce, and industry.

Alongside this system of administration existed a second, based not on the colonial civil service but on the pillar of colonial "indirect rule" in Lesotho, the hereditary chieftainship. Under this system, each village or village section falls under the jurisdiction of a village headman (*ramotse*), who is in turn politically subordinate to the area chief (*morena*) within whose area of jurisdiction his village lies. The local chief in turn is subordinate to one of twenty-two Principal and Ward Chiefs. Nineteen of these high-level chieftainships are held by descendants of Moshoeshoe I and two of his brothers. The other three have jurisdiction over incorporated communities of Tlokoa, Khoakhoa, and Taung, respectively. A total of 1,048 chiefs and headman are "gazetted," i.e. on the government payroll. (The titles "chief" and "headman" are somewhat arbitrary in this respect as some officials called "headmen" are gazetted while others called "chiefs" are not.) Chiefs are responsible for various matters concerning field allocation and grazing lands, as will be discussed in later sections.

These two administrative pyramids are formally linked at the top, in the office of the Paramount Chief. The Paramount Chief, or King, is the titular head of state, the immediate superior to the Ward and Principal

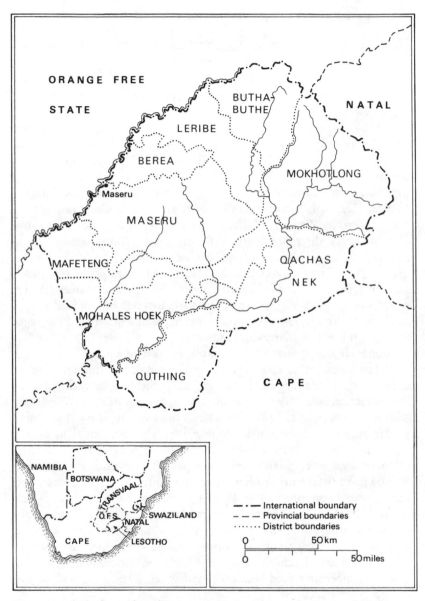

Figure 4.1. Lesotho and its districts, 1966. *Source*: van de Geer and Wallis 1982: 18.

Chiefs, and the nominal holder of title to all land in Lesotho. As head of state, laws are enacted in his name, and the national parliament is said to be speaking in his name. But "the will of the king" is legally decided by vote of parliament, so the executive authority nominally vested in the King is, as in other constitutional monarchies, legally exercised only by the legislative branch. "Liaison" between the civil service and the chieftaincy at lower levels is under the jurisdiction of the Ministry of the Interior, and has been the responsibility of District Administrators (before 1980) and Local Administration Officers (from 1980 to the present).

The formal political structure outlined above, however, has only a limited bearing on the way that politics is actually conducted in Lesotho. To understand why that should be so, and to understand the place of the formal system in the actual political processes that were confronted by the Thaba-Tseka Project, it is necessary to review a little recent political history.

Recent political history

When Lesotho became independent in 1966 it was under the leadership of the Basotho National Party, headed by Chief Leabua Jonathan, who became the Prime Minister. The Basotho National Party, or BNP, had won the elections of April 29, 1965, by a narrow margin of thirty-one out of sixty constituencies (the opposition Basotholand Congress Party [BCP] and Marema-Tlou Freedom Party followed, with twenty-five and four seats, respectively) and had captured only some 42 percent of the popular vote, against fifty-eight for the combined opposition. Notwithstanding the precariousness of Jonathan's electoral position, the British government refused opposition demands for new pre-independence elections, and granted independence to the Jonathan government on October 4, 1966.

In the 1965 elections, the National Party had found its most important points of support among chiefs, traditionalists, the Roman Catholic Church, and the South African government.[1] Organized in 1958, and originally conceived as a "Christian Democratic Party," the BNP offered itself as an alternative to the more radical African nationalism of the older BCP, which had been the early leader of the fight for independence. In its election campaigns, the BNP promoted a message of anti-communism, social conservatism, and friendly cooperation with South Africa. The BCP, or Congress Party, on the other hand, opposed the influence of the churches (especially the white missionaries), took a pragmatic but fundamentally hostile view of apartheid South Africa, and was in touch with powerful radical nationalist, pan-Africanist, and revolutionary currents elsewhere on the continent and beyond. Both the BCP and the much smaller Marema-Tlou Freedom Party took objection to Jonathan's close relationship with the South Africans and often portrayed him as little more than a puppet of the South African government (see Breytenbach 1977; Khaketla 1972; Spence 1968).

When Jonathan came to power, he put into effect the close cooperation with South Africa he had called for. His economic policies called for an open door to South African capital, and in 1967 he became the first independent black leader to go to Cape Town to visit South African Prime Minister Vorster. At the same time, important government posts in Lesotho were given to white South Africans sympathetic to the ruling National Party in South Africa. The Chief Justice of Lesotho, the Attorney-General, the Chief Electoral Officer, and a number of magistrates were all Afrikaners; the Commissioner of Police and the Commander of the para-military Police Mobile Unit were whites as well, as were many lesser officials and economic advisors (Khaketla 1972, esp. 120–1). In 1968, the government abolished the District Councils, which had become centers of political dissent and opposition.

New elections were called in 1970. The BCP, after being caught by surprise in the 1965 elections, campaigned hard throughout the country and rebuilt its strong local organization. The BNP, confident of victory, stood on its record. When the results came in, it became apparent that the BCP had won. Instead of yielding power, however, Jonathan declared a state of emergency and argued that the elections had been sabotaged by "communists." For the sake of "law and order," the present government would continue in power. Although the final results, which the government never released, showed that the BCP had won a clear majority (thirty-five seats for the BCP against twenty-three for the BNP and one for MFP, according to one source)[2], Jonathan's coup preempted the election (Macartney 1973, Khaketla 1972).

In the months which followed the coup, opposition figures were arrested and terrorized, newspapers unsympathetic to the government were closed, and political violence involving the para-military Police Mobile Unit (PMU) and members of the BNP Youth League ("Young Pioneers") took a heavy toll throughout the country. Mokhehle and other BCP leaders were imprisoned. A small faction of the BCP later agreed to participate in the "Interim National Assembly" set up by

Jonathan in 1973, but it was disowned by the greater part of the party, which refused to participate in the government on Jonathan's terms.[3] An abortive attempt to seize power by BCP loyalists in January of 1974 was harshly repressed by the police and the PMU. In the violence which followed, Mokhehle fled the country in fear of his life, and the BCP was split into two factions – an "internal wing," led by those who recognized Jonathan's government and sat in the "Interim National Assembly," and a much larger "external wing" under the leadership of the exiled Mokhehle. In 1979 an armed unit of the "external wing" of the BCP, calling itself the Lesotho Liberation Army (LLA), began a guerrilla campaign of sabotage and attacks on government installations.

The context of international alignments, meanwhile, had shifted significantly. From 1971 on, the Jonathan government had become more and more hostile to the South African government, perhaps in part because the anticipated benefits to Lesotho of a friendly relationship with South Africa had not materialized. Little technical or financial assistance was forthcoming, and the much publicized Oxbow-Malibamats'o hydro-electric scheme had fallen through. Instead of helping to promote Lesotho's industrial development, as the government had hoped, the South Africans had introduced subsidies for investment in "border" industries in the Bantustans, making it harder than ever for Lesotho to attract capital for industrial development. At the same time, as Jonathan scrambled to stay in power in the years following the 1970 coup, he was able to coopt the opposition to some extent with his increasingly hostile denunciations of apartheid South Africa. By 1979, the balance had shifted to the point where it was Jonathan's BNP government that was accusing Mokhehle's LLA of being supported by South Africa. The allegation was not proved, but neither was it regarded as entirely implausible by many observers on the scene.[4]

It was as the government turned away from its South African patrons that the pipeline of aid from the West began to open up. When South Africa closed the Transkei border with Lesotho after Lesotho refused to recognize the Transkei's "independence" in 1976, Western donors rushed in to pledge their aid in unprecedented amounts. From 1974–5 to 1979–80, annual foreign aid commitments to Lesotho rose from about R17 million to R95.5 million.[5] Relations with "frontline" black states improved, and in 1980 Lesotho became a member of the newly formed anti-South Africa economic grouping, the Southern African Development Coordinating Conference, together with Mozambique, Angola, Swaziland, Botswana, Zimbabwe, and Zambia.

On December 8, 1982, the South African Defence Force invaded Lesotho and attacked the homes of African National Congress (ANC) refugees in Maseru, killing some forty-two people, including Basotho nationals and women and children. The effect of this assault was to further alienate the Lesotho government from South Africa, and to provoke an unexpected response: in May of 1983 Chief Jonathan visited a number of communist countries and opened diplomatic relations with the Soviet Union, China, and North Korea, with the promise of links with other Eastern Bloc countries to come. This improbable-looking move by the erstwhile rabid anti-communist brought the political game in Lesotho around full-circle. Soon the Catholic church was attacking Jonathan for having dared to visit the communist countries, just as they had once attacked Mokhehle for going to China, and there was talk of the formation of a right-wing "Christian Democratic" party based on principles of anti-communism and friendly relations with South Africa.[6] In the countryside, villagers were treated to the ironic scene of BNP politicians uncomfortably defending themselves against the charge that Jonathan was a communist. Meanwhile, the LLA continued to be accused of receiving South African support, and it was widely rumored that Mokhehle himself was now based there. There were published reports, too, that the LLA was now accusing the ANC of supporting and collaborating with the Jonathan government. The growing tension culminated in January 1986 in a military coup led by Major-General Justin Lekhanya and precipitated by a South African blockade of the border. Although the new goverment featured many of the same old BNP faces, it quickly moved to establish warmer relations with South Africa, and to expel ANC and other refugees from the country.

Politics at the grass roots

In the mountain villages of what would eventually become the Thaba-Tseka district, all the political conflicts just described at the national level found local expression. Both major parties, the ruling BNP and the opposition BCP, had local organizations, and both were powerful forces at the village level, at least until the repression of the BCP after 1970.

In the 1965 elections and before, the mountain areas were generally BNP strongholds. The BCP was strongest in the towns, especially among workers and the educated; the BNP, with its appeals to traditionalism and its support from chiefs and the Catholic church, found its natural constituency in the "less sophisticated" rural areas, especially the mountains and other areas out of touch with the more radical political culture of the capital.

By 1970, however, the situation had changed. The mountain constituencies voted overwhelmingly for the BCP in the 1970 elections, reversing the pattern set in 1965 when they had voted solidly for Jonathan's National Party. In the campaigning for the 1970 elections, Jonathan had made much of the new roads and "development" projects he had brought to Lesotho – and this line of argument was persuasive enough in some places (for instance Leribe district, where the BNP picked up two constituencies in the 1970 elections, Weisfelder 1971: 126). But, whatever the merits of the government's new roads and projects, the mountain areas had seen no benefits from them. Khaketla suggests that the real needs of the mountain areas did not include tarmac roads and prestige projects in the lowlands, and that government neglect of and insensitivity to the concerns of the mountain dwellers accounts for their mass defection to the opposition:

As a horse-riding people, what [the mountain people] wanted and what mattered to them was the bridle-paths which had been allowed to go to ruin since the abolition of district councils [in 1968]. They wanted bridges across the numerous rivers which brought everything to a standstill during the rainy season. And they wanted jobs which would enable them to earn cash wages and not to receive payment in the form of mealie-meal. [This is a reference to the government's "Food-for-Work" program.] These were the things which mattered to the mountain people who, in 1965, had voted overwhelmingly for Chief Leabua [Jonathan]. At that time he had promised them bridges, bridle-paths, jeep-tracks, health clinics, hospitals and a host of other things. Although he had not carried out his 1965 promises he asked them to re-elect him, and once again he was promising them the same things he had promised them in 1965. To have expected them to continue to support him was too much. What they had seen of his administration was cruelty at the hands of the police. Several people had been arrested, and others even shot dead, by the stock-theft unit of the police force. Many had had their livestock – their means of livelihood – taken by the police and handed over to farmers in the Republic of South Africa who claimed the animals had been stolen. And in many cases these farmers were not even required to show proof that the animals belonged to them. It was enough for the farmer to say: "This is my cow" or "This is my horse." So the disenchantment grew.
(Khaketla 1972: 187–8)

After the events of 1970–4, the Congress Party was so severely repressed that it became impossible for it to maintain a public presence or to continue with its local organization. Leaders fled into exile and supporters were intimidated into silence. In the mountain villages, the BCP effectively ceased to exist as a public organization, though it persisted to a degree as a kind of underground. The BNP, on the other hand, was able to entrench its local political organization by converting its village-level election committees into permanent, state-sanctioned village organizations known as "village development committees" or VDCs. These "development committees" are important features of local political life in most villages in the Thaba-Tseka district.

Although official government policy stated that the VDCs were elective bodies which represented "the people" and articulated their "development" needs, it was an open secret in Thaba-Tseka when I did my field work there in 1982–3 that these committees were political organs of the National Party. The highest government officials in Thaba-Tseka confirmed to me that this was the case, and I encountered no one in either Thaba-Tseka town or the village where I was living who maintained otherwise. Officials told me that the committees had originally been election committees; then in 1970 "their designation only was changed" and they began to be called "Village Development Committees." Members of the VDC interviewed in one village all acknowledged that it was a committee of National Party members only, and stated that selection of members was presided over by a local BNP political official known as the Liaison Officer. Villagers opposed to the government regarded the committee as "the eye and ear of the ruling party" and declared that its function was to keep track of and report on villagers who opposed the government. "You see," one informant remarked, "I think that the name is not right; it is nicknamed this name of 'development', but you can see that it is a political body."[7]

In the BNP organization, the village committee is nominally responsible to a Polling Station Committee, which reports to a Constituency Committee. Above this is the National Executive Committee. In practice, the Polling Station Committee and the Constituency Committee are not active, and have not been since the last election. The real point of contact between the VDCs and the Party hierarchy is the government's Liaison Officer. There is one Liaison Officer for each constituency. In addition to meeting with the village committees, Liaison Officers, according to one source, "seem to have been appointed to play an entirely political role, i.e. they liaise with the party leaders in the district and may attempt to influence resource allocation in favour of party members" (Van de Geer and Wallis 1982: 51)

The other important political force at the local level is the military, which means, in Lesotho, the Para-Military Unit of the Police (the PMU – successor to the old Police Mobile Unit, also known as PMU). The brown uniforms of the PMU were in 1982–3 to be seen in numbers in all parts of Lesotho, and police road blocks and searches had become commonplace. Even in the rather remote village areas of the Thaba-Tseka District, which are far from the border and have little or no history of LLA activity, there was an extremely visible military presence, and it was common to see groups of men with automatic weapons patrolling the peaceful countryside.

Villages in the area were sharply divided over politics, but it was not a thing which was discussed openly. It was difficult to determine people's political sentiments because so many were afraid to speak about politics, but it is evident from material to be presented below and in later chapters that there existed substantial opposition sentiment in a highly charged political atmosphere. Government supporters feared the LLA, whose notorious deeds were rehearsed daily on the government's Radio Lesotho, and were suspicious of BCP supporters. Supporters of the Congress party were extremely reluctant to identify themselves as such, and in some cases even identified themselves publicly as National Party members to avoid persecution. The events of 1970 and 1974 were remembered well, and stories told of arrests, killings, and mutilations by the government forces suggest that they made a vivid impression. The highly visible presence of "Leabua's soldiers" (as the PMU troops were called) provided a constant reminder of the continuing relevance of this experience. One informant, after giving a detailed account of the 1970 election and the repression which followed and offering an opinion that in another election Mokhehle's Congress Party would again emerge victorious, asserted:

But now we are afraid to speak of that, because we will be shot dead. We can't say anything. And when they say *"Hloho!"* ["Victory!"; a BNP slogan] and raise their hands [in the "V" sign which is the symbol of the BNP] we also raise up our hands, for fear of being shot dead.

The labor reserve economy

Nobody really knows how many Basotho are employed in South Africa. Estimates usually range from 150,000 to over 200,000 out of a population of some 1.2 million, or about half of the adult male population. The South African government gives a figure for 1981 of 150,422, of which 129,508 are said to be employed in mining (SAIRR 1983: 85–6). The Government of Lesotho figures for the year 1978/9 estimate a total of 154,600 migrant workers, of which 124,578 are reckoned to be in mining. It seems likely that official estimates such as these underestimate the number of illegal migrants, who after all might be expected to avoid having their illegal migrant status recorded as a statistic.

The earnings of these migrant laborers dominate the local economy. The Government of Lesotho estimates that the total earnings of the migrant workers in 1977/8 was some R234 million, of which R118 million was figured to come home as remittances. Gross Domestic Product in the same year was only R176 million (GOL 1980). It had been estimated that some 70 percent of average rural household income is derived from wage labor in South Africa, while only 6 percent is derived from domestic crop production (Van der Wiel 1977). Table 4.1 compares the estimated income required for a minimum subsistence existence as of 1974 (as calculated by Marres and Van der Wiel 1975) with the estimated value of actual agricultural yields for the same year. "Subsistence" is, of course, an extraordinarily difficult concept to quantify, and it is not clear that the creation of arbitrary "Poverty Datum Lines (PDL)" does much to clarify things. Still, the exercise does give some crude idea of how far Lesotho's agriculture is from providing "subsistence" (taken from Makhanya 1980: 16). The villagers who make their homes amidst Lesotho's barren mountains, for all their rustic appearances, are nearly all dependent, directly or indirectly, on wages earned elsewhere. As Murray (1981) has remarked in his authoritative study of migrant labor in Lesotho "the population of Lesotho today is aptly described as a rural proletariat which scratches about on the land."

This was not always so. The story of the transformation of a booming agricultural export economy in the mid and late nineteenth century to the impoverished dormitory for migrant workers that is Lesotho today is a long and complicated one, and it is not necessary to review it in detail here. Colin Murray has given an excellent account of the evolution "from granary to labour reserve"; here I underline only a few points.

First, it is clear that poor agricultural production in Lesotho is neither

Table 4.1. *Net annual income from raising crops on an average farm*
(2 ha) assuming one crop each agricultural year*

Crop	Gross margin from yield Rands	P D L Rands	Deficit Rands
Maize	22.4	804.24	781.84
Sorghum	32.0	804.24	772.24
Wheat	41.4	804.24	762.84
Beans	101.6	804.24	702.64
Peas	90.0	804.24	714.24

*The actual average farm size in the study area was 1.7 ha.
Source: Makhanya 1980: 16.

an original state nor a very recent phenomenon. In 1863, Lesotho was described as "the granary of the Free State and parts of the [Cape] Colony" (Murray 1981: xi). Ten years later, after the discovery of diamonds in Kimberley in 1867, Basotho farmers were responding to the incentives of the expanding market "with such zeal and success that, on the one hand, the missionaries expressed anxiety lest their material prosperity endanger their spiritual progress ... and, on the other hand, the *Friend of the Free State* was moved to remark, 'Nowhere else in South Africa is there a more naturally industrious nation, as honest and as peaceable as the Basuto'" (Murray 1981: 11). In 1873 they exported 100,000 bags of grain and 2,000 bags of wool and imported foreign manufactured goods worth about £150,000. Yet by the 1930s the country was importing large amounts of maize, and agriculture was becoming increasingly marginal to the migrant labor which by then engaged most of the adult men. In this respect, the state of affairs described by the Pim Commission in 1935 does not appear drastically different from that which obtains today (see also Leys 1979, Palmer and Parsons 1977).

It is certainly true that agriculture has been in decline over most of the last century, and that wage labor has taken on increasing importance. But it is clear from the historical records that, although agricultural decline and migrant labor are related, the relationship is not a simple one. Migration of large numbers of Basotho in fact preceded the decline in agriculture by many years, and even in years of very good crop production, from the 1870s on intermittently into the 1920s, workers left the country by the thousands for work. In the early stages it seems migration was not related to a need to make up for poor food production but to buy guns, clothing, cattle, and other goods, and, from 1869, to pay taxes. Ashton, after observing that labor migration among the Basotho is "nearly as old as their contact with Europeans," reports:

By 1875, out of a total population of 127,325, of which the number of able-bodied men was estimated at 20,000, 15,000 men were getting passes to work outside the territory for long or short periods, and by 1884 this number had doubled itself. By 1908, 78,000 men out of a population of 350,000 "went abroad at intervals for work." They were not all away at once and the periods during which they were absent doubtless varied considerably and probably averaged no more than six months in the year; this means that about 39,000 were away at any one time. In May 1936 the census revealed that 78,604 men and 22,669 women out of a population of 660,546 were "absentees at labour centres"; in 1946 the corresponding figures were 58,634 men and 12,144 women out of a population of 624,605.
(Ashton 1967: 162)

Just as there were important reasons for migration before and beyond the need to supplement a stagnant subsistence agriculture, so there are important causes of the decline in agriculture beyond simply the increasing rate of migrant labor. Among the most important factors was the loss by the Basotho of most of their best agricultural land to the encroaching Dutch settlers during a series of wars between 1840 and 1869. Figure 4.2 illustrates the extent of this loss.

Although its immediate effects on production were apparently not great, this radical reduction of the resource base available to the Basotho farmers was to have profound consequences. In succeeding years, in the face of population growth (exacerbated by the 1913 Land Act, which forced South African Basotho off land in the Orange Free State), soil exhaustion, drought, and cattle disease, the slender strip of land at the foot of the Maluti mountains became a more and more precarious basis for agriculture. At the same time, other external factors intervened. Toward the end of the century, the market for which the Basotho had produced so vigorously in the 1860s and 1870s was undermined by protectionist measures – first by the Transvaal in 1886, then by the Orange Free State in 1893 – and by the importation of cheap American and Australian grain which was made possible by the construction of a new railway from the Cape to Kimberley. After a brief resurgence around the time of the First World War and after, the depression of

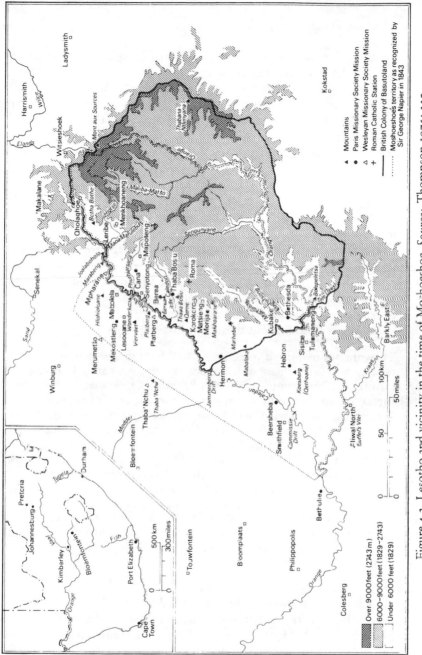

Figure 4.2. Lesotho and vicinity in the time of Moshoeshoe. *Source*: Thompson 1975: 330.

- ▲ Mountains
- ● Paris Missionary Society Mission
- ○ Wesleyan Missionary Society Mission
- △ Roman Catholic Station
- + British Colony of Basutoland
- ‒‒‒‒ Moshoeshoe's territory as recognized by Sir George Napier in 1843

- ▣ Over 9000 feet (2743 m)
- ▨ 6000–9000 feet (1829–2743)
- ☐ Under 6000 feet (1829)

the early thirties reduced the agriculture of Lesotho to a level of stagnation it has not been able to escape since.

In the years since, population growth, soil exhaustion through overuse and monocropping, and erosion of both crop and grazing land have contributed to a slow, steady decline in agricultural yields, while the number of landless in rural areas has gradually increased. The general state of agriculture, however, is not drastically different today from what it was fifty years ago. Neither the rise of migrant labor nor the stagnation of agriculture is a recent development, and accounts which suggest that migration is a response to a relatively recent "crisis" in agriculture brought on by population pressure are completely unsupported.

The most important recent transformations in the area have been not in agriculture but in the structure of employment. The establishment of border posts and influx control at the South African border in 1963, along with regulations introduced in 1968, resulted in a number of restrictions on Basotho migrant workers that had not previously existed. Murray summarizes these as follows:

> They are not permitted to enter South Africa for the purpose of
> seeking work: they may only engage in employment in South Africa
> through a labour contract made in Lesotho. Otherwise, they require
> special permission to be so engaged, under sections of the South
> African legal framework which specifically discriminate against
> foreign Africans. Such permission has been granted from time to time
> in the past but, in view of the prevailing level of structural
> unemployment, it is quite unlikely to be granted in the future (Spiegel
> 1979: 24). The period for which workers are recruited may not
> exceed one year, and in any case they must return to Lesotho within
> a period of two years. A worker may not become the tenant of a
> house in a 'prescribed' area of South Africa; and he may not be
> accompanied by his wife or children to be resident with him. Labour
> contracts are not available to women from Lesotho.
> (Murray 1981: 28)

At least two important shifts occurred as a result of the new regulations. First, there was a drastic reduction in the number of women able to work in South Africa. Secondly, there was a reduction in all forms of employment except those recruited from within Lesotho on a contract basis. In practice, this meant that the workforce was increasingly concentrated into a single industry, which was mining.

More recently, important changes have occurred in the mining industry itself that have had profound effects on the Lesotho labour reserve. During the 1970s, various political and economic pressures induced a general rise in mineworkers' wages, which had long been kept unnaturally low (Wilson 1972). The reasons for these quite substantial wage increases have been explored elsewhere (e.g., Murray 1981, Stahl 1979); here it is necessary only to note that relevant factors included the rising price of gold, the desire to "internalize" labor supplies, and a wave of strikes and political unrest throughout South Africa in the years 1974–6. Table 4.2 shows the suddenness and magnitude of these increases.

Two other important recent shifts are associated with this increase in wages. First, as a result of the new "internalization" policy, Lesotho's quota of recruitment has been reduced in favor of greater recruitment from the Bantustans. Secondly, because the high wages make it possible to make use of more skilled labor, and because the increasingly capitalized mines have more and more need for it, mine work has become increasingly "professionalized." See Figure 4.3 showing a sharp dropoff in new recruits along with rising or constant overall numbers. By 1982, instead of nearly all men spending their youth in the mines and returning to Lesotho after some years, which was the old pattern, fewer and fewer miners were being kept on for longer and longer terms. For the first time, one was beginning to find heavy unemployment among young men, and mine work was coming to be not merely a phase in the life cycle, but a life-long occupation available to some but not all.

Table 4.2. *Average annual cash earnings of black labor on the gold mines, 1972–1978*

Year	Average annual cash earnings (current rands)	Cost of living index, Lesotho (October 1972=100)	Index of real earnings (October 1972=100)
1972	257	100.0	100
1973	350	112.8	121
1974	565	128.4	171
1975	947	146.6	251
1976	1,103	162.1	265
1977	1,224	191.0	249
1978	1,476	211.0	272

Source: Murray 1981: 31.

The view from the village

The structure of economic life in the mountain villages of the Thaba-Tseka district can be illuminated by examining some statistics I collected through a comprehensive household survey of Mashai village in 1982–3. Demographic data alone tell a part of the story. Out of seventy-eight adult (18 or older) men under the age of sixty declared residents of the village, only twenty-seven were present at the time of the household census. There were forty-four men absent by reason of employment, along with four more migrant workers home resting at the time of the census. The demographic pyramid for Mashai (Figure 4.4) shows the

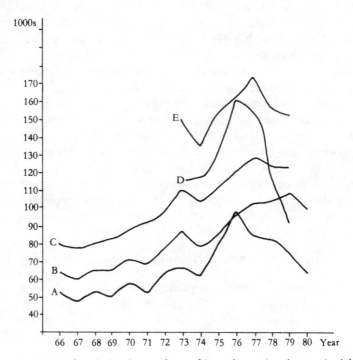

Figure 4.3. Annual variation in numbers of Lesotho nationals recruited for and on strength of South African mines. *Source*: Spiegel 1981: 5.
A = Total number of recruits forwarded by TEBA from Lesotho annually
B = Total number of Lesotho nationals on TEBA supplied mines at 31 December annually
C = Total number of Lesotho nationals on all S.A. mines annually
D = Total number of recruits forwarded from Lesotho into South Africa annually
E = Total number of Lesotho nationals employed in South Africa annually

extent to which the village is a repository for the very old, the very young, and the female.

Murray (1981) has analyzed village census data on absentees and employment by distinguishing six classes of person based on their status as absentees, migrant laborers, and paid employees. For the sake of comparability, this same classification will be used in presenting census data from Mashai. Figures 4.5 and 4.6 define the terms "absentee," "migrant laborer," and "paid employee"[8] and show the distribution of the six categories based on these terms for one lowland village surveyed by Murray in 1974 (Murray 1981: 52). For Mashai, where the number of households surveyed is, by coincidence, exactly the same (i.e. seventy-three), the picture is as shown in Figure 4.7.

Three main differences emerge between the two samples. First, the number of women working as migrant laborers in Murray's Ha Molapo sample was thirteen, while there were no migrant laboring women reported in Mashai. This is most likely due to Ha Molapo's proximity to the South African border, on the one hand, and to increasingly harsh influx control by the South African government in recent years on the other.

Secondly, while the number of absent employed men in Mashai was higher than in Ha Molapo (forty-four against forty-one), the number of men counted as "migrant laborers" is much lower (thirty-six to forty-seven). This greater number of "migrant laborers" in Ha Molapo is not a

```
Age                                Males│Females
70 and up                            XXX│XXX
65-9                              XXXXXX│XXXXXXXXXXX
60-4                               XXXXX│XXXXXXX
55-9                           - - - XX│XXXXXXXXX-
50-4                            - -XXX│XXXXXXXXXXXX
45-9                        - - - - -XXX│XXX
40-4              - - - - - - - - - -XXX│XXXXXXX-
35-9                          - - - -XXXX│XXXXXXX
30-4                    - - - -XXXXXX│XXXXXXXXXXX
25-9                      - - - - -XX│XXXXXXXXXXXX-
20-4        - - - - - - - - - - -XXXX│XXXXXXXXXXXXXXXXXXXXXX- - -
15-19          - - - - - -XXXXXXXXXX│XXXXXXXXXXX- - - -
10-14  - - -XXXXXXXXXXXXXXXXXXXXXXXX│XXXXXXXXXXXXXXXXXXXXXXXXXXXXX-
5-9      -XXXXXXXXXXXXXXXXXXXXXXXX│XXXXXXXXXXXXXXXXXXXXXXXXXXXX
0-4    - - -XXXXXXXXXXXXXXXXXXXXXXX│XXXXXXXXXXXXXXXXXXXXXXXXXXXXXXXX-
```

Figure 4.4. Distribution of Mashai population (1983) by sex, residential status, and age cohorts. Note: each 'X' represents one person present at time of census. Each '–' represents one absentee.

The "target population"

In Lesotho at time of census				In South Africa at time of census	
ABSENTEES elsewhere in Lesotho		Present in reference community		ABSENTEES	
1	2	3	4	5	6
Absent for reasons other than paid employment		Resting at home		Currently employed	Absent for reasons other than paid employment
			PAID	MIGRANT LABOURERS EMPLOYEES	

Figure 4.5. Schematic representation of absentees, migrant laborers, and paid employees. *Source*: Murray, 1981: 52.

matter of more workers in the mines – on the contrary, Mashai had thirty-three men employed in the mines at the time of census, against only twenty-seven for Ha Molapo – but of workers in occupations other than mining in South Africa. There were twenty men reported working in non-mine activities in South Africa in Murray's survey of Ha Molapo, while only three such men were found in Mashai. This reflects the increasing difficulty with which Basotho workers today find employment in South Africa in any industry other than mining, for reasons discussed above. At the same time, Mashai had nine men working out of the village elsewhere in Lesotho, while Ha Molapo had only one such employee, perhaps reflecting greater employment opportunities within the country due to the booming growth of its capital city.

The third major difference is in the number of locally employed persons: twenty-three for Mashai to only four for Ha Molapo. This difference is most likely due to the fact that Mashai, though not an extremely large village, is a center for many commercial, social, and governmental services, all of which help to generate more local employment than is typical of less centrally placed villages. Mashai village contains the government's local court and treasury office, a primary school, several small "cafe's," and a Protestant church. Government agricultural extension and nutrition officers are based in the village; it is also the seat of the area Chief and the original home of the late Principal Chief of Qacha's Nek. There is a large trading store and mill nearby, and a large Catholic mission with clinic and school not much further. This local prominence gives opportunities for local employment which might not exist in other villages such as Murray's Ha Molapo. It should be noted that this local employment is typically very low-paying compared to work in South Africa. A full-time worker at the Catholic mission, for instance, received R30 per month, as against the R256 per month earned by the average black underground worker in the gold mines in 1982 (TEBA, personal communication).

Box	Definition	Absentees	Migrant labourers	Paid employees	Ha Molapo. Oct. 1974 Male	Female
1.	Persons elsewhere in Lesotho for reasons other than paid employment	+			8	3
2.	Persons in paid employment elsewhere in Lesotho	+		+	1	–
3.	Persons in paid employment in reference community			+	2	2
4.	Migrant labourers temporarily 'resting' at home		+	+	7	2
5.	Migrant labourers currently employed in South Africa	+	+	+	40	11
6.	Persons in South Africa for reasons other than paid employment	+			1	3
Ha Molapo. October 1974		67	60	65	N = 73 households	

Figure 4.6. Distribution of absentees, migrant laborers, and paid employees identified as *de jure* members of Ha Molapo, October 1974. *Source*: Murray, 1981: 52.

Note: Plusses indicate whether the people in a given box are to be considered "absentees," "migrant laborers," or "paid employees." Persons in Box 2, for instances, are considered "absentees" *and* "paid employees," but not "migrant laborers."

Box	Definition	Absentees	Migrant labourers	Paid employees	Mashai, 1983 Male	Oct. 1974 Female
1.	Persons elsewhere in Lesotho for reasons other than paid employment	+			16	11
2.	Persons in paid employment elsewhere in Lesotho	+		+	9	1
3.	Persons in paid employment in reference community			+	10	13
4.	Migrant labourers temporarily 'resting' at home		+	+	4	0
5.	Migrant labourers currently employed in South Africa	+	+	+	32	0
6.	Persons in South Africa for reasons other than paid employment	+			0	0
	Mashai, 1983	72	36	69		

N = 73 households

Figure 4.7. Distribution of absentees, migrant laborers, and paid employees identified as *de jure* members of Mashai village, 1983.

The number of absentees in the village is dramatic, but the tale told by those present is equally clear. The extent to which migrant labor dominates the economic life of the men of Mashai is underlined when we look at the circumstances of the twenty-seven out of seventy-five men over the age of 18 and less than 60 who *were* present at the time of the census. Out of these twenty-seven, several were migrant workers home visiting from South Africa, or resting between contracts, while the rest were made up mainly of sick, disabled,[9] or recently laid-off miners, along with a few men with local employment. Consider the following list of adult working-age (over 18 and less than 60) men present at the time of the census:

Person #	Age	Employment situation or infirmity
#1	Age 23	Anthropologist

#9	Age 47	Primary school teacher.
#36	Age 23	Deaf mute, crazy.
#68	Age 22	Crippled arm.
#102	Age 32	Laid off from mines 1981.
#116	Age 28	Laid off from mines 1976 due to illness.
#120	Age 30	Home visiting from mines, will return.
#133	Age 51	Fired from mines and blacklisted after being hit on the head with a shovel in fight with white man.
#142	Age 38	Missing a leg.
#148	Age 38	Stopped working in mines in 1977 due to illness. Now better and hopes to go back next year.
#156	Age 48	Not right in the head.
#157	Age 22	Home visiting from mines.
#168	Age 30	Works at local mission station.
#177	Age 36	Home visiting from mines.
#185	Age 51	Laid off from mines 1978.
#211	Age 55	Ex-miner, due to illness.
#232	Age 45	Laid off from mines 1982 for back problems.
#239	Age 52	Laid off from mines after breaking hip in 1977. Now a cripple.
#249	Age 40	Laid off from mines 1983.
#275	Age 50	Lost an arm in mining accident, 1971.
#281	Age 43	Crazy.
#287	Age 40	Works at local court.
#298	Age 31	Laid off from mines last year.
#361	Age 25	Fired from mines for participation in a strike. Now blacklisted.
#362	Age 20	Attending local secondary school.
#364	Age 33	Laid off from mines 1981.
#373	Age 30	Home visiting from mines.

Fourteen additional men were over 60 years of age; all of these older men were present at the time of the census.

Those men who remain behind in the village, then, are first of all mainly the old, the sick, the disabled, and the unemployed. They, along with most of the women, form a great mass of dependants, seeking to eke out a living through some combination of mining remittances, farming, beer brewing, and selling minor goods and services to those privileged ones with direct or indirect access to wage labor.

Of the seventy-three households, fifty had at least one employed member. Ten of these households had only local (typically low-paying) employment. Forty households had a non-local employee; thirty-five households had a worker employed in South Africa, of which thirty-three were mineworkers. Only three households had more than one-local worker, and only one had more than one worker in South Africa.

Against this background of migrant labor and absenteeism, "subsistence" agriculture made only a small relative contribution to "subsistence." Fifty-seven of the seventy-three households held at least some land; thirty-nine of these owned some stock, too, while another five landless stock-holding households made a total of sixty-two of seventy-three households with either land or stock. But the information collected in Mashai suggests that there, as elsewhere in Lesotho, agriculture is not a very rewarding activity. The old colonial government used to estimate the minimum subsistence requirements for an average household at twenty bags of grain per year. In Mashai, the average yields reported for the staple crops harvested in the winter of 1982 were: 1.7 bags of maize, 1.3 bags of sorghum. In a hypothetical "good year," the expected yields were: 4.5 bags maize, 4.4 bags sorghum. The averages were only slightly higher when taking into account only field-holding households: 5.5 bags maize, 5.4 bags sorghum in a "good year"; 2.1 bags maize, 1.6 bags sorghum in 1982. "Good years" for crops in Mashai, it should be added, are more the exception than the rule, and drought years, of which 1981–2 was not an especially severe example, are quite common, sometimes estimated at one year in four.

A more vivid illustration of the marginality of agriculture is given by the responses to the question of how long the food harvested from the fields lasts before it becomes necessary to buy grain from the stores. For the average household, in a "good year" the field food will last about 3.7 months into the year; for field-holding households the average is still only 4.5 months. This implies that even those who hold land, and even in the best years, are able to produce only about one-third of their total subsistence needs of maize and sorghum.[10] For an average household in an average year, the outlook for agriculture is far worse even than this.

Livestock will be the subject of the following chapter, but it is appropriate to review a few general features of stock-keeping in order to locate their place in the local economy. The following generalizations will be supported in greater detail in Chapter 5 below. First, it is important to note that livestock in Mashai are not a major source of either cash income or subsistence goods, and that their chief function is to store wealth, not to produce it. The two most important exceptions to this rule are the provision of ploughing and dung for fuel by cattle, and income from chickens, which many households keep for the occasional eggs and meat. But apart from fowl (to be discussed in Chapter 5), the contribution of livestock to agricultural production is mainly the derived one of preparing land for crop farming, not the primary one of producing goods for consumption or sale.

Cattle are only very rarely slaughtered (almost always for a funeral or wedding), and are sold only in response to an owner's personal emergency or destitution. Cows, for lack of pasture, do not produce an appreciable amount of milk, and herds, left to themselves, do not increase, but decrease (see Chapter 5, note 28). Losses due to drought, disease, and theft are high. Sheep and goats are more often slaughtered for holidays and celebrations, but here, too, there is generally little or no "natural increase" so it is difficult to say that the herd is the source of much economic value. Wool is sold, but the amounts are small and the quality poor, so that the cash from sale of wool usually amounts to less than the cost of hiring a herd boy to look after the sheep, and only rarely makes a significant contribution to the household accounts. The income reported as produced by stock-keeping in national statistics is mostly derived from the selling of animals in time of desperate need. Where herds do not increase, however, the money gained in this way must be seen as a recovery of money invested long ago – like a withdrawal from a savings account – not as income produced by the keeping of livestock.

Wage labor and agriculture are by no means the only economic activities available to rural Basotho villagers, though one might well get that impression from much of the literature. There are a host of alternative or "informal" sources of income which may supplement or even exceed income from wages and crops. For the poorest households, these other sources may be all that stands between them and destitution and hunger. In Mashai, it was possible to find people making their livings not only through wage labor and farming, but by brewing beer for sale, working in government road gangs under the "Food for Work" program, baking bread and sweet rolls (*makoenya*), selling small knitted goods and handicrafts, sewing clothes, dispensing traditional and not-so-traditional medicines and cures, repairing shoes, fetching firewood or water; building houses, chopping tobacco into snuff, hauling stones, making furniture, renting houses, and even transcribing tapes for an anthropologist. Of all these pursuits, the first two – beer brewing and "Food for Work" are by far the most important; none of the others made substantial and consistent contributions to more than a few households.

Twenty of the seventy-three surveyed households in Mashai reported that they had worked in "Food for Work" road gangs at least three times in the last year. This form of work was not considered "wage labor" in the survey because it was done only intermittently, in blocks of fifteen days at a time, and because it was paid in kind, with only a small amount of cash thrown in to sweeten the deal. Workers were nearly always women, and it was usually only women from the poorest households who were willing to do such strenuous work for so little pay. Even so, there were always more workers than there were openings available. A prospective worker was obliged to sign up with the local Village Development Committee in advance; she would then be called when her turn came. Supporters of the BNP were more likely to have such work than others; whether this was simply because those in sympathy with the opposition refused the work (as many certainly did) or because (as some charged) the committee discriminated against non-BNP workers is difficult to say. After working fifteen days, a worker would receive a packet of food (donated by Western nations) which typically consisted of:

Item	Approx. value
Two 20 liter tins of maize meal	M10
Two bottles or one tin of cooking oil	M8
One small tin of peas or beans	M1
Six small tins of fish	M6

There was, in addition, a small cash payment which amounted to M7.50 at the time of the fieldwork.

This sort of work was usually a last resort for the destitute, and it was characteristically undertaken by those with few other options and no access to wage labor or remittances. It was one of the few recourses left for the old, the abandoned, and the penniless. This least powerful category of people consisted mainly of women, most of all old women. Anyone who has visited Lesotho in recent years has seen the gangs of aged women working on the roads with picks and shovels.

Thirty-eight of the seventy-three households in Mashai reported that they brewed and sold beer at least six times in the last year. Many brewed far more often than that, and some brewed once a week or even more. Brewing can bring in a significant amount of money. Most often about forty liters were brewed at a time, which could be sold for between M4 and M10 depending on the quality of the beer. The ingredients, which included a washbasin full of sorghum and a small bowl of maize meal for each forty liter batch, usually cost less than M1, so it was possible for a diligent brewer to net as much as M5, M10, or even more per week from beer. For many households which lacked wage labor, beer brewing was the main source of income (see Gay 1980a for an account of the economics and sociology of brewing in a lowland village).

Beer brewing, like many other economic activities through which women support themselves, must be understood not simply as a productive activity, but as a mechanism of redistribution. Beer is sold only to local villagers, predominantly men, and brewing is first of all a way of obtaining access to the cash earnings of employed men. Production of beer is directly stimulated by the presence within the village of men with money to buy it, and it is best understood as one of a number of possible ways for women to get a piece of that money. Brewing is thus very much a dependent or derived form of production; without migrant labor, the villagers of Mashai could no more support themselves through beer brewing than Mark Twain's famous townsmen could support themselves by taking in each other's laundry.

Understood in this way, it is easy to see why brewing is as much a social skill as a technical one, and why one's ability to make money by brewing is not a simple matter of the amount of beer one produces. Beer drinking is the main social event in the village for men, and it goes on in small or large groups every day. To sell a lot of beer a woman must be a cheerful and congenial hostess, and have a strong social position in the village. Making money on beer requires the same kinds of skills and social assets as throwing a successful party. It is thus a form of economic activity which is deeply embedded in the social relations of the village. I shall return to this point later.

There is one more activity that is of great importance in the economic lives of women, and here the economic aspect is embedded still more deeply in wider social relations. That activity is the taking of lovers, a practice which is widespread and goes under the name of *bonyatsi*. *Bonyatsi* is not prostitution, but it does characteristically involve cash gifts from a man to his *nyatsi* or lover. Information on such matters is extraordinarily difficult to obtain, but Gay (1980a) suggested that a figure of about M10 per month might be the norm. This economic edge to love affairs in Lesotho should be viewed in a larger perspective as part of the pervasive and extremely important economic content which suffuses virtually all relations between the sexes under the conditions of the labor reserve.

Economic classes and economic categories

In the literature on the rural periphery of South Africa, there exists a debate over how class analysis is to proceed in social formations such as that of Lesotho, characterized by heavy dependence on wage labor alongside a number of apparently "non-capitalist" or "traditional" features in a rural setting. On the one hand are those (e.g. Innes and O'Meara 1976, Spiegel 1979, 1980, Amselle 1978) who argue that occupants of the labor reserves must be considered proletarians pure and simple. Rural settings notwithstanding, the really significant relations of production are those between capital and worker, and an analysis which fails to recognize rural workers' status as proletarians simply falls prey to the rationalizations of *apartheid* (Spiegel 1980). On the other hand are those (e.g. Wolpe 1972, Meillassoux 1975, Webster 1978, van Binsbergen and Meilink 1978) who hold that the social formations of the periphery reveal not *only* the capitalist mode of production, but also other, pre-capitalist modes in "articulation" with capitalism. Thus Wolpe (1972) agrees with Meillassoux (1975) that pre-capitalist relations in the rural areas are selectively preserved in a way that is functional to capital. "Traditional" networks of social relations and "subsistence" production of food effectively serve to subsidize the wage which the capitalist must pay by making an independent contribution to the reproduction of the labor force.

For the adherents of the first view, the class position is clear: Basotho migrants are part of the Southern African working class, and they have the objective class interests which correspond to that position. If they differ from other sections of the working class (e.g. white urban workers) this is only at the political and ideological level, not the economic (Spiegel 1980:113; cf. Poulantzas 1973). The task of class analysis within Lesotho is to point out emerging class formation and to identify the different class positions that households can occupy (Spiegel 1980, 1981; cf. Innes and O'Meara 1976, Cooper 1980). Thus Innes and O'Meara (1976) draw up a typology of households based on differential access to land and wage-earnings, while Spiegel (1980) distinguishes between ordinary proletarian households on the one hand and entrepreneurial and salaried petty bourgeois on the other.

For followers of the second view, the situation is not so clear. It is true that capitalism is a commanding presence and that the societies on the periphery have been thoroughly "proletarianized." But the class position of people in the villages is complicated by a second set of relations of production, corresponding to a pre-capitalist mode. Migrant workers in Southern Africa are thus simultaneously related to both the capitalist mode of production, within which they are unambiguously proletarians, and to a second mode of production, articulated with the first, within which other relations of production obtain.

Both views, however, have problems when it comes to explaining the events and practices one would like to be able to explain. When one asks a simple sociological question about Lesotho, for instance, such as why people keep cattle the way they do, or why they vote the way they do, or why they have the religious beliefs they do, the socially relevant categories with which one is immediately confronted do not correspond to those identified by either variety of class analysis. Labeling the Basotho as "proletarians" may be accurate enough, but it does not go far toward explaining why proletarians in Lesotho behave so differently from proletarians in Pretoria, or New York City. Hunting the various "fractions" of the petty bourgeoisie, meanwhile, does not seem to take us much nearer to an answer. At the same time, it is not helpful to dissolve a set of social practices into "pre-capitalist" and "capitalist" components unless it can be shown that there exists some analytically separable sphere of "pre-capitalist" relations of production which generate or explain the apparently non-capitalist practices in question. No one has yet convincingly done this. Indeed, I will argue in the next chapter the exact contrary: that apparently "pre-capitalist" patterns of livestock holding in Lesotho must be related not to "pre-capitalist relations of production" but to the set of social relations linked to the modern, migrant wage labor system.

The entire discussion on class in the Southern African rural periphery seems to depend on the premises that the economically significant categories must be classes, that class is a relation of production, and that relations of production can be analytically separated from all other social relations and used to explain them. A reexamination of these premises may make it possible to conceptualize these problems in a slightly different way.

First, there is no reason to assume that relations of production will be analytically separable from other social relations. Even in advanced capitalist society this is a dubious proposition, as recent feminist work on gender has shown. The marriage relation, for instance, is not purely a relation of production, nor does it have separable "economic" aspects which can be isolated from social, religious, sexual, reproductive or other aspects. All aspects of the relationship have economic and political content and are significant to an economic and political analysis. Likewise, in Lesotho many relations of production are embedded in other, larger systems of social relations and are not generated by the production process. The relations of production involved in raising livestock, ploughing fields, taking a lover, or brewing beer cannot be separated out, nor should we wish to so separate them.

It follows from this that many of the most economically relevant categories are not purely economic. They have economic content, to be sure, but they are implicated in a whole range of economic and non-economic institutions, and can only be understood in that larger context. Again, this is not a peculiarity of the South African rural periphery, or of "pre-capitalist" social formations; it is true as well for advanced capitalist societies such as the United States. Race categories in the U.S., for instance, are economically relevant and have real economic content, but they are not generated by the production process, and they find many of their firmest points of attachment in realms which lie outside of the strictly economic sphere. The sterile debates over whether economically crucial categories based on determinations which lie outside of the production process (such as age and sex) are *really* classes or not (e.g., in Seddon 1978) are not only fruitless but unnecessary. If relations of production are not a separate realm, then we must take the economically relevant categories as we find them and reject *a priori* schemes which treat classes as natural objects instead of socially constituted categories.

With this much said, it must be noted that, if the economically relevant categories are not *simply* categories of production relations, they still must be specified, and the interests corresponding to them analyzed and made explicit. Such an analysis proceeds just as a more conventional class analysis would, except that the analysis of interests begins only *after* the relevant economic categories have been discovered. In place of class interest, then, I prefer to use the broader concept of "category interest," where a "category" occupies a certain specified structural position in society and possesses certain interests corresponding to that position.

The above discussion helps to clarify the position in Lesotho. First, a number of relevant economic categories do follow immediately from the production relations of the migrant labor system. The distinction between employed and unemployed is a crucial economic distinction, as is that between a dependent with access to remittances versus a person with no access at all to cash earnings. Spiegel's distinction (1980) between ordinary wage laborers and entrepreneurial (café owners, traders, etc.) and bureaucratic (chiefs, government civil servants) petty bourgeoisies is helpful here as well.

Distinctions based on landholding, on the other hand, are, at least in Mashai, not highly significant. Land is a form of property which can, according to law, never be bought or sold. Title to all land is vested in the nation, in the name of the King. Use rights to arable land (fields) are allocated to adult men by a "Land Committee," consisting of four elected members, three appointed by the Minister of Agriculture, and the area chief.[11] Traditionally a man had a right to expect three fields; today land shortage means that many must settle for one, or none at all. The new Land Act 1979 introduced for the first time legal inheritance of fields (though sons had always had a strong customary claim to their fathers' lands) and a rule of primogeniture to check the increasing fragmentation of plots.[12] Rights to fields are thus acquired through citizenship or inheritance, and fields cannot be bought up or monopolized by the wealthy.[13] Pasture land, on the other hand, is "communal." The grazing lands are divided into two types: cattle-post grazing and village grazing. Cattle-post grazing grounds are seasonal mountain pastures where herds from all over Lesotho are grazed throughout the summer by herdboys or herdsmen who travel with the herds and stay in temporary "cattle-posts." In the winter, the cattle are withdrawn to the "village grazing" areas surrounding their owners' villages, where the grazing has been reserved for the long winter. The cattle-post areas are under the control of the Principal and Ward Chiefs, while the village areas are under the control of local chiefs. In neither case, however, is the chief able to exercise anything like rights of ownership or to exclude commoners from grazing rights.[14]

Under this system of land rights, then, land-holding is relatively equitable, and there is nothing approaching landlordism. Some hold more land than others, but even the largest holdings fall short of providing regular and consistent subsistence, let alone a significant surplus, and holders of larger numbers of fields are not much less dependent on wage labor than anyone else. Exploitation of larger amounts of land is possible only by share-cropping, which is a matter of owning cattle and equipment, not land. Even landlessness fails to define a highly significant economic category, since the size and quality of existing fields means that nobody is really that far from being landless to begin with. Rather than being the axis of class formation, landlessness in Mashai is in most cases a disability of the young, those whose turn has not yet come to be allocated a field. But, since crop production plays such a small role compared to wage labor, landlessness is but a minor disability for a household with a migrant or even a local worker. Taking a synchronic view, most of the landless are actually better off than the land-holding, due to the fact that young men are most often employed while older men are not. Of the 16 landless households in the Mashai survey, only two reported members working in the "Food for Work" road gangs; compare this with eleven households on Food for Work out of the thirty-three households that lacked work outside of the village.

Generally, then, where one stands economically in Mashai is a matter not of land-holding but of one's relation to the local and non-local systems of wage-earnings. The most significant distinctions are between workers (high-paid migrant versus low paid local worker); between worker and unemployed, and worker and dependant; and between dependant with remittances and dependant without remittances. These categories all revolve around questions of wage employment and remittances.

But the situation is more complicated than this. As Murray (1981), Spiegel (1979) and others have shown, the shifting, temporary nature of the employment most commonly available to Basotho workers (contract labor in the mines of South Africa) gives a crucial temporal dimension to the most important economic categories. Because of the fact that migrant labor is not a lifelong career but a phase in a man's life cycle (and, as we shall see, because of the way that land and livestock are acquired), the economic position of individuals and households can change drastically over time. The structural relation of a family and its members to the system of migrant labor and to domestic productive resources changes over time as a result of the internal dynamics of household structure. For this reason, as both Murray and Spiegel have stressed, our attention must turn to the "developmental cycle" of household units.

Access to remittances by a household depends on the ability of the members of the household, most of all the men, to obtain wage labor; this, in turn, is highly dependent upon the age and health of the prospective worker. Thus a family which appears prosperous and even affluent at one stage may within a few years be reduced to poverty when the wage-earner is laid off at the mines due to "old age" (he may be 40), illness, or injury; at a later point, access to remittances may be reestablished, either directly through an employed son (occasionally daughter), or indirectly through receipt of bridewealth. Rights to land, too, come – if at all – only later in life, and the accumulation of livestock has, as we shall see, its own place in the succession of phases. If one takes into account the temporal dimension, one may find that the "poor" household one encounters is not an unchanging member of a lower class than its rich neighbor, but only an image of that neighbor's future; the spatial array of rich and poor families may represent not so much different strata of society as different temporal phases in the developmental cycle of the labor reserve household. To the extent that this is true, then, the position of a household must be related to its location in the developmental cycle as well as to its location in the overall economy. Households in Lesotho, in this perspective, are not simply rich or poor; they occupy, in Murray's incisive phrase, "different class positions both simultaneously and serially" (Murray 1981: 99).

It must be pointed out that there is a danger in such formulations of collapsing all economic differences between households into temporal differences between phases, and thus ignoring real differences lying at a deeper level than that of the developmental cycle. One finds, for instance, an increasingly large number of young men who are unable to obtain employment in the mines, while other, older miners are being kept on as part of the industry's move toward "professionalization." There thus arises an important division between young men who have prospects for long-term employment in the mines on the one hand, and those who are excluded from the start from such employment on the other. The new class of unemployed young men does not fit into the "typical" developmental cycle described by Murray, and is significantly different from the category of older unemployed ex-miners, who have had a chance to build up their economic and social investment in the village over the years (cf. Spiegel 1981).

But another, more fundamental, caution is necessary as well. All of the above approaches have taken "the household" as their unit of analysis and produced typologies of the economic or class positions of different households. It is of course important to be able to do this, but an economic analysis which takes households as its basic atoms and conceives economic or class interests and antagonisms only at the level of households will be blind to crucial economic category interests that cut across households. I am thinking here most of all of the categories of employed versus dependent; man versus woman; young versus old. Murray can be spared this criticism to a large extent, thanks to his sharp focus on the question of women's access to remittances and men's earnings, and women's economic place within the household (e.g., Murray 1981: 149–70). But too often (e.g., Innes and O'Meara 1976, Spiegel 1980) economic analyses of rural Southern Africa take the form of sorting households into "types" or "classes" without taking any account of the crucial relations and categorical antagonisms *within* households. These relations cannot always be conceived as production relations, but they are of the greatest significance to any serious economic analysis.

It must be clear already from the above discussion that, although strictly economic categories such as employed and unemployed are crucial, other equally important categories are not so easily derived from production. The most important such categories have been identified as old and young, on the one hand, and men and women on the other. It is true that both sets of categories take on much of their economic importance because of the demands of the production system – the mines recruit only young men, reducing the old and the female to the status of dependants – but it is equally clear that the categories have to do with a great deal more than economics alone and cannot be understood *simply* as relations of production. The different interests corresponding to such categories have economic content, but they are formed by a host of social institutions which can be reduced to "production" only at a loss to our understanding of them. Exploring the economically relevant categories of old and young, male and female, will therefore take us directly into the anthropology of a whole range of social relations clustered around these categories. The following chapter will attempt this in the context of an analysis of the form of economic activity with which the "development" apparatus in Thaba-Tseka was most centrally concerned: that is, the keeping of livestock.

5 The Bovine Mystique: a study of power, property, and livestock in rural Lesotho

Introduction

The Thaba-Tseka Project was originally conceived as a livestock/range management project, as was seen in Chapter 3. From the start the first and most fundamental of the many justifications for the project was seen to be the promise of increased livestock production. Through all the project's various phases, the idea of commercializing and "rationalizing" livestock production remained the heart of the planners' designs for "development" of the region. Since livestock occupied such an important place in the plans and programs of the Thaba-Tseka Development Project, it is appropriate to take an especially careful look at the role of livestock in the local socio-economic system.

It was not only the planners of the Thaba-Tseka Project who were concerned with livestock production; livestock has long been a preoccupation of colonial and post-colonial "development" planners, who have seen Lesotho's grasslands as one of the few potentially exploitable natural resources the country possesses.[1] But planners have been consistently frustrated by what they see as "traditional," "non-commercial" forms of stock-keeping. It has been observed that "the condition of the cattle 'industry' has virtually remained unchanged since the turn of the century despite the continuing efforts of colonial and other European specialists to commercialize it" (LASA 1978: VII–2). Various symptoms have been noted: Basotho livestock owners "tend to regard livestock more as a reserve asset or property of pride than as a commercial commodity" (GOL 1977: AG–17); "cattle are not held by the Basotho solely for economic gain" (LASA 1978: VII–15); "traditional reasons for keeping cattle, e.g. brideprice, prestige, investment, etc. make farmers unwilling to sell their surplus unproductive stock" (FAO 1980: 82); traditional herdsmen value "quantity rather than quality" (FAO 1980: 19); unproductive animals are "retained merely as status symbols" (GOL 1981); always there is "the traditional attitude against selling animals, particularly cattle" (FAO 1980: 19).

Attempts at explanation have tended to fall into one of two categories. First is the theory of the "dual economy." In its simplest form this argument suggests that Basotho keep livestock the way they do because stock are highly valued in Sotho culture for religious, social, and symbolic reasons, as well as economic. Livestock are thus "overvalued" (over their "true" economic value, that is), and it is for this reason that the Basotho keep so many animals and are so reluctant to part with them. These traditional values, the argument goes, are slowly dying out as the modern economy gradually penetrates the tribal world.[2]

A more sophisticated version of this argument appeals not so much to values as to the notion of "traditional" and "modern" sectors, or spheres of exchange (cf. Bohannan 1959). Sansom suggests an evolutionary scheme for the "Southern Bantu areas" of three phases:

The first step was the initial creation of dualism by the addition of a novelty cash economy to subsistence activities. In the second phase, the market economy increased in importance: it co-existed with subsistence production but the cash sector and the subsistence sector were maintained as separate spheres. The final phase is that of interpenetration, when two sources of income – wages and agricultural products – can be recognized, but when the distinction based on source of income no longer provides the basis for the separation of two seemingly autonomous systems for organizing labour and exchange.
(Sansom 1974: 168)

In this perspective, cattle keeping is "the last stronghold of traditional modes." Such things as reluctance to sell and exchange of stock at non-market prices are signs that "the final phase" of interpenetration between traditional and modern sectors, the "breakdown of the relative autonomy of cattle exchange" (Sansom 1974: 174), has not yet been reached.

Opponents of the dualist theory have argued that there is no dual economy, but that apparently "irrational" livestock practices are in fact rational economic choices made by individuals working within local circumstances and constraints. This view can be termed utilitarian. In the utilitarian scheme, if Basotho invest in animals which do not appear to give a good return on capital, this is due to the absence of other opportunities for investment of surplus; under the circumstances livestock may be a "rural bank" for investors who have no other outlets for productive investment. Or, if it seems that people are keeping large numbers of poor, unproductive stock rather than fewer, more profitable animals, it may be argued (*à la* Chayanov) that the investment decisions are being made rationally when one takes into account that the poor family's first concern is security and the survival of the herd, rather than merely maximum off-take. Or, again, if livestock owners are not willing to sell their stock, this is based on a rational appraisal of the use-values of the animals versus a particular amount of cash. And so it goes, with new explanations trotted out as needed on an *ad hoc* basis, always defending the economic rationality of the African.[3]

Data recently collected in Lesotho contradict both the utilitarian and the dualist view, and suggest a different interpretation. The first important finding is that the peculiarities of Sotho livestock keeping reflect a certain structuring of property which makes of livestock a special domain not freely interconvertible with cash. The first part of this chapter is an attempt to demonstrate this fact and to describe the rules governing the category of property, "livestock."

These cultural rules structuring property can never be accounted for by appealing to individuals and their rationality (or their "values"), for individual choices only occur within and in terms of a cultural order which is invisible to utilitarian theory (cf. Sahlins 1976). When I focus on decisions people make about livestock, as I will shortly, it is to illuminate the rules which structure the range of options, not to derive these rules from people's "rational" choices.

Dualist theory serves us no better, for, as I shall demonstrate, although there is a degree of "separateness" between livestock and cash, this can in no way be expressed as a division between "traditional" and "modern" sectors. In place of the vague formulas of dualism, which posit "two economies" or two "autonomous sectors" one can say quite precisely that what is at issue is rather a socially created "one-way barrier" between cash and livestock, and a prestige complex centering on the "livestock" domain so defined. This "Mystique," which makes livestock such a special sort of property, in fact owes its continued existence to a whole range of social forces and interests which transcend the dualist division, as I shall show in the second half of the chapter.

It is at this point that the question of power will be crucial. For it is not enough simply to demonstrate a particular structuring of property as an ethnographic fact (though this is how one must begin); one must go on to explain how this order is reproduced and transformed in practice, and such an explanation must confront the power relations at work in that process. Here utilitarian theory – which reduces a social practice to a sort of voluntaristic consensus of economic good sense – shows its weaknesses. Dualism, for its part, must either fall back on the mystical concept of "inertia" or make the argument (which, as we shall see, could not be more mistaken) that "traditional" livestock practices are maintained by "traditional," "tribal" forces and institutions and transformed by "modern" ones such as wage labor.

Instead, I shall try to explain the ongoing perpetuation and re-creation of "traditional" modes of stock-keeping by dissolving the dualist divide and focusing on the power relations, "traditional" or otherwise, that account for the way livestock practices are structured. I will argue that the "Bovine Mystique" in Lesotho can only be understood in relation to a set of cultural rules which define and valorize livestock as a special domain of property; and that these rules are maintained and re-created as a product of contesting forces articulated around the oppositions men/women (based on the division wage-earning husband/dependent wife), senior/junior (based on the division bridewealth receiver/bridewealth giver), and patron/client (based on the division livestock lender/livestock borrower).

The Bovine Mystique

In 1983 the village of Mashai suffered the loss of some 40 percent of its cattle due to drought. This event was not unforeseen; from the time the spring rains had passed so lightly over Lesotho in the late months of 1982 it had been clear that some such eventuality was likely. Beginning in January 1983 the Ministry of Agriculture was predicting widespread losses and urging livestock owners to sell off their stock before it lost its value through emaciation and, eventually, death. Extension workers in Thaba-Tseka district carried this message to the villages, and officers of the Ministry of Agriculture and the Thaba-Tseka Development Project traveled to remote corners of the district to lecture the people on the need for de-stocking in general, and the particular dangers of the then current drought. One could not help but notice, however, that in Mashai, at least, this exhortation seemed to have little or no effect. In July, when there could no longer be any doubt as to the severity of the situation, the local extension worker in Mashai confessed to me that no one in the village had yet sold any animals due to the drought, and she did not expect that any of them would. Many, many animals would die, she said, but people take such pride in owning stock they refuse to sell them, even when it is clear that they will likely die. They listen to her arguments politely, she noted, and seem to agree with her, but afterwards they just ignore her advice. This, she believed, was because they lack "understanding" (*kutloisiso*).

But the villagers certainly did not fail to understand that cattle were going to die; what had been a widely expressed fear in the spring had become an uncontestable certainty by the winter months of June and July, when it was almost universally acknowledged that cattle would die "in great numbers" in the coming months. Nor was it the case that livestock owners were ignorant of or unfamiliar with the cash market in livestock. Basotho have been selling livestock for cash for a very long time now, and the monthly livestock auctions held in Thaba-Tseka provided a convenient and well-publicized market-place. Livestock owners in Mashai knew about this market, knew how to use it, and usually knew quite accurately the prices being offered there. But whether or not these livestock owners lacked "understanding," it is certainly true that, as the extension worker claimed, no one in Mashai was selling off stock due to the drought. This was apparently the case throughout the district. See Figure 5.1, which shows monthly sales of large stock at Thaba-Tseka from October 1980 through October 1983.

One can see immediately that livestock sales in Lesotho are seasonal; animals are usually sold in the summer months from January to May, and only rarely in the winter and early spring.[4] But what is more striking here is that rather than showing a surge in sales as the drought set in, as one might expect, the figures reveal far *fewer* sales than in a normal year. For the key period from January, when the Government first started urging cautionary selling of stock, to September, when animals began dying off in numbers, total sales in 1983 were just 45 percent of the same period in 1982. This drop in sales was apparently the result of a decline in beef prices which plunged the Thaba-Tseka Market from average prices of 69 cents/kg for oxen in November 1982[5] to a low of 51 cents/kg in March 1983. This is confirmed by the very high proportion of animals offered but not sold at the auctions – more than half at some sales in this period – and by widely voiced dissatisfaction with the prices offered.

But there is something odd here: stock owners in Thaba-Tseka refused to sell because prices were low; but prices were low precisely because the market was being flooded with stock that ranchers all across Southern Africa were being "forced" to sell due to the drought. The effect of the drought on commercial ranchers was to force them to liquidate their assets or risk losing them, thus sales went way up, pushing prices down. In Lesotho, the economic logic of drought seemed to work backwards; instead of selling off stock to cut their losses, stock owners sold fewer animals than ever, responding to drought-depressed prices. The drought itself, meanwhile, was unimpressed by these ma-

```
        *     *                *
        *     *                *
      * *     *                *
      * *     *                *
      * *     *                * *
    * * *     *                * *
    * * *   * *                * *                  *
    * * *   * *            * * *   *                *
    * * *   * *            * * * * *                *
    * * *   * *            * * * * *              * *
      * * * * * *          * * * * *            * * *
  *   * * * * * *          * * * * *            * * *
    * * * * * * *          * * * * * *   * *     * * *
    * * * * * * *          * * * * * *   * *   *   * * *
  * * * * * * * *     *    * * * * * * *       * * * * *
* *   * * * * * * * * *    * * * * * * * *     * * * * *      *
* * _ * * * * * * * * * * * * * * * * * * * *  * * * * * _ _ * * *
O N D J F M A M J J A S O N D J F M A M J J A S O N D J F M A M J J A S O
  1980  |      1981       |       1982       |        1983
```

Figure 5.1, Monthly livestock sales at Thaba-Tseka, October 1980–October
1983
Note: Each '*' represents ten cattle sold. Figures taken from Thaba-Tseka
Livestock Marketing Program records, rounded to nearest ten. The symbol
'–' indicates that no sale was held for a given month

neuvers, and proceeded, according to its own logic, to decimate the
herds of the Basotho. And this, it must be added, came as a great surprise
to no one.

In August 1983, the following conversation was recorded with a
Mashai man who only two months later would lose over half of his large
cattle herd to the drought.[6]

It looks like the drought is very bad now.
Yes.
The grass is all gone. Are you afraid that your animals may die?
Yes, they will die.
They are skinny, aren't they?
Yes.
Don't you want to sell them? Some people think they should sell
them before they may die, then they buy more afterwards.
*If they're dead they're still dead, right? Maybe they will live, and so
they will still be there.*
Is it better to wait and see if they are going to survive or not?
Or I should keep on going with them to look for other places where

there is a little grass and water. Maybe the rain will give us water and they will live.
But perhaps they will die. You don't want to sell them?
Nope.
. . .
So it would be bad for people to sell off their stock?
Truly this would be a terrible thing, because they would be unable to plough. It would be very bad; not a person would even survive. You see, how would we plough? How would we complete the "thatho" ritual – this is a custom of ours – for these children of ours born and yet to be born? How could we live? We would be naked.
But the grass has run out.
Yes, the grass has run out.
But it is better to keep the animals?
These animals – although the grass may run out, better that we people should all be wiped out [i.e. rather than live without animals]. Then we are finished because if the grass should run out then we, too, are finished. There is no other way.
It is a difficult problem.
You see, by the custom and the habit of the Basotho people, we must keep the principles which raised us and not be caused to give them up; it would be a difficult thing. The white people, you see, I might strip my body completely naked – a white person, a Caucasian.
Like me.
Yes. Then this person might strip completely naked like this, right? This is a lady, a woman, she might strip her body naked, and then she has to stay there dressed like that. But this breast of hers, this breast . . . You know it is a very bad thing if this breast of hers is exposed. It is a terrible thing; it is not a thing that can even happen. It is not forgotten. It is their custom and their culture. Now we, too, in the same way, if we should run out of all animals it is a very bad thing. It means our entire way of life is finished. Now that would be to destroy our culture and all that is proper for us.
. . .
So in Sesotho culture livestock are very important.
They are terribly important. They are the most important thing.

This, then, may perhaps serve as a first introduction to the Bovine Mystique. The reader may start to gather that it is true, as economic dualists argue, that livestock in Lesotho are not treated as simple "economic" goods (i.e., commodities); it is true, as well, that they occupy an important and highly embedded place in Sesotho culture. But this is not, as some seem to think, the place to end the explanation. It is, on the contrary, precisely the place to begin it.

In the pages that follow I will attempt to make sense of livestock practices in Lesotho by *explaining* the "Bovine Mystique," not by invoking it. To do this it will be necessary to explore the way the cultural rules make of livestock a special domain of property, and to analyze the social forces which maintain that domain by perpetuating both the rules which give it form and the ideological mystique which surrounds it. Let us consider first of all property.

Property

Property, it has long been observed, is not a relation between people and things. It is a relation between people, concerning things. And if property is always a social relation, one can state as a corollary that property is always structured – always, everywhere, property is structured. The "free market" in commodities of advanced capitalism, of course, is itself a structure, a structure characteristic of and maintained by a particular form of social organization. "The market" is never the absence of a structure, the "natural" on to which culture and power graft themselves as externalities; it is a social institution, like any other, constituted by social forces. Where the constellation of social forces is different, one may anticipate the possibility that property may be structured differently. Such is indeed the case in Lesotho.

Certainly an extremely well-developed market in commodities does exist in Lesotho. The mainstay of the rural economy is cash remittances from migrant laborers in South African mining and industry; capitalism is well established. The economy is highly monetized and has been for at least a century.[7] Buying and selling are basic activities of daily life in Lesotho's villages. But while an item such as a transistor radio or a bar of soap may appear to be subject to the same market mechanisms of pricing, supply, and demand as it is anywhere else, other classes of property are subject to very different sets of rules. Rights to land, for instance, are allocated to heads of households by a land committee (in former times by a chief). With the allocation comes a set of rights and responsibilities over the land, but in no case may the land be bought or sold; legal "ownership" is vested in the Basotho nation, and fields are not commodities.[8] Other domains of wealth may also be distinguished, based on other sets of rules which set them apart from simple commodities. The domain which concerns us here is that of "livestock," which is, in Lesotho, a very special kind of property. (Note that "livestock" is used here as a kind of shorthand for grazing stock only. Pigs and fowl are treated differently, as we shall see.)

Livestock and cash

The first clue that livestock was something other than an ordinary commodity came in the course of investigating bridewealth payments in cash and livestock. Bridewealth in Lesotho is traditionally paid in cattle, but small stock and/or cash are very often substituted in negotiations between the two families concerned.[9] Curiously, however, the rate at which cash is equated to cattle in these transactions is much lower than the going market price. In recent marriages in Mashai, for instance, a typical rate would be M100 or M150[10] to equal one head of cattle, while an average price for the same animal on the cash market might be more like M300. This phenomenon has been noted before (e.g., Sansom 1976) and Murray (1981: 131) has suggested it is due to an "inevitable lag" in the response of bridewealth reckoning to inflation in market prices. It is not clear why such a "lag" should be inevitable. People in Mashai know current market prices for livestock quite accurately; why should this knowledge not be reflected in bridewealth negotiations? In any event, if the differential is due merely to a lag, one might expect people to try to take advantage of the lag, or at least to take it into account. That is, all other things being equal, one would expect that a payer of bridewealth would prefer to pay in cheap cash-units rather than much more valuable cattle-units. Likewise, one would expect bridewealth receivers to prefer to be paid in real cattle (easily convertible to cash at monthly auctions at a rate of something like M300 per animal) rather than in cash-units of M100 or M150. In fact, however, this is not the case. Many bridewealth payers opt to pay in real cattle. This, it could be argued, might be simply because a marriage with real cattle is generally considered of higher standing, "good Sesotho." But it is more puzzling that bridewealth receivers very often prefer to receive cash-units, worth far less than the cash value of the livestock units. When one asks why, one is invariably told that it is because the person in question needs cash, and has little use for cattle. This is a strange answer; in such a case one could take payment in cattle, sell them promptly, and net two or three times as much cash. But a bridewealth payment is an extremely involved social transaction, and one can imagine any number of complicating factors entering into such a simple calculus. The point can be clarified by asking a different question.

No longer speaking of bridewealth, but, in a simple hypothetical choice, I asked: if you were offered a choice between having a fine ox[11] (*pholo e ntle*) or M150, which would you take? Again, large numbers of people – most, in fact, both men and women – chose the cash. This continued to be the case for many even when the amount of cash was lowered to M100, and for some even M50. This, it was explained, was because cash, even a small amount, was more useful to them in their current circumstances than an ox would be. This ranking of use values surprised me – particularly when it came from owners of what the government likes to call "unproductive stock" who were refusing to sell them even in the face of a menacing drought. Such preferences certainly seemed odd, but they hardly suggested an emotional "over-valuing" of cattle for cultural or symbolic reasons – on the contrary, they revealed a systematic *undervaluing* of cattle, side by side with a refusal to part with them. Let us look at the way one interview proceeded as I tried to get my informant, an unemployed young man with a family, to explain this curious undervaluation to me. I began by posing a hypothetical choice in a bridewealth transaction between M150 and an ox (*pholo*); my informant chose the cash. The interview continued:

If you sell an ox at the livestock auction, how much do you get, these days?
If it is big, I might get two hundred pounds (M400).

This is a realistic estimate for a large, fine ox, looking at actual prices offered in this period at the Thaba-Tseka auction. This accurate knowledge of market prices in livestock is widespread in Mashai, especially among men. The interview continued:

Now if someone comes up to you and says "Sir, today I will give you either this fine ox, or this M150 in cash," now which will you choose?
Between an ox and M150 cash?
Yes. Which do you prefer?
I prefer the cash.
Yes. Not the ox?
No.
Why?
The cash can help me with many of my needs.
Yes, I see. It's more useful than the ox?

It is more useful than the ox.
Yes, I understand. But if you want cash, why don't you want to take
the ox and then sell it?
*It would be a big job. Maybe I won't be able to get as much as M150 –
it may be less.*

This was a common answer in such cases. In fact, there is no way a "fine
ox" could fail to bring much more than M150. Even at the time we were
speaking, when the drought had depressed prices and reduced the
animals being sold to walking skeletons, the price being paid for an
average ox at Thaba-Tseka was over M250, and these animals could by
no stretch of the imagination be called "fine." Was my informant really
so ignorant of the market? I doubted it, especially given his earlier
estimate. I pressed him on the point, but he stuck to his story, insisting
that the market price for a good ox could vary between M150 or less and
M400, depending on "luck." It seemed improbable that he really believed this. I tried to make it more improbable by reducing the amount
of cash in the hypothetical choice. Between an ox and M100, he still
preferred the cash. Only when the figure was reduced again to M50 was
he willing to take the ox instead.

So now my informant prefers M100 to an animal he estimates could be
sold for four times that amount. At this point it is hard to avoid the
suspicion that selling the ox is in fact not a real option for him – that the
ox can only be compared to the cash as one use value to another, and that
how much he could sell it for and how easily is not really the point. This
suggests a line of questioning that would not ordinarily come to mind.
Later in the interview:

If someone gave you an ox, now, today, would you keep it?
I would keep it.
Now perhaps you have the ox right now. The person has already
given you the ox. Now it is yours. Now after some weeks someone
comes to you and says: Sir, I want to buy your ox. I will give you
M200. I want that ox. Now what will you do?
Yes ... he wants to buy it?
Yes.
And it is mine?
Yes. It is your ox, and then someone says: I want to buy it. Do you
want to sell it? What will you say?
No. No, I will not sell it to him.
Why not?
I will be already in possession of the ox. Now it is true that I should

only go for money, that I should abandon the ox and go for money.
Only in some other way, not by the method of selling the ox.
That is, you want money more than cattle, but you don't want to sell
the ox?
Yes. Yes.
Why? Because I already know that you think that M200 is more
beneficial than an ox, right?
Yes.
But you don't want to sell it when someone will give you M200.
No. I don't want to.
Why?
Eh . . .
Are you unable to sell it?
I will never sell it if I already own it. I will never sell it.
That is, after the ox is yours you will keep it. You don't want to sell
it?
My ox?
Yes.
Yes. If I have it I will keep it. I will not sell it. I will never sell it if it
is mine.

Here is revealed the barrier between livestock and cash, the social rule
that restricts selling, clearly exposed for the first time.[12] There was
nothing exceptional about this informant. He was young, intelligent,
and widely experienced; he was neither conservative nor especially
enamoured of livestock. The livestock-cash barrier shown in his testimony was evident in nearly every one of the scores of interviews I
conducted on livestock in Mashai. (The exceptions will be discussed
later.) Sometimes it was even more striking, as in the case of a man[13] who
said that he would much prefer even M50 to an ox, since the cattle were
all dying anyway. This was so even though he owned a large herd of
cattle (most of them soon to die, it is true) which he refused to sell, and
had stated that if given an ox he would keep it and not sell it, even if he
were offered market price for it.

It is clear, then, that the fundamental fact here is not that livestock are
very useful economic investments (though they certainly are for many
people) or that they are greatly loved and valued for their symbolic
connotations (though this, too, is often the case) but that livestock and
cash are not freely interconvertible. There exists what one might call a
one-way barrier: cash can always be converted into cattle[14] through
purchase; cattle, however, cannot be converted to cash through sale,

except under certain conditions, conditions usually specified as a great and serious need for money which cannot be raised any other way, a situation arising from an emergency or from poverty.[15]

This is confirmed by two small surveys that were done by the live-stock marketing program of the Thaba-Tseka Development Project in 1978 and 1979, which asked livestock sellers at auctions their reasons for selling. The reason "need to buy food" was given by 85 percent of all sellers; this was followed by "need to buy clothes" and, farther back, "pay for school fees." The project decried the lack of a "production mentality" and noted, quite correctly, that livestock was not being primarily used to generate income, but to store it. But what must be emphasized is that once resources are "stored" in the form of livestock, they cannot be liberated at will, but only under circumstances at which the above figures hint.

A person who chooses M150 over an ox "worth" M300 is choosing a free and untied asset of M150 over "stored" assets of M300. But the way property is structured, these "stored assets" can be liberated only if and when that person should fall destitute; in the meantime, the ox is merely an ox, with whatever use value a particular user may place on it, which may die or be stolen at any time. With the drought on, the range exhausted, and thievery widespread, many people quite sensibly opted for the cash. Others, in choosing the ox, were expressing their convic-tion that the use value of the ox (which is considerable for many people) plus its value as insurance in case of need (when the "stored assets" can be liberated) outweighed the benefits of M150 in cash.

The Bovine Mystique in Lesotho, then, is not a matter of some emotional overvaluing of livestock (indeed, it often generates an *under-valuation* of animals), nor is it a simple resultant of economic individuals rationally allocating their resources as they please (since a man who refuses to sell an ox for M300 may often, according to his own testi-mony, be of the opinion that the benefits of owning an ox are worth less than the rewards of having even a third that amount in the bank). It is, rather, the result of the fact that "livestock" is constituted as a special domain of property in Lesotho by cultural rules, the most important of which establishes a "one-way barrier" between the domains of money and livestock. I have up to now been concerned only to establish the existence of this rule as an ethnographic fact, and to show that it has far-reaching consequences. In the sections to come, I will try to move on toward an explanation of this particular structuring of property by showing some of the interests and social forces which help to establish and maintain this one-way barrier between livestock and cash. To do this it will be necessary first to discuss certain other cultural rules which help give the domain of "livestock" its peculiar shape, as well as the general social setting (household, community, and regional economy) in which the issue arises; and secondly to show the way these rules are challenged and defied by some but defended, enforced, and en-shrouded in a mystique by others in a process that is considerably more complex and dynamic than the discussion up to now has perhaps implied.

Livestock and the household

Our understanding of the situation of the household[16] in the Lesotho labor reserve economy has been revolutionized by the recent work of Colin Murray and other anthropologists influenced by the "new histo-riography" of Southern Africa.[17] The most important aspects of this new understanding have been discussed in the last chapter. Here it is only necessary to review very briefly three main points which have a central bearing on the argument to be advanced here concerning livestock.

First, and most obvious, is the absence of working-age men. The system of labor control known as *apartheid* decrees that a working-age Mosotho man must typically spend ten or eleven months of the year in a South African mining compound hundreds of miles away from his wife and children. This characteristic situation, in which a physically absent man is structurally present as a household's "head" and (usually) as its main source of subsistence, is reflected in the distinction customarily made in Lesotho statistics between "*de jure*" and "*de facto*" members of a household.

The second aspect to be emphasized is the way the structural relation of a family to the system of migrant labor and to domestic productive resources changes over time as a result of the internal dynamics of household structure: the "developmental cycle." Access to remittances by a household depends on the ability of the members of the household, most of all the men, to obtain wage labor; this, in turn, is highly dependent upon the age and health of the prospective worker. Thus a family which appears prosperous and even affluent at one stage may within a few years be reduced to poverty when the wage-earner is laid off at the mines due to "old age" (he may be 40), illness, or injury; at a later point, access to remittances may be reestablished, either directly through an employed son (occasionally daughter), or indirectly through receipt of bridewealth. Rights to land, too, come – if at all – only later in life, and the accumulation of livestock has, as we shall see, its own place in the succession of phases. The corollary to all this is that the position of a household must be related to its location in the developmental cycle as well as its location in the overall economy.

It may be stated as a general proposition that economic dependence of women on men is the sign not of a general and essential female passivity but of structural constraints on the economic freedom of action of women. Nowhere is this more true than in Lesotho, and it is this point I should like to emphasize as the third aspect of family life in the labor reserve. Income earned from migrant labor dominates the rural economy of Lesotho; it is estimated that 70 percent of rural household income is earned by migrant workers in South Africa (Van der Wiel 1977). Yet wage labor in South Africa is, as a rule, not available to women. Not only do the principal employers, the mines, hire only men, but it is actually illegal for Basotho women to enter South Africa to work or to look for work. This does not always prevent them from doing so; nevertheless it is an extremely severe constraint on women's economic options.[18] Rural Basotho women thus most often find themselves dependent – sometimes almost completely dependent – on their access to the earning power of their husbands, lovers, or sons.[19] Claims by dependent women on the earning power of absent men, then, are an extremely important aspect of the rural economic structure, and the gender division thus takes on a fundamental economic importance such as we are more used to associating with class.

Having shown something of the economic structure of the household, let us now look at the form which property relations take within the household, paying special attention to the domains of money and livestock. Money in the household generally falls into the category of "household property," a class of property in Sesotho law and custom "jointly administered by the man and his wife, her authority being subordinate to his" (Ashton 1967: 180). Ideally, the disposition of this money is decided by agreement between husband and wife; legally, the husband has executive authority, which is balanced in part by his legal responsibilities to provide for his wife; in practice, it constitutes a *domain of contestation* between husband and wife and a frequent cause of disputes and even physical fights and beatings. Women have acknowledged legitimate claims on this money to support the family and to provide for their own maintenance, claims which they press forcefully, and they are critical of men for wasting money on beer, tobacco, and, often, on what they regard as useless stock. Men, on the other hand, accuse women of wasting money, of spending it indiscriminately, or even of giving it to their lovers. They are often frustrated by the fact that as soon as their earnings enter the realm of "household money" they are set upon by dependants and quickly depleted. These disputes are a constant and ongoing feature of village life.

Not all money, however, is "of the household" (*ea lelapa*). Women may have their own funds of money which are recognized as theirs and theirs alone, over which the husband is usually conceded to have no authority. This is cash that is acquired through practice of a special skill or trade (e.g., a herbalist), through occasional brewing or baking for sale, or from the keeping of "women's animals."[20] "Women's animals" are pigs and fowl, which are fed, cared for, and owned exclusively by women. This money is outside of the "domain of contestation"; if a woman makes M10 from selling chickens and wants to buy a dress with it, she can do so whether her husband likes it or not.

The other way in which money may lie outside of the "domain of contestation" is for it never to arrive in the household in the first place. Men working in the mines often maintain other women and even families in South Africa in the vicinity of the mining compounds. These may constitute a second "domain of contestation," competing for resources with the first. Along with this is the habit of some Basotho workers of keeping money in secret bank accounts in Maseru or elsewhere as a personal store of cash "for their own enjoyment" (*ea boithabiso*). It is in this context that one should understand the fact that migrant workers, as a rule, never tell their wives how much money they earn.

One has, then, a domain of household money, over which the husband has general authority and the wife strong legitimate claims (the

Women's money	"Domain of contestation"		
	Household money	Illicit second "household" (RSA)	Husband's private fund
Money within household		Outside of household, not always present	

Figure 5.2. Money and the household

"domain of contestation"), a private fund for women ("women's money"), and sometimes a secret or extra-household private fund for men, in the form of a private bank account (see Figure 5.2).

Livestock, as already noted, is culturally divided into men's animals – the grazing animals, which I have referred to in short-hand as "livestock" – and women's animals – pigs and fowl. This is not only a symbolic association; as we have seen they constitute two different categories of property. "Women's animals" are the personal property of the woman. She may sell them if she likes and spend the money as she pleases. "Men's animals" are household property, and firmly under the authority of the husband.[21] If a woman should buy a sheep, for instance, with her own personal money, the sheep will not be her personal property (as would, for instance, a chicken); it will be household property and she will be said to be buying it "for her husband." Should that sheep be sold, the cash would be household property, and no longer her own (personal).[22]

Men's animals are classed as "household property" but they do not constitute a "domain of contestation" in the way "household money" does. Certainly the wife and other dependants have certain claims to the use of the animal and its products, but the actual resources invested in the animal are secure and out of the realm of contestation, and this due to the barrier that restricts their conversion to cash. If a man comes home from the mines with M300 in his pocket, the money will be set upon by his dependants; his wife may present him with a demand to buy her a new dress or furniture for the house, the children may need new blankets. If, on the other hand, he comes home with an ox purchased with that M300, the question will not arise. It is in this sense, then, that there is no "domain of contestation" when one speaks of livestock, only a sexual division of rights and responsibilities over different kinds of animals, as Figure 5.3 indicates.[23]

Women's animals (pigs, fowl)	Men's animals (cattle, sheep, goats, horses, etc.)
Women's property	Household property

Figure 5.3. Livestock in the household

Livestock and the community

Livestock is never the concern of one household alone. Of all types of property, it is the most embedded in the social relations of the rural community. Bridewealth payments, of course, are one form of this embeddedness, and nearly every household is in this way linked to other households through long-term, ongoing bridewealth debts and credits reckoned, if not always paid, in livestock. (There will be more to say about this later.) But bridewealth is not the only way that households may be linked through livestock. It is common in Lesotho for owners of livestock, particularly owners of large herds, to place animals with friends, relatives, and neighbors on a long-term basis.[24] The recipient is expected to care for the stock and to return them to their rightful owner on demand; in exchange he or she receives the use of the animals and all the proceeds and profits arising from them (such as sale of wool), and usually some or all of the offspring of such animals. Through such arrangements, livestock owners can take advantage of distant pastures, relieve themselves of management responsibilities, and establish re-lations of clientage with the recipients of the loaned animals. In this way, the owner of a large number of livestock can come to be a "big man," both through the patron-client relationships so established, and by the ostentatious display of his animal wealth throughout the village and beyond. A man with animals may also establish himself in the com-munity by helping others with various chores or rituals that may require animals, or, less altruistically, by share-cropping the fields of those unable to plough by themselves. Livestock are always embedded in these relations of dependence, and, whenever one finds an animal per-forming a technical task, one will usually find that it is performing a social task as well. In all these social tasks, too, the *number* of animals is of more importance than their "productivity" in the narrow economic sense.

A man who is wealthy in livestock (known in Sesotho as a *morui*, plural *barui*)[25] thus regards his herd as a resource which is at once social and economic. If a man needs a sheep, for instance, he may go ask a *morui* to help him by selling one to him. The price asked in such cases is said to vary greatly depending on why the man needs the sheep, how much money he has, and what sort of relationship he has to the *morui*, leading one informant to claim "a sheep has no price," meaning that the "price" might be M10 or M60 depending not on the sheep or the market but on the social situation.[26] Livestock are nearly always involved in these relations of patronage and a man with many animals is for this reason greatly respected – he is a man "who can help the people."

This point must be emphasized. The *morui* is respected not merely as someone who is wealthy, but as someone possessing a particularly social *form* of wealth, which "belongs," in some sense, to the whole community. One is respected not only for the amount of one's wealth, but also for its "sociability." Most informants insist that a man who owns many livestock will be more respected than another man who owns a comparable amount of cash or consumer goods (furniture, clothes, radios, etc.). (Though, as we shall see, there are important divisions of opinion on this point.) "He is a chief," it is said, "he is a *morui*"; and this may be the case even where the man in question is, apart from his livestock, obviously poor. People describe with some fondness the stereotypical figure of the *morui*, who only cares about animals and lives like a pauper. I asked one informant if a man rich in other things might not be respected as well. There followed:

Yes, he is a rich man (*morui*), but you will not hear him praised as a *morui*. The one who is praised is the one who has the animals, even though they continue to be equal [in richness]. Often, some of these *barui* – you will find that he has acquired all these animals, he has no house, he has no chair, he has deprived himself of clothes, wearing just a plain grey blanket, he has no shirt – but the cattle are many!

Informants explain that respect is due a man with livestock because livestock help the whole community. I suggested to one informant that a man with money in the bank had made a good investment, since it would increase with interest. "Yes," he replied.

that is correct, only it is increasing for him alone and not for the mutual help of all we Basotho. Because with the cattle, he will hire me with them, so that he ploughs for me or does various things for me with these animals. Now I, too, am able to live. Well, when someone can see how he, too, may survive, truly that is fine... With money, he is not going to help me with it. It is something which is just closed up (deposited) there, and it will work for his household alone.

Cash and cash goods are a selfish, household-centered form of wealth. The possessions of a man who is wealthy in this way are:

merely nice things. He has no animals, if you visit him, he doesn't give us milk, he doesn't loan us the animal with which we will plough. Now the *morui*, we will respect him because when we go to borrow, he lends me an ox, he lends me a horse.

A man with money "only helps himself"; a true *morui* "knows the poor."

Livestock and migrant labor

The above discussion has already indicated that livestock practices in Lesotho are inextricably bound up with the migrant labor system and the rural institutions of household and community which are its product. Here it will be shown that the connection between "traditional" livestock practices and "modern" wage labor is even more direct and more immediate than has yet been indicated (see Tables 4.2 and 5.1).

There is reason to be suspicious of official livestock figures; nevertheless, the general trends are certainly clear. When the dramatic wage increases of the 1970s took effect, Basotho miners seized the opportunity to invest in livestock, especially cattle, in unprecedented numbers. At the same time, the influx of cash meant that fewer households were placed in situations where they were obliged to sell off stock – hence the dramatic decline in exports (see Table 5.2).

Two points must be emphasized here. First is that livestock in Lesotho, however useful and necessary they may be, are less an "industry" or a "sector" than they are a type (however special) of consumer good. They are purchased when times are good and sold off only when times are bad. A drop in exports, as in Table 5.2, is the sign not of a depressed

Table 5.1. *Imports of livestock, 1970–1978*

Year	Cattle	Sheep	Goats
1970	4,730	12,416	446
1971	6,869	16,194	59
1972	5,028	6,202	124
1973	4,067	3,313	378
1974	3,046	3,068	137
1975	31,756	6,152	213
1976	33,821	9,134	102
1977	47,673	17,519	179
1978	57,787	36,138	223

Source: Taken from GOL 1980: 172.

Table 5.2. *Exports of livestock, 1970–1978*

Year	Cattle	Sheep and Goats
1970	11,408	16,143
1971	8,656	10,867
1972	8,918	31,766
1973	12,894	31,211
1974	9,225	19,141
1975	3,503	7,035
1976	1,250	2,267
1977	1,223	533
1978	574	486

Source: Taken from GOL 1980: 173.

"industry" but of a rise in incomes; a "boom" in exports, on the other hand, would be the mark of a disaster. Although the Mystique declared that "Basotho make their livings with their animals," and another mystification posits livestock as an "industry" which is "the mainstay of the mountain areas,"[27] one must observe that contrary to appearances Lesotho is, in these times, a net *importer* of livestock, and that the Basotho are not livestock producers, but livestock consumers.

This is even more clear when one notes that, in spite of far more imports than exports, "[a]n examination of livestock population changes in the last twenty years suggests a declining trend" (GOL 1980:171) with cattle numbers remaining nearly constant. With the range badly degraded and terribly overstocked, it seems that the national herd exceeds not only the optimum "carrying capacity" (generally put at less than half the current population), it exceeds even the literal biological carrying capacity of the land. Imports are necessary even to maintain current numbers, and the herd, left unsupplemented by imports, would see no natural increase at all, but more likely a "natural decrease."[28]

The second point is that the resources that I have argued are "stored" as livestock are nearly always wages earned in South Africa; the two are indissolubly linked, as the above figures indicate. Livestock cannot therefore be considered in any way a separate "sector"; still less should stock-farming be seen as an alternative to migrant labor. Rather, one should speak of a single livestock/migrant labor complex, in which the funds for buying animals, as well as many of the reasons, derive from migrant labor.

I have already shown that one of the things that makes livestock such an attractive investment is its ability to establish social bonds between a man and the larger community. But the reason these social bonds are so important and so difficult to maintain in other ways is precisely because most men spend large parts of their working lives in distant South African mining compounds. Murray has shown that this need of the migrant worker to invest in the rural homestead and community is a central fact of economic life in Lesotho. In these terms he has analyzed the modern meaning of bridewealth in Lesotho, and shown that it represents a socially and economically necessary form of investment under the conditions of the labor reserve, and to his analysis I have nothing to add (Murray 1981, 1977). I point out only that, even where livestock is not used as bridewealth, it performs similar functions, insofar as it: (1) establishes the legitimacy of a husband's claims to be legal "head" of a household (and its children) by providing tangible and visible support to dependants, even in the husband's absence; (2) serves as a "placeholder" for the absent man, in the household and the community, symbolically asserting his structural presence even in the face of his physical absence; and (3) involves the absent man in relations of patronage and reciprocity with other villagers and establishes for him a prestigious social position and a large social network in the village to which he will, one day, return unemployed.

The general pattern is this: a man builds up his herd during the years he works in the mines, during which time the animals are of use to the man's family and many others in the village, and structurally "hold his place." After leaving the mines, the man returns to the village to "scratch about on the land" (Murray 1979: 337) and to try somehow to survive. This is the point at which livestock begin to be sold, in response to absolute shortages of minimum basic necessities such as food and clothing. Left to itself, as noted above, a herd will do well even to maintain its size in the degraded and crowded rangeland of Lesotho; if animals are being regularly sold for basic necessities, even if the rate of such sale is low, herd size declines, and tends toward zero. Livestock is thus acquired when working and used up when laid off – a sort of special "retirement fund" for migrant laborers, a role for which livestock as a domain of property is specially suited, as we shall see in the next section.

This mode of livestock keeping, in which stock-holding is an appendage to wage-laboring, is in fact the dominant one in Lesotho. Not all livestock owners are current or former migrant laborers, it is true, but nearly all of them owe their stock, if not to their own wage labor then to a link with someone else's (through bridewealth, for instance). The traditional figure of the *morui* with thousands of animals who lives the pure Sotho life and subsists on his animals is almost never encountered in real life, and the genuine commercial stock farmer seems a rarer sight still.[29] Certainly there are some very large herds, and some people for whom livestock provide a way of making a living within the country, but these are very few. According to the 1970 Agricultural Census, 92 percent of all cattle in Lesotho are in herds of twenty-five or less; 63 percent are in herds of ten or less. Seventy percent of all sheep are in herds of 200 and less, and the remainder are concentrated in the hands of only 2 percent of the households.[30] For the vast majority of the population, these smaller herds are storehouses for wealth earned elsewhere.

One can see from this how wrong it is to consider livestock keeping and migrant labor as separate unrelated activities, or to conclude, as the Thaba-Tseka Project did, that the fact that surveyed livestock sellers reported no source of income other than agriculture means that they are "serious stock farmers" as opposed to "migrant laborers." Investment in livestock is not an alternative to migrant labor but a consequence of it. The sale of an animal is not "off-take" of a surplus, but part of a process which culminates in the destruction of the herd. Buying and selling stock are activities characteristic of employed and unemployed miners, respectively; they are phases in the migrant laborer's life cycle.

The re-creation of tradition

In the preceding sections, I hope to have shown that the apparent oddities of Sotho livestock keeping derive from the fact that "livestock" is a type of property set apart from ordinary simple commodities by cultural rules which establish a one-way barrier between livestock and money and a prestige complex centering on the domain of property so defined. We are now in a position to ask a more productive question than those generated by utilitarian or dualist paradigms, namely: what social forces account for and maintain this structuring of property and its associated prestige complex? We may approach this question by looking at the way the divergent interests of different categories of people are arrayed around the question of the Bovine Mystique.

First, let us consider the different interests at work within the household. A man at work in the mines of South Africa is laboring under two economic necessities: first, he must support his wife, children, and other dependants back in the village; and secondly, he must secure, economically and socially, his own future "retirement." Investment in livestock can help to accomplish both these things. It maintains his place in the household by providing real material support (from the proceeds and labor of the animals), a symbolic placeholder in his absence, and insurance against calamity (when the "stored assets" are liberated). It maintains his place in the community, as I have shown, by creating for him a network of social relations of reciprocity and patronage and a prestigious and respected social position, even in his absence. Finally, and crucially, it establishes a fund of savings which simultaneously lies within the household (and lends support to it) and is inaccessible to it under most circumstances. Livestock can thus constitute a special sort of "retirement fund" which is effective precisely because it cannot be accessed.

Other means of storing wealth are less effective (from the man's point of view) not because they offer less "return" on the investment, but precisely because they are not "protected" the way livestock is. Resources in the household which are not invested in livestock necessarily fall within the "domain of contestation," where male control is compromised by the legitimate claims of dependants (see "Livestock and the household," above). Money, even money in the bank, does not have the same resistance to the everyday needs of the household. It is not "well saved" as are livestock ("*Ha e bolokehe joalo ka liphoofolo*"). "Money does not stay with a person," runs a Sesotho saying often invoked in explaining this point. This does not only mean that it can be frittered away on frivolous things; even money soberly and carefully saved in the bank will run out, for a fund of cash must respond to claims from which livestock is exempt. Money disappears, one man told me, not only because of women's reckless spending (a common complaint) but "because a child is sick, or in need of clothes, or we want to build houses." The interview continued:

But if you have livestock will you keep them? Won't you sell them to buy the other things?
I may just sell one in a year. This little money might last me two years or more. I am still left with the others, they go on breeding, they go on doing work, they keep going.
They won't run out?
Oh, no. Animals will not run out.

This is not true, of course (though it is commonly asserted by promoters of the Mystique) – the animals *do* run out, as nearly any older man in Mashai will tell you if you ask him why he doesn't have any. But one can see from this the way that livestock is protected from the legitimate claims (e.g. a child is sick, a child is unclothed) that can be made on money. And this protected status derives, as we have seen, not simply from the practical difficulty of selling an animal, but from a socially created barrier, in the form of a cultural rule.

The ability of livestock to effectively serve as a "retirement fund" therefore depends on the maintenance of the barrier separating livestock and cash. Without the Mystique, livestock would lie squarely within the "domain of contestation," and would no longer be protected against the claims and ordinary needs of household life which make of cash such a fleeting asset. Every time an animal is sold, resources leave the domain of livestock for that of money; they leave a protected enclave of men's property for an exposed, contested position in the midst of the intra-household struggle over the disposition of men's earnings. In the same way, when the livestock-cash barrier is challenged, it threatens to throw the entire domain of livestock into that same contentious realm.

Under the terms of the Bovine Mystique, resources invested in livestock can be expected to stay there and patiently wait for the migrant's return to the village without being eaten away by the real but less than compelling needs of his dependants. At the same time, they visibly support his family, symbolize his own presence, and establish his place in the community as a secret Maseru bank account could never do. To the extent that this system works well for migrant-laboring men, one may begin to speak of a category interest on the part of men in maintaining the rules and ideology which make it work. I speak of a "category interest," as suggested in Chapter 4, in a way analogous to the usual conception of class interest, where a "category" occupies a certain specified structural position in society and possesses certain interests corresponding to that position. It is true that not all men are migrant laborers, but migrant labor looms so large in the lives of male Mosotho villagers that it may be said to possess determinant force in shaping the interests of a "category" (men) that is in fact defined by gender and not simply a relation of production.[31]

If men have an interest in preserving the inviolability of livestock-as-retirement fund, women have an interest in destroying and eroding this privileged domain. Where men build up the mystique of livestock-owning, women tear it down; where men protect their stored assets for the future, women lay siege to them with claims for the present. It is not that women have no concern for the future, only that they are occupied most immediately with the real and often pressing needs of the present. We have already seen that household money is quickly set upon by the claims of dependent women; this same pressure is brought to bear on the domain of "livestock," and for the same reasons. This is not to say that wives are necessarily opposed to their husbands keeping animals. When a man comes home with livestock his wife will be glad to see them; she will be glad to see *any* resources coming into the household sphere, since (in her view) such resources are more often squandered on beer and other women. And few women would oppose the purchase of a certain number of cattle for ploughing, since this makes an important contribution to the maintenance of the family. But the overriding interest of dependent women in getting access to men's earnings to meet the immediate needs of themselves and their children can give rise to a female challenge to two key aspects of the mystique surrounding "men's animals."[32]

First, and most common, is an ideological assault on the prestige complex. It is not women who sing the praises of the *morui*, and the accumulation of large numbers of stock is often described by women as foolish and wasteful. The "traditional" pride in stock is denounced as old-fashioned and lacking in "understanding," while the virtues of wealth in money are extolled. Money in the bank is safe and gives a good return; large herds of useless animals only give one trouble, and anyway there is no grass for them to graze, so they will only die, or if not that end up getting stolen. Between a *morui* with lots of animals and a second man equally wealthy in money and consumer goods, but with no animals, who will be more respected? Most men argue for the man with livestock, citing the peculiarly "Sotho" character of wealth in livestock, as well as its "sociality," as shown earlier. Women interviewed on this point rarely agreed. They argue that the two will be equally respected, or even that the man with money is more respected, and go on to reel off the familiar merits of money as against livestock, laying particular emphasis on the assertion that the man with money "lives better" than the *morui* who is unable to properly clothe and house himself and his family in spite of his great wealth in animals. In this way, the male prestige complex of the Mystique is continually eaten away at by the ideological attacks of women.

The second challenge to the Mystique posed by women is at the level of actual economic practice. Not surprisingly, women who challenge the prestige complex in general ideological dispute also attempt to discourage their husbands from buying what they regard as useless animals with "household money." Sometimes, however, women seem to be willing to go even further: to advocate violation of the "one-way barrier" restricting sales. This may be, as above, in the form of encouragement to the husband, as: these sheep are all going to die or get stolen one day, and they do us no good, why don't we sell them and put the money to use? This type of exhortation, however, is not likely to succeed; it is precisely this request that the Mystique guards against so well. For the husband in such a case to sell would not only violate his own "retirement fund," it would (as we shall see) be seen as an unsociable gesture to the community, and a humiliating sign of destitution as well. Women are in a much better position to challenge the system when it happens that they own stock themselves. This is easily seen in some of the hypothetical scenarios I used to reveal the one-way barrier in the first place. Most often when given a choice between M100 or M150 cash and an ox, women choose the cash, reflecting the high value they place on money and their realization that the ox's cash "value" of M300 is irrelevant as long as it, as a "men's animal," is unsellable and out of the "domain of contestation." But sometimes a woman given this choice will opt for the ox and explain that she will then sell it and net a greater amount of money which she will then put in the bank.[33] With married women such answers must be understood as wishful thinking: the woman would have no right to sell such an animal without her husband's assent, which would not, as a rule, be given. With widows, however, it is a very real question, and the only case I know of where "men's animals" were actually sold in cold blood, out of a simple preference for money and not as a last resort in time of need, did in fact involve a widow.[34] One widowed woman, when I asked how it was that she could, in the cash/ox scenario, so coolly sell off her hypothetical ox for cash when others were so reluctant to do this, explained that men have such pride (*boikhohomoso*) in owning animals that they will not sell them, even when they need or want the money they could get from them. Someone like herself, on the other hand, who has no pride in animals, can take the ox and sell it for the extra cash.

Such tensions between husbands and wives are usually to be found where livestock, or even the idea of livestock, is present. They are part of the larger contestation over the disposition of men's earnings which is so much a part of family life in Lesotho. But what is at issue is not only where the earnings will go, but what rules will govern the form of property in which they have been invested. It is not only a matter of whether a particular ox will be sold, or whether a particular herd of sheep is really a waste of money; at issue is the Mystique itself. One must understand these sometimes petty-sounding quarrels for what they are: real arenas of contestation in political, economic, and ideological practice, arenas in which "traditional" rules and valuations are invoked, to be sure, but simultaneously challenged, renegotiated, and re-created in the course of daily life. In this way the Mystique is constantly at issue, and its perpetuation owes nothing to "inertia" or primordial "Sotho" sentiments and everything to real contemporary social forces.

The forces brought to bear by the category interests generated by the relation migrant laboring husband/dependent wife, and articulated around the gender division men/women, are indeed crucial, but the picture is more complex than such a simple schema might imply. I will now try to indicate some other social forces which come into play as "traditional" livestock practices are challenged, defended, and reestablished.

We have seen that the economic position of individuals and households can change drastically over time, chiefly because migrant labor is not a lifelong career but a phase in a man's life cycle. An obvious consequence of this is the tremendous concentration of earning power in the hands of younger men, leaving the older generation often impoverished and dependent. It is in this context that one can begin to speak of a divergence of interest between the younger, wage-earning generation (juniors) and an older generation of unemployed men and dependent and/or widowed women (seniors), a divergence which may play a part in the re-creation of "traditional" livestock practices.

It seems to be the case that the main channel for the flow of remittances from the junior to the senior generation is bridewealth. Marriage payments involve a great many households and a substantial amount of resources. Murray cites a study finding that "for nearly one fifth of households, annual *bohali* [bridewealth] transfers (in or out) represent about one third of the median household income" (Murray 1977: 84). Ordinary cash remittances from married men, on the other hand, are apparently sent nearly always to wives, and only rarely to parents or grandparents (Van der Wiel 1977; Gay 1980a). Unmarried sons and daughters may make a greater contribution to the parents, but here, too, a son's first priority is his own household, for which he prepares by saving up bridewealth. The most important intergenerational transfers of wealth, then, occur not between son and parents but son and parents-in-law, in the form of bridewealth. This is the key to how generational interests are brought to bear on the cultural rules governing livestock practices.

Murray has argued (1981: 147) that the senior generation has an interest in high levels of bridewealth and that the power of the seniors helps maintain prevailing customary levels which seem extremely high from the point of view of the actual earning power of a young man in these times.[35] In the same way, I would like to argue, the senior generation has an interest in promoting and protecting the special status of livestock against its detractors. This is so because livestock is a category of wealth preeminently suited to bridewealth payments, to which the senior generation consequently has a particularly strong claim.

To understand why this is the case it is necessary to remember that in Lesotho bridewealth is not a single transaction or ceremony, but a series of payments made over many years. A marriage is not a yes or no proposition, but a process of becoming, in which the marital bonds are strengthened and given legitimacy with the passage of time and the payment of bridewealth over many years.[36] The amount of bridewealth required to nominally "complete" a marriage is so high that, in Mashai, at least, marriages are rarely actually completed, and most married men never fully pay off their nominal bridewealth debts to their wives' families. Thus the wealth of young men is constantly the object of more or less legitimate bridewealth claims on the part of in-laws – claims which may or may not be successful but must always be reckoned with.

Under these circumstances, the cultural identification of livestock (and especially cattle) as the proper currency of bridewealth takes on new importance. If a married man comes home from the mines with a new radio, his in-laws will have no special claim to it; if, however, he returns with a cow, they may have a very good claim to be given that cow, or at least its progeny. One may thus speak of an interest on the part of the senior, bridewealth-receiving generation in valorizing the domain of livestock over and above all other kinds of property. Likewise, when an animal is sold, it leaves a sphere of property to which elders have special rights (through bridewealth) for the private, household-oriented domain of money and consumer goods. It is true that bridewealth is often paid in cash, and that in-laws may be said to have claims to a migrant's cash savings as well as his livestock. These claims to cash, however, are not as strong as claims to cattle, since cattle are specifically defined as the currency of bridewealth, and – more cynically but perhaps more to the point – because money may be hidden or denied, whereas livestock are a highly visible and public form of

163

wealth.[37] The senior generation thus has an interest in defending the prestige of those who accumulate livestock, and in preventing resources already stored in livestock from being siphoned off into other domains to which it has no special claims. The junior generation, all other things being equal (which, of course, they never are) may be expected to have opposing interests for the same reasons.

It must be noted that this set of interests (seniors vs. juniors) cross-cuts the men/women division discussed earlier. The positions of older women and younger men are in this respect ambivalent. Where older women are dependent on cash remittances from a wage-earning son or other man, their interests are, like those of wives, opposed to the Mystique. Where the main channel of access to the earning power of younger men comes through bridewealth, however, older women, like older men, have an interest as seniors in promoting the Mystique. Younger men, too, are pulled in both directions. On the one hand they have an interest, as we have seen, in protecting, valorizing, and investing in livestock as a "retirement fund"; as soon as they do, however, they find the immobilized resources which are so well protected against claims from within the household set upon by claims from without, on the part of in-laws and (as we shall see) others. The positions of senior men and junior women, on the other hand, are unequivocal, with senior men strong supporters of the Mystique, junior women its constant attackers.

It should be noted, in passing, that the fact that young people are more often hostile to the Mystique does not imply that "traditional" practices are inevitably dying out with time. The loyalty of the older generation to "traditional" livestock customs is rooted in real economic interests which they, as a category, possess, and is in no way simply a "holdover" from old pre-capitalist days (particularly since the "old days" in question were not pre-capitalist in the least). Young and old occupy different structural positions, and thus have different interests. It is true that in twenty years the "conservative" "traditional" old people of today will be dead – but there will still be old people, and if their structural position has not changed they will continue to support the customs which are in their interests, for which they in turn will be characterized as "traditional" and "conservative." An intergenerational struggle is not necessarily an indicator of coming change, and it need not signal the death of tradition. It is a contentious, dynamic process, but it is through precisely such contentious, dynamic processes that tradition is, and always has been, re-created.

One more set of interests bearing on the question of livestock practices is generated by the relation livestock lender/livestock borrower, which one might also term patron/client. We have already seen that livestock is a particularly "social" form of wealth, which participates in the economic life of the community in a way that more "personal" forms of wealth such as money do not. A man with a large herd may place animals with friends and relatives on a semi-permanent basis, and even smaller herds are usually enmeshed in networks of reciprocal favors, patronage, and dependence. Thus, although livestock is legally the property of a single household, it is a kind of property to which many dependants, and in fact the entire community, may be said to have some sort of claim. It is because livestock is a social, shared domain of wealth that livestock borrowers may be expected to promote the prestige complex that makes the *morui* a "big man" to be respected. Likewise, these dependants have no interest in valorizing the accumulation of "selfish" forms of wealth such as money and consumer goods, since they will have no access to these. Again, when stock is sold, an animal to which many clients had customary rights is converted to private resources which will help only their owner. Clients can be expected to resist such an occurrence, and thus to support the "one-way barrier." It is not clear how much power clients have in such a case, but it is certain that an unnecessary sale of an animal is regarded as an anti-social gesture. One man told me that he could sell a certain ox at auction "if nobody here wants it." I assumed that he meant "if nobody here wants to buy it," but it soon became clear that he meant "if nobody here wants to use it"; it seems he would not sell without the permission of his clients.

If livestock borrowers have an interest in supporting the prestige complex and the one-way barrier that constitute the Bovine Mystique, what of the livestock lenders, the patrons? It might at first seem that livestock owners have an "economic" interest in relieving themselves of their constraints by destroying the one-way barrier and freeing themselves to do what they like with their property, even if that means selling it and reinvesting their wealth in less social ways. But such reasoning applies only to some sort of fictional "ideal capitalist"; in fact, the whole logic of the system runs the other way. It is not only that most livestock owners, as men, have an interest in maintaining livestock as a men's "retirement fund"; what makes the Mystique work is a prestige complex of which the livestock owner is the beneficiary. It may be true that the rules governing livestock obstruct a wealthy stock owner's road to capital accumulation, but at the same time they make him a *morui*, the most respected man in the community. Livestock lenders, even more than their clients, have an interest in promoting the Mystique.

The opponents of the Mystique, then, are neither the patrons nor their clients, but those who neither lend nor borrow livestock but earn a cash income and base their claims to prestige on assets other than animals. Livestock's most vociferous detractor in Mashai was a relatively wealthy man who owned no livestock at all, but had invested instead in building the village's largest and most modern house, complete with stereo and other luxury goods.

I have argued that "traditional" livestock practices in Lesotho are supported and attacked by a range of cross-cutting category interests based on the oppositions men/women, seniors/juniors, and patrons/clients. The Bovine Mystique is thus continually being challenged, fought out, and renegotiated – in ideological practice, as the Mystique is defended and attacked in daily argument, oratory, and conversation – and in economic practice, as couples and communities come into conflict over actual decisions concerning their animals. Such conflict is not a sign of disintegration or crisis; it is part of the process of maintaining and recreating "tradition," and "tradition" is never simply a residue of the past. If the cultural rules governing livestock keeping in Lesotho persist, it is because they are *made* to persist; continuity as much as change must be created and fought for. These rules may be "traditional," and they may be resistant to change, but they are not inert; they are perpetually challenged and always at issue, and always there is something at stake.

Conclusion

In the above sections I have described the way that livestock practices in rural Lesotho are structured and suggested some explanations for this. The explanations offered are tentative and may need to be revised or abandoned as we learn more about this neglected area. The account here has attempted only the necessary preliminary task of describing the rules that make of "livestock" a special category of property and source of prestige, and showing some of the interests which maintain these rules and make them work, along with other, opposing interests which introduce ambiguities and resistances. This preliminary analysis may perhaps make it possible to achieve an informed understanding of the events which occurred when a "development" project attempted to commercialize livestock keeping in the Thaba-Tseka District. Chapter 6 below represents an attempt to reach such an understanding.

Part IV
The deployment of "development"

6 Livestock development

From the very start, the Thaba-Tseka Project was conceived as a live-stock and range management project. "Livestock," declared the 1975 FAO/World Bank Preparation Mission, "must play the major role in the development of the mountain areas." Given the scarcity of arable land in the Thaba-Tseka area, and the fact that more than 90 percent of the total area is suitable only for ruminant grazing, it seemed clear that "the contribution which can be made by the mountains in Lesotho's economic development will largely depend on livestock development" (FAO/World Bank 1975: Annex 1, 10–12). A 1978 CIDA appraisal written just before the launching of Phase Two of the project noted that the project "was predominantly mounted on the premise that the exten-sive range and livestock population of the area represented by far the greatest potential asset to be developed in the mountain region gener-ally." The original project planners, the report observed, had felt that successful "Mountain Development" would be possible only through the development of a commercial livestock industry, which would in turn depend on the achievement of the following five aims:

1 Developing appropriate marketing outlets for livestock and convincing farmers to market their non-productive stock.
2 Controlling the use of grassland to permit a regeneration of the natural climax of grasses suitable for grazing.
3 Developing and maintaining a program of grassland improvement and utilization to maximize productivity of the natural sward.
4 Reducing the arable acreage required to sustain an adequate output of subsistence crops for local consumption.
5 Increasing arable acreage given over to the production and conservation of fodder to support livestock production during seasons of limited growth. (CIDA 1978R)

The report went on to note that:

After some five years of project planning and development the options as determined by the kind and amount of resources available remain as restrictive as first conceived. If anything, the direction indicated above now stands out even more clearly as the only way to proceed to accomplish the social and economic objectives established

for the project.
(CIDA 1978R: 2)

The heart of the Thaba-Tseka Project, then, was its program for livestock development. It was here that the planners placed their strongest emphasis and their greatest hopes. Indeed, the prospect of the development of a mountain livestock industry was the principal justification for the entire project. Yet it was in just this area that the planners suffered their keenest disappointments and encountered their worst frustrations. It is therefore of the greatest importance for our purposes to understand what happened when the plans produced by the "development" problematic described in Part II encountered the elaborately structured local livestock system described in Part III. This chapter will describe and analyze the experience of the Thaba-Tseka Project's livestock development initiatives under three headings: (1) Range Management; (2) Livestock Marketing; (3) Improved Stock and Fodder Production. A discussion of some more general issues raised by this experience follows.

Range management

Chapter 3 has already described the proposals for range management proposed in the original planning documents for the Thaba-Tseka Project. The core of the scheme was the division of the 32,800 hectares of cattle-post grazing land in the project area into eight controlled grazing blocks of about 4,000 hectares each. On three of the eight blocks grazing associations were to be established in which members possessing improved stock and adhering to recommended management practices would be given exclusive grazing rights. The remaining five blocks would be left "open," but overgrazing would be controlled through the introduction of resting and rotational grazing. Extension, research, seeding and fertilization, and other range activities were to be carried out within the framework established by the system of grazing blocks. This scheme at full development was supposed to allow the project area to support twice its current animal population, with animals running some 20 percent heavier, "producing at a much higher level" (FAO/World Bank 1975: Annex 2, 17). Incremental production resulting from the Project was projected at 500 tons of carcass weight meat, 40 tons of wool, and 10 tons of mohair annually (FAO/World Bank 1974: 14).

The range proposals described in the early planning documents, however, were never put into effect, and the grazing-block system was not implemented by the field staff who started work in Thaba-Tseka beginning in 1975. The main reason for this was simply that the project had no legal power to restrict movement of livestock, limit numbers, or restrict access to grazing. The planners seemed to have assumed that the project could divide up and regulate the rangeland in any way it pleased, but under the laws of Lesotho it had no such right. As was observed in Chapter 4, the cattle-post rangelands of Lesotho are legally held by the nation and administered by the Principal and Ward Chiefs on behalf of their subjects. Stock owners are free to graze the open range, and there is no private ownership of land. In this context, the project had absolutely no authority to implement any of the grazing-control measures the early documents had proposed.

For the first two and a half years of the project, this obstacle deterred range management personnel from making any attempt at controlling grazing, and energies were concentrated on research on rangeland seeding, fertilization, and weed control, as will be discussed later. It was only in 1978 that the project reevaluated the situation and approached the Principal Chief of the area for permission to try to start a single grazing association on a much smaller area of land "for purely experimental, demonstration, and in some ways political reasons" (TTDP 1981B: 139).

The grazing association

In May of 1978, the Principal Chief of Rothe gave the Thaba-Tseka Project permission to start a grazing association for owners of small stock on 1,500 hectares of rangeland near the new town of Thaba-Tseka. By 1979, the area had been fenced, and a CIDA evaluation was able to claim that "the introduction of the first Graziers' Association in August 1979 in the mountains of Lesotho is considered to be an outstanding achievement of the TTIRDP" (CIDA 1979: 57). By the end of the next year, the fence had been cut or knocked down in many places, the gates had been stolen, and the association area was being freely grazed by all. The office of the association manager had been burned down, and the Canadian officer in charge of the program was said to be fearing for his life. In 1982, when I arrived on the scene, the project was being described by project officials as "a complete disaster." It is necessary to explore here how such a result came about, and why.

The idea of the grazing association was to restrict grazing within an allocated area to the stock of progressive, commercially minded farmers who would be willing to keep fewer but better-quality animals on well-managed rangeland. These progressive farmers would keep improved purebred livestock and follow recommended management practices, thus earning significant cash incomes from their animals while at the same time demonstrating the high potential for commercial livestock production to their peers. A stock owner who wanted to join the association, according to the constitution which was drawn up, had to have animals which were "improved or on the trend of improvement," as certified by the Livestock Division. Furthermore, the prospective stock owner had to agree to have his flock examined annually by an officer of the Livestock Division, and to remove any animals deemed not to qualify for the association. Finally, an association member had to agree to "improve and care for his livestock according to advices given by the Livestock Division." All who could not qualify or who refused to apply for membership would be excluded from grazing within the fenced 1,500 hectare enclosure.

On these terms, ten stock owners registered to join the association in June of 1978. The fencing was not complete until March of 1979, so it was not until the grazing season beginning at the end of 1979 that the association area was to be occupied. But in November, only five stock owners actually agreed to put their stock into the enclosure, although many others had sufficiently good stock to qualify for the association. Many meetings held by project and Ministry of Agriculture officials failed to convince stock owners to commit their flocks to the association.

In the meantime, the grass within the fenced enclosure was growing, and the few animals that had been put into the area were not nearly enough to keep it in check. By the end of the 1979/80 grazing season, the grass had grown so high that snakes, jackals, and liver flukes had become problems. The contrast with the bare, overgrazed land on which the majority grazed their hungry animals was stark.

By the start of the next grazing season, in October 1980, the outrage of the excluded stock owners was reaching its boiling point. Fence-cutting – a sporadic problem up to this point – became common, and large and small stock of non-members entered the enclosure and violated the association's grazing monopoly. The association fought back by having trespassing animals impounded and held for fines. Tensions ran high. The fence continued to be attacked, and gates were stolen from the entrances. The project-built office of the association's manager was burned down, and fear was expressed that more violence might follow. But, as it happened, the conflict was to reach its climax quite peacefully, in court.

In November 1980 a man whose livestock had been impounded for trespassing within the grazing association took his case to the Thaba-Tseka Local Court. The Court, much to the project's dismay, decided in his favor, ruling that the grazing association did not in fact have exclusive rights to the allocated grazing area. It was not possible to obtain the official record of this case, but participants recall that the ruling was based on two points: (1) the fact that the grazing association was unregistered and hence had no legal "standing"; and (2) the fact that the Principal Chief of Rothe, in allocating the land, failed to give the association the "Form C" document required to obtain an allocation of public land. Following this ruling, the fence fell into complete disrepair, and the association land became common grazing. In the months following the decision, Project attempts to restart the association on a better legal footing met with a conspicuous lack of cooperation from Central Government, the Principal Chief, and the local stock owners. The last meeting with "the farmers" on this issue seems to have been in May of 1981, when a large number of stock owners turned out to oppose the continuation of the association.

It is easy to see why stock owners with poor-quality animals resisted the grazing association. They were not eligible to join the association without making major changes in the structure of their flocks, selling off poor animals to buy improved ones, and ending up with perhaps half as many animals. Apart from the restrictions on the sale of stock described in Chapter 5 above, the prospect of halving the size of one's flock is not an appealing one for most Basotho. But, without taking such drastic action, such stock owners had no way to obtain access to the controlled grazing land. The result of the grazing association was for them a net loss of 1,500 hectares of good grazing land to which they had previously had customary rights. In a time of scarce grazing, such a loss was not inconsiderable. Stock owners excluded from the fenced area were forced to invade other, already over-grazed, lands in search of pasture. Conflicts soon arose in neighboring grazing areas between the new invaders displaced from Thaba-Tseka and the Principal Chief of Matsieng, who sought to preserve the grazing for his own subjects. As a result, the Principal Chief is said to have resorted to burning down cattle posts in the Lesobeng area when herdsmen from Thaba-Tseka moved in with their livestock.

Those excluded from the grazing association thus had good reason for opposing its establishment, as the project clearly recognized. A 1979 discussion of the costs and benefits of the strategy of creating fenced grazing associations and concentrating extension and veterinary care on these controlled areas noted the following drawbacks:

1 Accelerated depreciation of general cattle post [i.e. cattle-post grazing land outside of the grazing association areas] as more animals are forced onto less land.
2 Decreased productivity of general livestock because less feed is available per unit and because there will be less veterinary services outside grazers' associations.
3 Increased pressure and agitation of general livestock owners not participating in programs of controlled grazing.
4 Increased pressure on Parliament and Cabinet to stop government activities controlling grazing.
5 Higher incidence of unsupervised grazing control violations in traditional cattle posts and dip tank areas. Marginally greater likelihood of epidemics among general livestock not incorporated in grazers' association.

Given this analysis, no one at the Project can have been very surprised that the establishment of the association provoked resistance from those whose animals were forced off the newly fenced land to struggle on the over-grazed remainder. What is more surprising, and what the project failed to anticipate, is that even those farmers with large, relatively good quality flocks who were invited to join the association for the most part refused to do so. In 1983, one of the five original members of the association was able to list twenty stock owners off the top of his head who owned good-quality flocks and were eligible to join the association but did not. Even the area chief who had given permission for the land to be allocated in the first place refused to place his own sheep in the enclosure.

In exploring this matter, it became clear that the grazing association was a topic which many people decidedly did not want to talk about. Mention of the subject provoked suspicion from bureaucrats and villagers alike. A high official in the district actually attempted, with some success, to obstruct my attempts to discuss the matter with local stock owners, and advised the local chief not to cooperate with my investigations. Stock owners, for their part, often denied any aversion to the association in principle, and explained that they refused to enter their animals into the association simply because they feared the liver flukes (*maphele*) their stock might get in the high grass of the enclosed area.

Such explanations, however, were not very convincing. First, because liver flukes are easily treatable and only a minor inconvenience; secondly, because the grass grew so high only *after* the association had failed to recruit a sufficient number of members; and thirdly, because when the stock owners rebelled against the association, they tore down the fences and eagerly grazed their flocks on the very rangeland they claim to have feared. Apparently, few wanted to admit to having opposed the idea of the association, at least not to a foreign researcher with unknown affiliations. Supporters of the association, both in the project and in the villages, were unanimous in claiming that *maphele* had nothing to do with the refusal to join the association, and suggested a number of other reasons.

The first reason concerns the reluctance to sell animals which has been discussed in the last chapter. By putting one's animals in the association, one was agreeing to keep them according to commercial principles, and to accept selection, culling, and timely marketing as recommended by the Government's Livestock Division. This was a condition that even the few stock owners who did join the association resisted, and it is clear that the prospect of mandatory culling of stock provoked enough fear and anger to keep many stock owners away from the grazing association.

The second reason, perhaps the most important, stems from the perception that a stock owner who becomes one of the few allowed to graze in the association enclosure is betraying the many who are forced out of it. This is an attitude which has its roots in the strongly held principle that the land belongs to the entire people (*sechaba*), and that every Mosotho has a right to grazing land. It is also related to the idea discussed in the last chapter, that livestock is properly a social, shared domain of wealth and not a private, selfish, or unsociable domain like cash. A man who is wealthy in livestock, we have seen, is expected to be a benefactor, a friend of the people, a man one can turn to in time of need. Both his livestock and the range they graze on are considered public, socially available resources, and the prestige of the large livestock owner depends on his ability and willingness to extend patronage to his clients. It is not in keeping with the image of the *morui* to push others off of communal grazing land for his own economic gain.

On a less ideological level, it was often claimed that stock owners refused to join the association because they feared that if they did their animals would be stolen or vandalized in retaliation by the angry majority who were excluded from the enclosure. This possibility suggests an objective reason why livestock in Lesotho must remain a highly social domain of wealth and cannot be turned to narrowly self-interested uses as easily as other kinds of wealth; it is physically visible, exposed, and highly vulnerable. A Mosotho stock owner is not a capitalist rancher; he must live in a village community in which his livestock are deeply embedded in a network of social relations from which they cannot be easily removed. So long as his wealth is in such a visible and vulnerable form as livestock, anti-social behavior is not a viable option. A *morui* who lives amongst enemies will not long remain a *morui*.

A third reason for the refusal of stock owners to enter the association concerns the general suspicion of both the government and the project prevalent in the Thaba-Tseka area. While the grazing association apparently did not become a highly partisan political issue, the fact that it was instituted by an unpopular government in a region considered to be an opposition stronghold cannot be considered irrelevant. A stock owner who did join the association stated that others had refused because they did not like the ruling government and did not want to cooperate with it. The project officer in charge of the association, meanwhile, noted that "the farmers have always seemed to be somewhat suspicious of [the project], Government, and the fence itself," and noted that many stock owners endeavored to remain "as uninvolved with the Government as possible" (TTDP 1981B: 140–1).

Grazing control and range research

Besides the grazing association, the Thaba-Tseka Project initiated or helped to initiate several other programs aimed at the improvement and management of rangeland. From the start, the project had wanted to control both the movement of livestock and the number of animals in the project area, as we saw in reviewing the original planning documents of 1975. But, with no legal power to control grazing, the project was forced to focus its energies in the early years on researching other ways to improve the range. Experiments were done with overseeding of various grass varieties, along with limited tests of fertilization and weed control. The results of this research showed that all the seeding, fertilization, and weed control methods were prohibitively expensive, but that the range could recover very nicely by itself in the space of only two or three years if protected from overgrazing. The natural climax sward was found to be very good-quality forage and it was determined that rest alone could restore the Thaba-Tseka range to high quality grazing land.

Meanwhile, the Thaba-Tseka Project and CIDA had been pressuring the Government of Lesotho to take some action on grazing control. The lobbying contributed to the formulation of a new national law on grazing control, passed in 1980. The new law empowered chiefs, in consultation with the staff of the Ministry of Agriculture, to close overgrazed areas to grazing, to determine the stocking rate allowable in a given area, and to forcibly remove excess stock through culling. Chiefs were empowered to enforce these regulations through the hiring of grazing control supervisors and the levying of fines. To date all efforts under the new law have focused on the temporary closing of overgrazed areas; no stock limitation or culling has been attempted.[1] During the period of fieldwork, 1982–3, the Thaba-Tseka Range Management Division was busy compiling stocking rates and convincing chiefs to close the most badly degraded areas to grazing. In 1982, the Range Officer at Thaba-Tseka told me that some 109,950 hectares of cattle-post grazing land had been closed to grazing. Range Management staff travelled to public meetings throughout the district during the fieldwork period to explain the new regulations to the people and to urge their obedience and cooperation.

The closing of overgrazed areas was unpopular with the people of Thaba-Tseka District, just as it has apparently been unpopular all across the country. There is widespread agreement in the villages, at least in principle, that land is overgrazed, and that it is good for it to be rested. But objections are commonly raised on two counts. First, since grazing is so scarce, taking large amounts of land out of circulation gives the displaced stock nowhere left to go. There is a fear that, as one informant put it, "the Government is trying to deprive us of our animals by forcing them into an area where they will be unable to find enough food, so they will die." Secondly, there are charges that the chiefs who control the grazing lands take advantage of closed areas to graze their own stock, as well as that of their friends and those who are wealthy enough to pay the bribes. I was not able to determine how prevalent a practice this may be, but the Range Management Officer at Thaba-Tseka confirmed that such cases are known to occur. At any rate, it is widely believed in the villages. Once the rich and powerful are observed (or believed) to violate the grazing grounds, of course, it is but a short step to say, as one informant explained, "Well, if they are going to continue to keep their animals in that place, then we, too, will graze our stock there."

These attitudes, combined with rugged terrain and a shortage of paid staff, make it almost impossible to enforce the grazing control regulations. Prescribed areas are very commonly grazed, and apprehending offenders is difficult and sometimes dangerous. The prevailing attitude toward the control measures is perhaps best illustrated by the protest of a man at a public meeting on grazing control held in February of 1983 in Sehonghong, near Mashai. He understood the measures, he explained politely, and appreciated the reasons for them. "But," he objected, "these fines are too high! How will I manage to pay that much money when my animals are apprehended!"

Nearly everyone involved with the grazing-control program admitted that it cannot work without the simultaneous enforcement of de-stocking – that is, a reduction in the total number of livestock in the country. In Thaba-Tseka, the District Agricultural Officer, the Project Coordinator, the Range Management Officer, the Livestock Officer, and the Livestock Marketing Officer all agreed that it is useless to talk about grazing control in Lesotho without a program for effective and compulsory de-stocking. The country, it is generally agreed, currently supports somewhere between two and three times its rated "carrying capacity." With overgrazing as bad as it is, the temporary closing of one area only leads to the further denuding and erosion of other areas, which must absorb the surplus. The 1980 law gives Principal Chiefs the power to issue grazing permits in accord with the "stocking rate" determined by the Ministry of Agriculture staff. But, as the District Agricultural Officer in Thaba-Tseka observed, "If there are 20,000 animal units and the stocking rate allows 10,000 – what will you do with the other 10,000?" In practice, the chiefs give permits to all who apply.

The law does provide for mandatory culling of surplus stock, but to date no attempt has been made to implement this measure. It is not difficult to see why. Such a measure would be extremely unpopular and would almost certainly provoke violent resistance. For reasons discussed earlier, possession of and control over livestock is a highly emotive issue in Lesotho, as elsewhere in Southern Africa (see Beinart 1984, Beinart and Bundy 1981); forced de-stocking, with its implications of eroded rural security and its connotations of diminished male honor, would be perhaps the most politically dangerous thing the government could possibly do in Thaba-Tseka district. Several officials involved with the range management program in Thaba-Tseka suggested that a culling program could be enforced only by calling in the army. Speculation as to what might happen in such a case is moot, however, for none of the parties involved has any real interest in attempting such a thing – least of all the staff of the Ministry of Agriculture (90 percent of whom, in the estimate of one well-placed observer, keep stock of their own, often in large numbers, for "traditional" reasons). For this reason, all the talk about grazing control has up to now remained little more than talk.

Livestock marketing

It was observed in Part II that the problematic within which the Thaba-Tseka Project was conceived and planned insisted, for reasons of its own, on seeing Lesotho as an isolated, historically backward society, cut off from the cash economy and modern capitalist development. In Part III, we saw that non-commercial attitudes toward stock-keeping and an anti-market ethic where livestock is concerned are important parts of the local economic system, rooted in the network of local power relations generated in a labor reserve economy. Given these circumstances, it was perhaps inevitable that the project should interpret the non-commercial livestock practices prevalent in the area as symptomatic of isolation and lack of contact with the cash economy.

For this reason, livestock markets took on an extraordinary importance in the thinking of project planners and staff. Regular markets were of course a pre-condition for the mountain livestock industry the project hoped to establish. But more than that, the "introduction" of livestock markets was itself expected to dramatically transform the way in which people held stock. It was imagined that the provision of market outlets for livestock would make it possible for the first time for stock owners, previously isolated from the cash economy, to evaluate their animals in terms of monetary profit and loss. Markets would bring with them commercial attitudes, and people could begin to use their animals as sources of income, instead of simply crowding the overgrazed range with them. Markets were even expected to bring about de-stocking. It was explicitly stated time and again, both in documents and in interviews, that making more markets available to stock owners would reduce overall numbers in livestock, since it would make it possible for "farmers" to sell off their burdensome older, poor quality, and "non-productive" stock.

With these considerations in mind, the project began running a regular cattle auction, which was later expanded to include small stock as well. The first sale was held in August 1976, and additional sales were held at intervals thereafter, at a rate of about four a year. The sales were popular and attracted a good number of sellers. Between August 1976 and May 1979 a total of 606 cattle were sold at project-sponsored sales. In 1980, it was decided that sales would be held monthly, on the last Tuesday of each month. In Fiscal Year 1982, 548 cattle and 334 small stock were sold at the Thaba-Tseka auction.

The establishment of monthly auctions and the growing numbers of animals sold there have of course pleased project planners, and have led to the touting of the livestock marketing program as one of the project's great successes. It has been widely stated that the marketing program is bringing about de-stocking and helping to get low-quality, unproductive stock off of the range. It is also believed to have helped effect a transformation to a modern, commercial, cash economy; the success of the auctions, according to a "Review of Accomplishments" put out by the project in 1981, "reflects increased awareness of commercial agriculture and the increased demands of the cash economy."

Such assessments are badly mistaken for a number of reasons. First, there is nothing novel about livestock markets to the people of Thaba-Tseka, who have been selling livestock at auction for as long as anybody can remember. Before the project began, auctions were set up by the government's Livestock Marketing Corporation (L.M.C., now Livestock Produce Marketing Services, L.P.M.S.) periodically at different sites in the mountains, including Thaba-Tseka. The sales were advertised by radio, and through government extension workers and livestock improvement centers, and buyers in South Africa were alerted to the sale and driven or flown to the site by the L.M.C. According to buyers from South Africa, such sales have been held throughout the country since at least the 1950s, though the L.M.C. itself dates back only to 1973. Sales were held several times a year in the Thaba-Tseka area, and apparently substantial numbers of animals were sold. At the last auction before the project took over, for instance, in May 1976, 110 cattle were sold, and a 1978 project report claimed that "in the recent past auctions at Thaba-Tseka have prompted farmers to make available upwards to 300 cattle for sale" (CIDA 1978R: 30). Sales were also held in other mountain areas adjoining Thaba-Tseka, and stock owners looking to sell were used to taking their animals to quite distant auctions. Project officials noted with pride that their auctions drew stock owners from as far away as Mokhotlong and Qacha's Nek; in the same way, prior to the monthly auctions at Thaba-Tseka, auctions at Mokhotlong, Qacha's

Nek, Sehonghong, and Mantsonyane were available to people from the Thaba-Tseka region.

Another, older, system of marketing in the days before the project was in the hands of larger traders (e.g., the Frasers' store in Mantsonyane). A merchant would bring in a shipment of young cattle from South Africa, and trade a young animal plus some cash for a larger but older ox belonging to a local stock owner. The stock owner thus obtained cash to cover his needs without being obliged to reduce his herd. The merchant, for his part, sold the oxen for beef in South Africa at a profit. This is said to be a very old system of marketing in Lesotho.

A third marketing channel that pre-dates the project is direct sale by stock owners to buyers in South Africa. From Mashai, for instance, villagers commonly crossed over into Natal at Sani Pass and sold animals to white farmers there. This was one of the most common ways of selling cattle reported in Mashai. The distance involved is formidable, but not prohibitive, as Basotho herdsmen are accustomed to traveling long distances with their stock. Such direct marketing of livestock is illegal, and deprives the Government's L.P.M.S. of its usual 8 percent cut on every sale, but it seems to be very common. The same is true for the marketing of wool and mohair. A CIDA evaluation, even while making the usual claims about the absence of markets, noted that many farmers illegally sell their wool directly to traders, either in Lesotho or South Africa, instead of through the government woolshed at Thaba-Tseka. The report observed:

It is estimated that fifty percent of the wool and mohair produced in Lesotho is marketed illegally in the RSA. Farmers trek their animals into the RSA and the produce is sold to traders. Payment is made in cash and the price is relatively good, often 20 to 30 cents higher than the price offered by other buyers. Farmers will trek their animals for many miles to the RSA for the higher cash payments offered to them by the RSA traders.
(CIDA 1978E: 50)

The picture that emerges, then, is not one of backward subsistence farmers cut off from or baffled by the cash economy, but of canny market operators who make intelligent use of state marketing channels when it is in their interest to do so, and find alternatives when it is not. The Thaba-Tseka Project did not introduce livestock markets to the mountains, still less the cash economy, and there is no reason why the project's auctions should have any more effect on the de-stocking of the range, the establishment of commercial ranching, or the creation of a livestock export industry than any of the other auctions the area has seen in decades gone by.

But the fact that livestock markets and the cash economy got to Thaba-Tseka before the "development" apparatus did is not the only problem with the project's interpretation of the livestock auctions. When we look at the reasons people had for selling at the project auctions, the suggestion that the market is stimulating a "livestock industry" becomes even less credible. For the people who sold animals at the project auctions did not do so for "commercial" reasons, in order to realize a profit by selling surplus production. Neither did they sell them, as project personnel sometimes wishfully suggested, in order to be rid of old, useless, and non-productive stock – as if people had previously been burdened with more animals than they wanted simply because they had no way to get rid of them. The animals sold at the Thaba-Tseka auctions were neither "off-take" nor culls; they were highly valued property sold only out of desperation. As we saw in Chapter 5, the project's own survey found that, when asked their reason for selling, 85 percent of surveyed sellers cited "need to buy food," followed closely by "need to buy clothes" and, further back, "pay for school fees."

The place of livestock marketing in the local livestock economy becomes more clear when one recalls the discussion of the "bovine mystique" presented in Chapter 5. To recapitulate briefly: since livestock is culturally constituted (for reasons we have explored) as a kind of property that is not to be unnecessarily converted into cash, it is usually sold only in response to dire need or personal emergency. The usual pattern is that a man's herd is built up during the years he is employed (most often in the mines). When some years have passed and the man is no longer able to find work, the animals very slowly begin to be sold off, one by one, to meet urgent needs for such basic items as food and clothing. The sale of an animal in this system is thus not the "off-take" of a surplus but part of a process which culminates in the destruction of the herd.

Sale of stock under such circumstances, then, is a disagreeable and humiliating necessity. It is an insult to a man's pride and a public admission of his destitution. It is for this reason that auctions at Thaba-Tseka are such grim and solemn occasions. There is little of the zest and excitement so often associated with market places; indeed, a livestock auction in Lesotho is about as much fun as a funeral. Given these realities, the number of livestock sold is a better index of the number of men fallen on hard times than it is of the commercial "output" of a presumed "livestock industry."

This basic structure of livestock keeping in the area was not changed by the project auctions. Animals continued to be sold for the same reasons, in the same condition, and by the same sorts of people as at other auctions prior to the project. It is possible that the monthly auctions slightly boosted net sales, but there is no good evidence that this is so. Certainly more animals were sold at Thaba-Tseka than before, but it is likely that some, if not all, of these animals would have been sold elsewhere in Lesotho or South Africa even without the project auctions. At any rate, it is difficult to speak of a "de-stocking function" here – first, because the 500 or so head of cattle marketed annually through Thaba-Tseka hardly put a dent in the hundreds of thousands of cattle that graze Lesotho's mountain areas; secondly, because it is generally acknowledged that imports ran much higher than exports during the project period, for a net *increase* in livestock population, not a decrease.

Given this analysis, what are we to make of the widespread propagandizing in the villages by project and Ministry of Agriculture staff in favor of selling off "non-productive" stock? It was clear during fieldwork in Mashai that no one was going to sell any stock simply because the government advised him to do so, or because he had been told there were too many animals on the land. The few who reported selling stock in recent years cited extreme poverty and personal emergencies as reasons. Extension workers preached long and hard at public meetings periodically held in the villages, but their arguments did not appear to move anyone any nearer to making an unforced sale of an animal. The District Agricultural Officer in Thaba-Tseka made the same point, in the course of making an argument for a mandatory culling program. "It is not a matter of education," he declared. "There have been thousands of *pitsos* [public meetings in the villages]. People understand perfectly well what the issues are, what needs to be done – they just refuse to do it!"

In Mashai, meanwhile, the pro-marketing propaganda was greeted with considerable skepticism. It was widely believed that the prices paid in Thaba-Tseka were too low, that the government was exploiting the livestock sellers, and that the government's desire to have them sell their livestock was self-interested. In this context, the "educational talks" given by the agriculture experts were often interpreted simply as advertisements on the part of a profit-making business, much like the commercials on the radio.[2]

The livestock marketing program of the Thaba-Tseka Project succeeded admirably in establishing a regular, reliable, accessible market place for livestock in the Thaba-Tseka area. The new monthly stock auctions are unquestionably a great convenience to many stock owners. Thanks to the Thaba-Tseka Project, a man looking to sell an animal may now not have to walk so far or wait so long as he would have had to previously, and no doubt a great deal of shoe leather has been saved. But the consequences of the establishing of this market were neither as dramatic nor as far reaching as project planners imagined. Because the project area had never been isolated from the cash economy, and because non-commercial livestock practices in fact persisted for reasons having nothing to do with the presumed "lack of markets," the establishment of a monthly auction at Thaba-Tseka failed, as it had to fail, to transform "traditional" livestock practices, to de-stock the range, or to create a commercial livestock industry.

Improved stock and fodder production

We have seen that livestock marketing occupied a very important place in the project's plans for livestock commercialization. But the marketing program was in fact intended only as one part of a larger and more ambitious program to put livestock keeping throughout the region on a commercial, businesslike basis. This larger program required not only that stock owners be willing to sell surplus or non-productive stock, but also that they should make drastic changes in the structure, care, and management of their herds. The transformation envisioned depended on the adoption of two key elements: improved stock and fodder production.

The argument went like this: the animals, especially the cattle, owned by local stock owners are of poor quality, and are not efficient producers. By selling off these poor stock and replacing them with good quality purebred animals (even if the total number were fewer), even a small herd, properly managed, could be made to produce a substantial cash income. Improved stock, though, are not as hardy as the local strains; they would need to be fed supplementary feed in order to produce at optimum levels. For this reason, it is necessary to convince farmers to begin growing fodder on at least part of their crop land. By keeping good-quality cattle, feeding them with home-grown fodder, and selling milk, off-take, and culls as recommended, a stock owner could make a good cash living from his stock.

Project planning documents suggested that agricultural improvements would make it possible for a farmer to give up land to fodder production without losing food security. The 1982 revision to the Project Plan of Operations, while finally acknowledging that "options for the sale of surplus cash or food crops to lowland markets is [*sic*] marginal," still insisted on the viability of a strategy of "providing sufficient food on less land and diverting the use of surplus arable land to fodder production for commercial livestock output" (CIDA 1982). Project and Ministry of Agriculture staff in the field, however, were realistic enough to admit that there was no question of "surplus arable land"; if fodder was to be grown, it would be at the expense of food.[3] But, the argument went, the increased income from livestock production would more than make up for the lost food production. This was the argument that was carried out to the villages by extension staff and put before the people at village meetings throughout the fieldwork period in 1982–3.

There was, however, very little response in the villages to the push for improved stock and fodder. Extension workers noted with frustration that people listened politely to their arguments, and seemed to agree, but afterward refused to follow the advice they had been given. In Mashai, at the end of 1983, after several years of fairly intensive propagandizing by Thaba-Tseka officials, not one farmer had bought improved stock or switched to growing fodder crops,[4] and even the local extension worker held out little hope that attitudes would change in the near future. The response in other areas was apparently not much more enthusiastic.[5]

In Mashai, stock owners were usually reluctant to oppose the idea of improved stock in principle, but cited particular reasons why such a move was inappropriate for them. Several reasons were commonly cited. First, improved stock were said to be less hardy than the local animals – they would easily die off up in the mountains or when grazing got scarce. Secondly, they would need to be fed fodder, which would be very expensive. To grow one's own fodder, one would have to give up badly needed food, and in any case the animals would require more than could be grown on the small amounts of land available. Then there were arguments about numbers: ten poor animals were better than five improved ones, said many, citing the ability to form ploughing teams and the ability to pay bridewealth as reasons. For others, it was the mere idea of selling their stock that made the scheme unappealing. One man, after heartily agreeing with each step in the experts' line of argument, was asked why, then, he did not sell off his own rather large herd of inferior animals to buy improved stock. He smiled, shook his head, and said simply "I am too attached to them" (*Ke li qenehetse*).

Thaba-Tseka officials almost invariably recorded this opposition as a lack of understanding. Time and again I was told by officials (whose own claims to power and authority, of course, rested on their education or technical expertise) that villagers who opposed their schemes lacked education, that they did not understand the proposals, that matters needed to be explained better. However many village meetings had been held, they argued, they were obviously not enough, for the villagers still failed to understand. If stock owners continue to refuse to convert to purebred stock and commercial practices, this only means, in the words of one official, that "they must be educated, in order to understand."

Villagers in Mashai well appreciated the effects of this maneuver, whereby their substantive opposition was recorded as ignorance. One man tried to explain to me why the assembled villagers at the public meetings always went through the motions of agreeing with the officials who lectured them on their livestock practices:

If you don't do this, it is taken as the proof that you don't understand. You may not like to do it [i.e. pretend to agree], but you are forced to by the government.

A second man joined in at this point:

I don't like to do it, but out of fear I will do it, falsely ... If I don't agree, I am afraid to say to you: "No! I, for one, will not do this thing [i.e. switch to improved stock]". We understand very well what they are saying; we simply don't agree.

But if the project's proposals for commercial stock raising were rejected by most stock owners, this is not to say that they had no effect, or fell on deaf ears. For the arguments about the relative merits of improved versus local stock, a few good animals versus many not-so-good ones, and livestock as a commercial business versus livestock as use value and store of wealth fell right into the middle of another, larger argument that was ongoing in the villages, the argument over the "Bovine Mystique" discussed in Chapter 5. The Thaba-Tseka officials who lectured so long and hard at the village meetings were, without particularly intending to, entering into a long-established ideological dispute over the privileges and protections granted livestock as a category of property. And, again without particularly intending to, these officials, all men, entered this dispute on the side of the women.

We have seen that an ideological challenge to the supposed virtues of accumulating and hoarding wealth in animals, and on the prestige complex associated with owning many stock, was a part of a broader challenge by women to the Mystique of stock ownership. We have seen, too, that women often attempted to erode and break down the barrier that kept livestock, as men's property, distinct and not freely interconvertible with money and the "domain of contestation" within the household. The arguments of the Thaba-Tseka experts were seized upon by women as proof that men who insisted on the Mystique were foolish and old-fashioned, as they had argued all along. The men, for their part, received the arguments of the "developers" as a hostile attack on their only form of long-term security, and responded with ideological counter-arguments of their own.[6]

Opponents of the Mystique thus regularly appropriated the project's criticisms of such "traditional" livestock practices such as refusal to sell stock and pride in accumulating numbers, for reasons of their own. But some were willing to go even further, and endorse the experts' positive conception of a commercial livestock industry as well as their negative judgement of "traditional" practices. Women, especially young women, were often enthusiastic supporters of the idea of keeping fewer animals of better quality, feeding and caring for them, and selling animal products and herd "off-take" on the commercial market. Women, it must be recalled, were not opposed to animals in general – they were opposed only to animals held as inviolable and non-remunerative stores of men's wealth: opposed, in short, to the Mystique. The idea that livestock could be raised on commercial principles was appealing to women precisely because it challenged the Mystique and promised to make "men's animals" an asset that could be freely manipulated to maximize household income. This is in fact exactly the way "women's animals" are already treated. There is no mystique surrounding chickens and pigs; they are raised for food and for sale, and they are freely converted to cash by any buyer who offers a good price.[7]

One young woman, after describing "traditional" practices in rather unflattering terms, then went on to contrast the virtues of improved stock.

Some people just like to have a lot of animals, even if they are not good ones, because they haven't considered how good they are. They haven't paid any attention to their quality, they have only considered the number ... They look at the size of the herd, they don't look to see if the herd is any good, if it will give them any money. What they look at is the number, so that they can have more than the others. I think that is the only correct answer I can give you for why they keep so many animals that are not of good quality. They will not exchange them to get a few, better animals.

Would you, yourself, prefer to have improved animals?

Yes.

How many animals do you have now?

We have no sheep. We have 10 cattle, with calves, and 3 horses.

Would you want to sell your cattle to buy improved stock?

Truly, I would sell them to get improved stock, because now I have these ten – not that that is so many – but they are quite enough. But they are of no use, they don't provide the children with milk because they aren't improved. I have these animals, yet my children do not get any milk. And I see that if I can get five improved cattle, it will be better. The children will get milk.

And when they multiply, you can sell them and get money.

Yes!

On this point, of course, wives are likely to come into conflict with their husbands. Fewer animals are less "sociable," can help fewer people, can stand for fewer "head" of bridewealth, and can thus secure less prestige. For this reason, men value numbers: "quantity over quality," as has been often observed. At the same time, livestock as "retirement fund" must above all be hardy – they must survive many years and maintain their numbers with little attention, as the "improved stock" promoted by the government never could. The very idea of raising animals for sale, too, is a direct challenge to the "one-way barrier" which protects livestock from being converted to cash. Women who seemed genuinely interested in selling off numerous animals to keep fewer more productive ones were frustrated by their husbands' refusal to sell or to reduce their herds. The young woman in the interview above went on to explain why she has not been able to sell the ten cattle to buy the five improved ones as follows:

I have often seen that it seems that [my husband] is a person who loves wealth in animals. He will not agree easily. Because – I mean, even with the horses, here I continually tell him that I, for my part, don't want these horses when they are so many, because they will be too much for us. We will not be able to look after them, they will get lost, while you are at the mines and I am at work. Whey don't we get rid of these horses? He doesn't want to. He doesn't want to. He refuses, although there are people willing to buy them. I see that he is one of those people who likes numbers of animals.

The effect of the project's efforts to promote improved stock and fodder production was thus to enter into and intensify a dispute that was already ongoing within rural mountain society. But the project's intervention, although it did manage to stir up considerable ideological dust, did little to actually alter the balance of forces within the village bearing on the question of the Bovine Mystique. Until something does alter that balance (and there are a number of possible candidates here[8]), it is reasonable to suppose that "traditional" livestock practices will endure.

It must be added that, even if entirely commercial practices *were* adopted, there are some doubts that the improved stock scheme could work under the existing circumstances. The claims made for the potential income to be earned from keeping purebred livestock in the mountains are supported by the opinion of the experts at Thaba-Tseka, but there is little hard evidence for them. A small demonstration dairy farm run by the project and featuring the recommended Brown Swiss breed of cattle managed only to lose money for several years running, in spite of the fact that it had a guaranteed market for its dairy products at the project's own Farmer Training Center.[9] A sheep demonstration project ran in the red as well. And, although the project grew its own fodder for its animals, as it advised farmers to do, I was told in 1983 that it was never able to grow enough and was forced to spend a considerable amount of money purchasing expensive imported feed. A livestock expert attached to USAID in Maseru told me that in his opinion improved stock were a poor investment under such degraded range conditions, since they would require such large amounts of extra feed, which would have to be bought at uneconomical prices. The problem, in his view, had little to do with the genetic quality of the stock, but rather centered on the conditions under which they were raised. Such testimony raises at least some doubt about the wisdom of major investments in improved stock so long as the range remains so badly overgrazed, and suggests that many of the objections to the scheme raised by local stock owners may have been well taken.

Livestock commercialization in perspective

For all the project's efforts over the last ten years, few significant changes have occurred in the way that livestock is kept in the Thaba-Tseka region. The range is as badly overgrazed as ever, and the commercial livestock industry the project was intended to "develop" is nowhere to be found. The project has successfully provided agricultural and other services at a level of quality and convenience not previously available, but the novelty of such services should not be exaggerated. While project planners liked to make much of the region's isolation and lack of services prior to the arrival of "development," the basic livestock services of veterinary care, dip tanks, cattle auctions, woolsheds, and stud facilities were all available in Thaba-Tseka before the project began. The key measures the project relied upon to bring about a dramatic transformation of "traditional" livestock practices all failed to achieve what was asked of them: attempts to create a grazing association and to bring about de-stocking of the range were rudely defeated; attempts to convert stock owners to commercial practices through extension, "education," and browbeating were simply ignored.

The District Agricultural Officer in Thaba-Tseka admitted as much in a 1983 interview. "Our extension work has been a failure," he confessed (agreeing here with the equally pessimistic assessment of the Range Management Officer). It was not a matter of more education. "People understand perfectly well what the issues are, what needs to be done – they just refuse to do it." Mandatory measures for de-stocking he saw as the only answer. But, interestingly, he declared at the same time that he could see little or no prospect for such measures actually being imposed in the foreseeable future, noting that the issue is "very touchy politically," and would be nearly impossible to enforce.

The DAO's assessment captures nicely the dilemma which confronted the Thaba-Tseka Development Project, and continues to confront those who would attempt to commercialize livestock keeping in Lesotho. Caught between the ineffective and the impossible, the project had chosen for itself a task that it never had the wherewithal to even begin to carry out. To have actually executed its plan and created a successful livestock industry would have required major political and economic realignments that the project was never intended to be able to put into effect.

Project planners came eventually to realize the impossible position they occupied. The "technical measures" the project was competent to implement, a 1978 appraisal noted (CIDA 1978R: 25–6), were of "little significance" without far-reaching structural changes that were beyond the power of the project to effect. Without "essential organizational and institutional changes," the report went on, "the whole concept of mountain development and justification for the project would remain in doubt." The chief "organizational and institutional changes" the planners meant were: (1) implementation of an effective program of de-stocking; and (2) creation of means for the privatization or semi-privatization of range land, through changes in land tenure law or the establishment of grazing associations. Without headway on these key issues, the other measures promoted by the project would be futile, or even counter-productive.

The dilemma thus at Thaba-Tseka has been one of the futility of encouraging individual farmers to improve husbandry practice when competition for limited grazing was such that a greater intake of higher quality roughage simply was not possible. Improved measures of health and breeding under such circumstances could only serve to increase the competition for natural pasture at a time when economic prospects for cultivated fodder production and intensive feeding were far from certain. Hence, no matter what formula would be developed to improve husbandry, inadequate feeding would be the constraint limiting any progress that might otherwise be achieved in other areas. In order to improve the feeding situation on a broad scale, destocking in the first instance largely represents the only viable alternative. (CIDA 1978R: 29–30)

Yet time and again, when the project looked to the Government of Lesotho for support in effecting de-stocking or privatization of range land, the Government refused to take the kind of action that would have been required, as we have seen. On the question of de-stocking, it was noted that the political costs to a government that enforced any manda-tory sale of stock would be very high. Since one of the principal aims of the Government in launching the Thaba-Tseka Project in the first place was to bolster political support in the mountains and establish a beach-head there for political control (we will return to these points in sub-sequent chapters), it had no interest in igniting the political wildfire which was sure to follow from a serious attempt at de-stocking. Jona-than's government, besieged from within and without, had enough problems without that. On the question of privatization of range land, it is clear that in this area, too, the Government did not share the enthusiasm of the "development" planners for measures to fence and parcel out the range, either to private parties or to grazing associations. Again, politics raises its head: if grazing associations or private ranches are established, the political backlash created by those excluded from the privatized land would be formidable. At the same time, keeping live-stock outside of the grazing associations will become more and more difficult, and more and more people will be forced to give up owning stock. This is of course the precise intention of the planners: that stock raising should be professionalized, and that people who are "not serious farmers" should get out of the business of keeping animals. But (and we will return to this point again in Chapter 8 when the question of crop development arises), the prospect of hundreds of thousands of "non-serious farmers" leaving the land is not an appealing one to any of the established interests in the region, least of all the Government of Lesotho. The current system does an admirable job of keeping people on the land and out of Maseru, and this political function weighs heavily upon all considerations of commercialization and capitalization of agri-culture in the country.

The commercialization of livestock keeping thus turned out not to be a matter of implementing a simple technical solution, but of bringing about a wrenching political-economic transformation. The project, for all its technical expertise, had no ability to bring about such a transform-ation; the Government, which arguably possessed the power to effect such a change, had no real interest in doing so.

Conclusion

The failure of the Thaba-Tseka Project to effect a transformation in livestock practices reveals two distinct contradictions between the vision of livestock development that emerged from within the "de-velopment" problematic and the actual political and economic struc-tures that govern livestock keeping in Lesotho's mountains. The first contradiction involved the presumed characteristics of the "target population." The project proceeded on the assumption that the inhabi-tants of the Thaba-Tseka region were backward subsistence farmers, cut off from markets and the modern cash economy and adhering to ana-chronistic, "traditional" livestock customs due to lack of knowledge and an absence of necessary technical inputs. In fact, the villages of the region were all deeply embedded in a modern, capitalist labor reserve economy, and non-commercial livestock practices found their principal points of support in the local power relations generated within that labor reserve economy. The system of livestock keeping the project imagined to be simply due to ignorance and the supposed unavailability of technical inputs such as markets and improved stock, was in fact strongly supported by an array of entrenched interests at the local level. For this reason, the provision of technical inputs and education did not have the revolutionary effects that were envisaged. More direct attempts at transformation, meanwhile, such as the grazing association and the attempts to promote de-stocking, improved stock, and fodder production by exhortation, were simply rejected.

It is possible, of course, that the more ambitious of these direct attempts to impose a transformation to commercial ranching could have been successfully implemented if a greater amount of coercion had been applied. But it was precisely at this point that the second major contradiction appeared. For just as the "development" problematic had misapprehended the economic structure of the "target population," in the same way it failed to appreciate the larger political-economic situation of the project itself as an instrument of the Government of Lesotho. For reasons we have explored (and we have seen that they were largely political), the far-reaching measures that would have been required in order for the project to accomplish the task it had set itself had long- and short-term implications that were not in the interests of those who alone had the power to implement them.

Without the support of the local coercive apparatus, and armed only with the standard "development" package of technical agricultural inputs, the project could not bring about the economic revolution in livestock it had promised. The fact that it was ever imagined that it could is a testimony to the power of the conceptual apparatus reviewed in Chapter 2.

7 The decentralization debacle

Introduction

It was seen in Part II that a key construct in the "development" problematic is a principle called "governmentality" – the idea that societies, economies, and government bureaucracies respond in a more or less reflexive, straight-forward way to policies and plans. In this conception the state apparatus is seen as a neutral instrument for implementing plans, while the government itself tends to appear as a machine for providing social services and engineering economic growth. Because this principle is firmly entrenched in the conceptual apparatus of "development" (for reasons reviewed in Chapter 2), "development" planning in Lesotho seems to take little or no account of the fact that "government" is always the exercise of a power – the activity of rulers, not servants. Instead, a peculiarly de-politicized conception of the state – and, of course, of the development project – almost inevitably prevails.

According to formal models, of course, the Government of Lesotho is indeed set up to be a provider of services, a facilitator of economic growth, and a keeper of the peace. These formal models are not the whole story, of course, but they are not entirely false. In Lesotho, as in most states, the bureaucracy does in fact engage in tasks that can be described in these terms. But alongside these formal models, and intertwined with them, are a host of instrumental uses to which the state apparatus is put, on behalf of individuals, cliques, factions, and class interests. Here the power of the state apparatus is put to use to the benefit of some, and to the detriment of others; the bureaucracy becomes the vehicle for the exercise of a particular kind of power; and this not as some kind of mistake or pathology, but as an essential part of what the bureaucracy in fact is, what it is all about.

These two sorts of function are in fact always mixed, but this may not always be so easy to see. In the nature of things, formal structures are visible and maintain a high profile; the other uses and purposes of the state structure are characteristically unseen and unacknowledged, particularly in the "development" industry. For this reason, "development" planners are likely to take the bureaucracy at its word, and to ignore what from another perspective would be a fact so obvious as to go without saying: that the state is a political apparatus.

The confrontation of plans drawn up by the "conceptual apparatus" of "development" with a real, live state bureaucracy is well illustrated by the following case from Thaba-Tseka. The case involves the project's attempt to introduce a rationalized system of "decentralized," "integrated," local administration in the Thaba-Tseka District.

Decentralization and integration

During Phase I, from 1975 through 1978, the Thaba-Tseka Development Project had a clear, well-defined place within the Government of Lesotho state apparatus: it was an area-based development project within the Ministry of Agriculture. Like other area-based projects before it, the Thaba-Tseka Project did not fall into any one of the Ministry of Agriculture's divisions, but was treated as a separate division of its own, under the direct supervision of the Permanent Secretary of the Ministry. Funding from donors came through the Treasury to the Ministry of Agriculture, from where it was then passed on to the project. During this phase, there was little contact with other Government Ministries. A "Project Coordinating Committee" including the Permanent Secretaries from the Ministries of Finance, Interior, and Works, along with the Permanent Secretary of Agriculture and the Project Director,[1] was set up to handle any interministerial coordination that might prove necessary. The formal organizational structure is summarized in Figure 7.1.

From the beginning, the Government of Lesotho had intended that the project would eventually lead to the creation of a long-planned tenth administrative district, with its capital at Thaba-Tseka, to be carved out of the mountainous center of the country. By 1978, when planning for the new Phase II of the project began, preparations for the creation of the new district were already in the works. With the construction of the road and township nearing completion, the time seemed to have come to begin thinking of the project as part of the larger process of founding a new district. In this coincidence of the creation of a new administrative district with the continuation and expansion of the project into a new, "integrated" phase lay the germ of an idea.

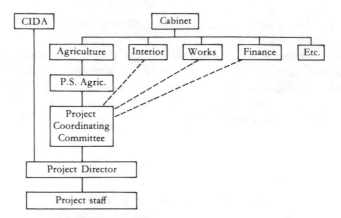

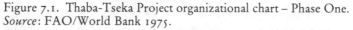

Figure 7.1. Thaba-Tseka Project organizational chart – Phase One.
Source: FAO/World Bank 1975.

The plan

In 1978, the Government of Lesotho was in the process of creating a new
district in Thaba-Tseka, but it possessed few facilities for administering
it. In creating a district administration and establishing government
services in Thaba-Tseka, most Ministries would be starting from
scratch. The most significant government presence in the area was the
Thaba-Tseka Development Project, which was an agricultural improvement project. But planners contemplating a second phase for the project
were already envisioning an "integrated" project of much wider scope,
encompassing programs in health, education, sanitation, training, and
other rural development activities to go along with the focus on agriculture. Why not, the argument went, build the new district administration
around the new Phase Two of the project, instead of setting up a whole
new, parallel structure with all the redundancies that would imply?
Instead of having each Ministry field its own staff, make its own policies,
and determine its own priorities in Maseru, why not have the Ministries
vote funds and forward personnel to an integrated district program,
which could improve efficiency by coordinating all "development"
activities at the district level and better direct district policies and
priorities than Maseru bureaucrats less in touch with local realities?

This idea, which seems, like so many others, to have originated with
the Project Director of the period, had the good fortune to strike a
responsive chord in certain quarters in Maseru, where proposals for
"decentralization" were at the time much in fashion. The old Project

Coordinating Committee, which had fallen into dormancy, was re-habilitated and emerged, after a March 1978 meeting of Permanent Secretaries, as the new Thaba-Tseka Coordinating Committee, intended to coordinate all Ministries and Government services involved in Thaba-Tseka. The Committee also had the task of reviewing and approving the plans for Phase Two of the project, or, as it began to be called, the Thaba-Tseka Integrated Rural Development Programme.

The plan that emerged called for a broader focus in Phase Two, continuing to concentrate on livestock and crops, but expanding to include "raising of educational participation and training opportunities, construction of vital village organizations, and improving sanitation and health." The plan called for the participation of a number of different Ministries under the umbrella of the project, or, as it was now called, the programme. The Government of Lesotho pledged to make available staff and resources from the Ministries of Agriculture, Works, Rural Development, Education, and Health to support specified programme activities. This coordination of resources from different Ministries at the district level was meant to be a model of "decentralized administration." The Phase Two plan thus intended:

To enable the Thaba-Tseka Mountain Development Project to continue over the next five years to function as a model of an integrated rural development scheme on a district level and to develop with the Government of Lesotho a model for district administration and development.
(CIDA 1978P)

The organizational chart as shown in Figure 7.2 was approved. A somewhat simplified version of this chart appeared in CIDA documentation in 1979 (see Figure 7.3).

Both these charts illustrate the two key features of the proposed new administrative system. First, field staff from all the Ministries involved in the "development" effort in Thaba-Tseka would be organized and divided up according to the functional "Divisions" of the Thaba-Tseka Integrated Rural Development Programme, not the Ministries of Central Government. These staff, whatever Ministry they may have come from, would work as part of the integrated District Programme. Field staff from Health, for instance, would report to the Ministry of Health only indirectly, through the programme and the Coordinating Committee. The Division Heads Committee, made up of the heads of each of

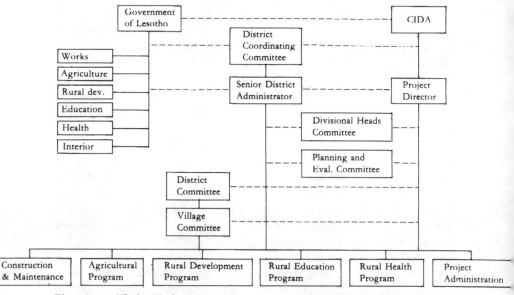

Figure 7.2. Thaba-Tseka Project organizational chart – Phase Two Plan of Operations. *Source*: CIDA 1978P.

the programme divisions, would meet monthly to coordinate activities between the divisions. This was "integration."

The second key feature is the existence of a policy-making apparatus at a district level. Instead of policy being made at the national level only, and implemented at the district level by the field staffs of the Ministries, in Thaba-Tseka, through the programme and the Coordinating Committee, policy measures could be undertaken at the district level and implemented by the district-wide programme. This was "decentralization."

The new system was supposed to be better in touch with the needs of "the people," since it would allow policy-making and executive decisions to take place at the local level. In this respect, the District Development Committee (DDC), a body of elected and appointed representatives of "the people," was intended to provide a channel for communicating popular needs to the government. The DDC was to be "advisory," and was granted no executive authority, but it managed nonetheless to occupy a rather imposing position on the organizational charts. (The DDC will be discussed at greater length in Chapter 8.)

"Integration and decentralization" was also supposed to be more efficient. Planning and executing programs at the district level would

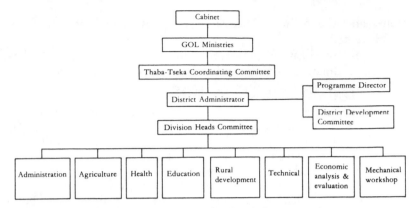

Figure 7.3. Thaba-Tseka Project organizational chart according to CIDA (1979).

make it possible to rationalize local administration and eliminate redundancy between Ministries. It was noted that roads, for instance, were built and maintained by three completely different authorities in Thaba-Tseka. First was the Ministry of Works, which was responsible for the main mountain road; second was the Prime Minister's Department of Community Development (later the Ministry of Rural Development), responsible for the Food Aid roads and tracks; and finally the Thaba-Tseka Project, which had its own road-building program. By coordinating all activities within a single district-wide authority, such redundancy could be avoided. In the same way, where cooperation was required between the staffs of different Ministries, disputes and delays arising in Maseru need not interfere, if all district staff worked together as part of an integrated program. Better coordination of day to day field activities, too, would bring about savings. Vehicles and other equipment could be pooled, instead of each Ministry keeping its own, reducing overall costs.

One additional consideration in favor of the new system of "decentralization" was no doubt among the most important (at least in some minds), though it nearly always went unspoken in official documents. The consideration was this: the new organization would allow proposals to be approved, funded, and implemented without having to go through the bureaucratic tangle in Maseru, where delays of many months and even years regularly handicap local government operations. If all the district funds were forwarded directly to the district administration each year, no one would be left waiting for funds or approval from Maseru. Effective executive decisions could be made there on the scene, and the dreaded Maseru bureaucracy would be effectively circumvented.

The "decentralization" idea received the strong support of the Thaba-Tseka Coordinating Committee. In a series of meetings in 1978, according to one source, it was ultimately agreed:

That the project would co-ordinate the implementation of Rural Development Activities under the District Administrator as subject to the policy guidelines and direction of the co-ordinating committee. In order to facilitate development at Thaba-Tseka, it was agreed that budgetary responsibility for the rural development program be decentralized to permit direct control at the District level and that responsibility for planning and implementation of programs also be concentrated at the district level. A resident economist from the Central Planning Office would co-ordinate Thaba-Tseka Regional Plans with National Plans and Programs.
(CIDA 1978R:15)

At the June 17 meeting of the TTCC, the issue was put quite clearly. According to the minutes of that meeting

A point was stressed that once officers are assigned to Thaba-Tseka they will fall under the jurisdiction of the S.D.A. [Senior District Administrator]. Ministries must become aware of the administrative innovation and relinquish the customary control of field staff from Maseru.

By the end of 1978, the Thaba-Tseka District had been officially gazetted, the plan for Phase Two had been officially approved, and all seemed to be proceeding smoothly. By 1979, a CIDA evaluation could conclude that "the integration of the Thaba-Tseka Programme into the administrative structure of the GOL and the decentralization of authority to the Thaba-Tseka District is considered an outstanding achievement of the programme and of the Ministries involved" (CIDA 1979:8).

But the evaluators had spoken too soon. In the next few years, things would become much more complicated.

Resistance to the plan

Although the decentralization plan had the blessing of the Thaba-Tseka Coordinating Committee, it soon became clear that the commitment of the various Ministries to the plan was less than complete. First was the matter of the budget. Although it had been intended that all Ministries active in "development" in the Thaba-Tseka district should be funded through a single District Authority, and that all Ministries should agree to vote funds to and work with the programme, this idea proved difficult to put into effect. Instead, the programme continued to get its funds through the Ministry of Agriculture, and other Ministries retained financial control over their own staff. At a November 1978 meeting of the TTCC, the Chairman explained that:

> although it would be advisable in the long run to allocate the budget requests by Ministry, in view of the present time constraint it would be possible to present the budget request through agriculture as long as Finance is aware that the additional funds requested are for other ministries as well. Prior to creating a rationalized budget proposal next year, it is necessary to get the GOL to specify exactly the nature of the new District Authority. The Chairman recognized the revolutionary approach embodied in TTDP will require Cabinet to set up a new administrative procedure. To this effect he had already submitted a position paper to Cabinet.
> (TTCC Minutes, November 30, 1978)

But by the end of 1980, the position had not changed. At the October meeting of the TTCC, the Chairman reportedly:

> told the meeting that in the past preparation of annual budgets for the Project were [*sic*] very easy as they concerned only two parties, the Ministry of Agriculture and the donor concerned.
> The new developments call for integrated budgeting for all government Ministries at district level. The budget has to originate from the District and be submitted to Central Government for approval. Talks have been held with [the Ministry of Finance] which concurs with the new system.
> The meeting made the following conclusions on this issue:
> 1. That the new system is acceptable.
> 2. However, the request came late.
> 3. As a result, the new system can only be employed for the financial year 1982/3.
> (TTCC Minutes, October 10, 1980)

This was the last time the matter was discussed. By the time 1982/3 came around, integrated budgeting was a dead issue, and the TTCC, in any case, was no longer around to discuss it, as we will soon see.

The deployment of "development"

But resistance to a decentralized budget was not the only snag the new plan was encountering. The Ministries that were supposed to be "integrated" under the authority of the District Programme persisted in maintaining their own control over their field staff and making unilateral decisions on actions in the district without consultation or agreement with the programme. As early as 1979, complaints were voiced that the Ministries in Maseru were refusing to integrate their staff, vehicles, and resources into the programme. The CIDA evaluation of 1979 noted conflicts between the Technical Division of the project and the Ministry of Works, and noted that "the question of decentralization and of integration into the Programme has not been addressed at the policy level by the MOW" (CIDA 1979: 113). At the TTCC Meeting of May, 1980, the district management reported that:

the [Ministry of Rural Development] official (Cooperatives) based in Thaba-Tseka has to date not integrated his programme with those of other divisions. He continues to act like an "independent agency." He has his own schedule and continues to use the government vehicle as he wishes.
(TTCC Minutes, May 9, 1980)

At the same meeting, it was observed that the Ministry of Education had decided to develop a technical school at the Paray Mission secondary school in Thaba-Tseka, ignoring the decision of the TTCC favoring an alternative plan involving the project's own technical school. This showed, according to the minutes of the meeting, that "MoE does not recognize the legitimacy of the TTCC and hence its indecision or indifference." At the next month's meeting (June 6, 1980), it was reported that the Permanent Secretary for Education had retorted that the project's technical school was "an imposition on the Ministry of Education by the Ministry of Agriculture and the Canadians."

The same meeting carried a report of an ongoing feud between the programme and the Ministry of Water and Energy Resources (WEMIN). WEMIN had never acknowledged the authority of the District Programme, and its representative to the TTCC finally declared as much at the June meeting. The minutes report:

The representative of WEMIN reported that it is the *exclusive right* of his Ministry to decide who should get water and who should not get it. To them this is a sensitive political issue which warrants unilateral decision. This report was reiterated in the letter written to

the District Management by WEMIN.
(TTCC Minutes, May 9, 1980)

The minutes go on to note:

This report was not only alarming but also disconcerting to the
TTCC at large. The report departs from the important concept which
the TTCC has been developing and nurturing for the last two years –
"Integrated Planning and Integrated Development." Several examples
were cited to show that the concept of integrated planning is the
centre that holds together ... Unilateral decision is totally
unacceptable to TTCC as this is at variance with the concept of
integrated planning which is a prerequisite of successful integrated
rural development. No pressures will cause TTCC to deviate from
the right direction.
(TTCC Minutes, May 9, 1980)

Such brave declarations notwithstanding, WEMIN, Rural Development, Education, and other Ministries continued to resist or refuse
"integration" with the programme. At a June 25, 1980 meeting of the
Division Heads Committee of the programme, the Project Director
reiterated that "Government acknowledges the operations of Thaba-
Tseka [Development Programme] but does not cooperate through its
Ministries." As a solution, it was suggested, characteristically, that the
Ministries were "to be educated on the Thaba-Tseka District." But, as
future events would show, the issues raised by the conflicts over "integration" were not of a sort to be resolved through any amount of
"education."

The new director and the district coordinator

Much of the opposition to the programme and its plans for decentralization was couched in the idiom of resistance to "the Canadians" and
"their Project," seen as trying "to push everyone else around." The
supporters of the decentralization plan, Canadian and Basotho alike,
were of course distressed by such thinking. The whole idea had been to
take the organizational structure developed by the project and turn it
into a permanent system for decentralized district administration. This
new structure was no longer to be a "Project," but an ongoing District
Programme – and no longer a Canadian venture, but an integral part of

the governing apparatus of Lesotho. Canada still had a key role to play, of course, as the principal donor; but it seemed clear that the identification of the programme with "the Canadians" was an obstacle to achieving the cooperation of other Ministries that would be essential to the success of the plan for decentralization and integration.

It was with these considerations in mind that the programme management decided to find a Mosotho candidate for the post of Programme Director. The plans had been laid as early as the end of 1979, when the move to appoint a Mosotho Director was described as "a major step in testing many critical elements of the institutional experiment in decentralization and integration" (TTDP Quarterly Report, October–December 1979: 54). The step was explicitly acknowledged as a tactic to defuse opposition to the new decentralized administration. The same report declared: "The resiliency of the central government's ability to adjust and cope with the district development program must be explored by hiring an indigenous challenger to the status quo." A candidate, the then District Agricultural Officer, was selected and groomed for the job by programme management, and it was intended that this "indigenous challenger" would be approved as the new Director in time to take over from the Canadian Director when his contract expired in August of 1980. In August, the TTCC approved the proposed Mosotho candidate as "Acting Director," but declared that the final nomination would be made by Government at a later point. CIDA, after initial reservations, supported the nomination as well. A Canadian was forwarded in October to serve as "Deputy Director," in an advisory role. Everything seemed to be going according to plan.

But the Mosotho candidate never received his anticipated final confirmation as Director. In January, he was abruptly withdrawn as Acting Director and given a day's notice to transfer to Maseru. CIDA was then informed that the Government of Lesotho desired a Canadian Director, and the Canadian originally designated as Deputy Director was swiftly confirmed as the new Director. These events were intimately connected with the arrival of the new District Coordinator in December of 1980.

The "District Coordinator" was a new office created by the Government of Lesotho in 1980 as part of a much-heralded nation-wide "decentralization" reform. The office of the District Coordinator, or DC, largely replaced the old "District Administrator" (or DA) post, but with important differences. The DA had been an official within the Ministry of Interior, in charge of general administration and coordination of Government activities in the district. But the DA did not have a direct link to the center of power in Maseru, reporting instead through the Ministry of the Interior. At the same time, the DA's authority over the staff of other Ministries was unclear. The office of the District Coordinator, on the other hand, was a much higher-ranking post than the old District Administrator's office had been. The DC was designated as the highest Government official in the district, at a rank equivalent to Deputy Permanent Secretary, with authority over the district heads of all Ministries and Departments on "day to day matters." The DC was mandated to report directly to the Senior Permanent Secretary, without going through any Ministry, and it was said that a DC could report directly to the Prime Minister himself on important matters. The stated function of the DC was to supervise all day to day activities of Government staff in the district, to coordinate the activities of the different Ministries, and to see that Government activities in the district conformed to the National Development Plan.

The introduction of District Coordinators was stated to be a move toward decentralization, placing greater executive authority in the districts and allowing greater coordination at the district level. In practice, matters are more complicated. It is true that the DC has authority over all government staff in the district on "day to day matters," but on "financial, technical and professional matters" staff must still report to their Ministry in Maseru. Yet "day to day matters," even under the old system, were never handled out of Maseru, but were the responsibility of the highest-ranking local officer in each Ministry. The shift in authority here is thus not from Maseru to the districts, but from the district heads to a central District Coordinator. Financially, as well, the Ministries in Maseru seem to have lost none of their powers to the DC. Budgets continue to come from the capital, and the DC has no power to construct an integrated district budget such as the Thaba-Tseka Programme had envisaged.

The creation of the new office of the District Coordinator thus did not transfer much real power to the districts. But the change was not without its effects; it did rearrange power within the districts, and provide a new channel for central control of the district machinery. Central control over all staff in the district was made possible by creating a high-ranking post outside of any one Ministry, capable of overseeing all Government staff throughout the district. At the same time, the direct link between the DC and the highest power centers in the capital made it possible for Cabinet to have much more direct control of goings-on in the districts whenever that might be necessary.

For all the talk of "decentralization," the creation of the post of District Coordinator thus had two important "centralizing" effects: (1) power within the district was centralized through the creation of the District Coordinator, or, as one informant preferred, the "District Czar"; (2) the power of the true political center (Cabinet) was enhanced *vis à vis* the outlying Ministries by the creation of a high-ranking district "watchdog," reporting directly to the highest levels.

The place the DC was to occupy in the ostensible "model district" of Thaba-Tseka was never well specified. The programme pictured the DC coming to take the place of the TTCC, and perhaps eventually the Project Director as well, as head of an integrated district development program, along the lines pioneered by the project. But the organizational structure actually approved by the TTCC at an October 1980, meeting was not so clear (see Figure 7.4, the organizational chart approved at that meeting).

At least three key points were left unspecified in this organizational model. First, the role of the TTCC itself was left unclear. The TTCC is mentioned on the chart, but only in a curious juxtaposition with the Permanent Secretaries, as if the two were interchangeable. Minutes of the Committee meetings from this period reveal considerable uncertainty about what the future role of the TTCC might be. In the face of this uncertainty, the chart hedged its bets: it did not definitively state whether the Committee would continue to exist at all; and if it did, whether or not it would have executive authority over the DC. The key

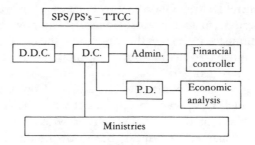

Figure 7.4. Organizational chart approved by TTCC, October 1980.
Note: SPS = Senior Permanent Secretary
　　　PS's = Permanent Secretaries
　　　TTCC = Thaba-Tseka Coordinating Committee
　　　DDC = District Development Committee
　　　DC = District Coordinator
　　　PD = Programme Director

question of whether there would continue to exist a policy-making body at the district level was not resolved.

Secondly, it was not clear what sort of authority the DC actually was to have over the field staff of the Ministries. Was the DC to be the head of a District Development Programme, actually directing operations and making policy for all departments and divisions, as the Programme Director had been intended to do originally? Or was the DC to be merely a general overseer and coordinator, along the lines of the old DA, leaving policy planning and finance in the hands of the Ministries in Maseru?

Finally, the plan approved by the TTCC gave no indication of the place of the programme's divisions in the new structure. The chart does not indicate anyone at all reporting to the Programme Director, but indicates three of the programme's divisions (Administration, Finance, and Economic Evaluation) at various other points on the chart. Were these divisions to be taken out of the Programme Director's responsibility? What about the other divisions, such as Agriculture, Technical, Health, and Education? Were they to be merged with the "Ministries," or would they remain under the umbrella of the programme, alongside the corresponding Ministries, creating a redundant parallel structure? What was to happen to the programme's "Division Heads Committee"? If the two structures were merged, would it be according to the "decentralized" and "integrated" plan, with all staff in the district divided and administered according to the programme's divisions, or would it follow the model of Lesotho's other districts? All of these major issues were left unresolved by the TTCC's deceptively simple looking organizational chart. They would be resolved in practice in the months to come.

When the new District Coordinator came to Thaba-Tseka in December of 1980, he entered a bureaucratic setting rife with structural ambiguity, in which lines of power and authority lay waiting to be drawn or redrawn. He arrived, as well, it seems, with a well-defined political agenda, centered on the task of gaining effective control of the district as swiftly as possible. Informants recall that he immediately perceived the programme as a threat to his legitimate control of the district, and commenced a series of measures that resulted in the isolation and alienation of the programme and its divisions from the rest of the Government structure within the district.

The first of these steps was the abrupt removal in January 1981 of the newly appointed Mosotho Acting Director, and his replacement by a

Canadian Director. It is difficult to know exactly how the decision to fire the Mosotho Director was arrived at, and useless to speculate on the basis of available information. But it is clear from informants' recollections that the switch was brought about in conformity with the wishes of the new DC, undoubtedly with active support at higher levels of the Government of Lesotho. Canadian officials involved in the negotiations are unequivocal that the switch was *not* made at the request of CIDA, which backed the nomination of the Mosotho candidate, but was insisted upon by the GOL. At the time, the decision was explained to CIDA officials as a matter of the lack of qualifications of the nomi nated Mosotho. GOL officials reportedly stressed his lack of seniority and insufficient "polish" for a position that involved dealing with foreign donors. Others close to the case suggested that a lack of suitable political connections might have been a more important consideration.

But what is most interesting here is not the rejection of a particular individual nominee, but the rejection of the *idea* of a Mosotho nominee, and the specific preference for a Canadian Director. We have seen that proponents of the decentralization plan first suggested a Mosotho Director in the anticipation that the organization reforms they were proposing would be strengthened by heading the new structure with "an indigenous challenger to the status quo" (see above). It seems likely from the events described above that others in the Government (whether the DC or his superiors, it hardly matters) had the same perception, and moved to head off such a possibility. As long as the programme remained a "Canadian" venture, headed by Canadians and funded by short-term foreign funding, there could be no danger of it taking over the district, or actually bringing about a "decentralization" of power away from the bureaucracy in Maseru. Insisting on defining the would-be "Programme" as a foreign "Project" made sure that it could pose no threat to the larger governmental structure and the entrenched interests supporting it.

Once the new Canadian Programme Director was in place, the stage was set for a series of disputes and struggles between the programme management and the District Coordinator. The old disputes over the "integration" of the Ministries with the programme had never been resolved, and now became even more fierce. The Ministries in question, chiefly Works, Interior, Rural Development, and Education, still refused to vote funds to the Programme, and for the most part denied any programme authority over their staff. This was a continuing sore spot for the programme management, but there was nothing new about it;

the staff of these Ministries had never been very effectively "integrated" with the project except in theory. But now, with the arrival of the DC, the lines between "Project" and "Non-Project" became more clearly drawn, and the polite fiction of integration began to break down completely.

With the "participating Ministries" no longer even paying lip service to the idea of integration, the project began to try to close off access to project resources to the uncooperative Ministries. The project had built housing which it supplied to all participating Ministries under the "integration" plan; it also presided over a vehicle pool intended for the use of an integrated district administration, as well as a horse stable, and common stores and supplies for all divisions. The Ministries which refused to "integrate" their staff with the project nonetheless enjoyed the privileges of the pooled resources in housing, vehicles, and so on. Project management grew increasingly resentful of what it saw as an exploitative relationship and tried, in the interests of cost containment, to limit access to "integrated" project resources.

A great many disputes followed from this. The issue of pooled vehicles was perhaps the most contentious of all during this period. Ministries not cooperating with the project refused to place their own vehicles in the project vehicle pool, yet they regularly expected to use the project vehicles whenever they needed them. When disputes arose over such issues, the DC inevitably took the side of the uncooperative Ministry, not the project. Such disagreements went on constantly throughout 1981, and often became quite heated. Witnesses recall that such disputes went so far as to involve breaking into offices and stealing keys to disputed vehicles, and at one point it is said that guns were even drawn. When these disputes between the "Programme" and the DC were appealed to higher levels, the DC inevitably received the firm backing of his government.

The conflicts in this period, however, did not only involve the non-integrated Ministries, but even the project's own divisions. In the period following the arrival of the DC, many of the non-agricultural divisions of the project came under attack, and project management lost control over many of what had been considered the project's own components. The case of the Health Division is particularly interesting here, as it illustrates nicely both the process through which control was wrested away from the project as well as some of the reasons why something like the Health Division should be such a contested resource in the first place. The account which follows has been pieced together from the testimony of several informants with good knowledge of the history of the case. This information, gathered second hand and at a distance of two years or more, may well contain some errors of detail or omission. In its broad outlines, however, the story was well confirmed through the fieldwork interviews.

The Health Division was established in 1978 as a division of the Thaba-Tseka Project. The division included a District Health Inspector, a Public Health Nurse, and a District Medical Officer. The District Medical Officer, a Canadian, headed the Division, and reported to the Project Director. The only link between the Health Division and the Ministry of Health in Maseru at this point was by way of the TTCC, in line with the "decentralization" ideal.

In 1980, a vehicle was donated by UNICEF to the Ministry of Health for the new Thaba-Tseka Health Division. The vehicle was delivered to Thaba-Tseka and placed in the programme's transport pool, in keeping with the policy of "integration." The Public Health Nurse in the division objected to this use of the vehicle and insisted that the vehicle should be for the use of the staff of the Ministry of Health, i.e. herself, not "the Project." Disputes arose over the vehicle, with the Nurse charging that the vehicle was improperly maintained and urging the Ministry of Health to withdraw it from the pool. The character of these disputes is well illustrated by the following excerpt from the project's "Transport and Mechanical Workshop Monthly Report for November, 1980."

Y19598 was booked for by Health Division to go on clinic inspection trek commencing on 7th November to the 12th of the same month which was on the date on which the vehicle should have returned to base. The trek was meant to cover [certain areas] in the Mokhotlong district ... Rather than covering only those areas indicated on the reservation form, the Health officer and the driver decided to take a tour around the country and only on 18th November the vehicle came back to base with the spare wheel missing and the vehicle in poor condition because it was overdue for service ...

The total mileage for this round-Lesotho trip is 1277 km which at 45c/km Health Division should pay R574.65 transport costs. It is the feeling of the Division Head for Health that it is not justified that his division must pay for this luxury tour. It looks like the only fair way of doing it is to make both the involved Health officer and the driver pay for the transport they so much enjoyed.

In the past there has been an allegation that our Division does not

properly maintain this vehicle which is a contribution by central
Ministry of Health to facilitate health activities in the Thaba-Tseka
district, and as a result Health Ministry threatened to withdraw the
vehicle. To us it seems like this officer misused this vehicle double
beyond its set service schedule only to prove the point that we
neglect maintenance of the said vehicle, so that when the vehicle is
scrabed [*sic*] she can go back to Health Ministry and say "that is what
I told you."

It is clear from these disputes that while the District Medical Officer
and the project management considered that this Nurse was merely an
employee of the project's Health Division, and a junior one at that, she
saw herself acting not simply as a project employee, but as a representative of the Ministry of Health, the rightful owner of the vehicle. By
trying to separate the Ministry of Health and its resources from the
project, she was apparently attempting to give herself more autonomy
and power *vis à vis* her superiors in the Health Division.

It was only one month after the above report was written that the DC
arrived on the scene for the first time. This new development effected a
decisive shift in the balance of power that had up to then prevailed. The
DC quickly took the side of the Public Health Nurse, and on his own
executive authority in the district ordered the contested vehicle to be
removed from the project's transport pool. From that point on, the
Nurse bypassed the Canadian "District Medical Officer" and reported
only to the DC. The DC cooperated closely with the Public Health
Nurse, and endorsed not only use of the vehicle, but setting up courses
and spending Health Division money without the consent of the project's Head for the Health Division.

Both the District Coordinator and the Public Health Nurse were
described as "very staunch supporters" of the ruling National Party,
and both reportedly took a strong interest in the political uses to which
the Health Division might be put. On the one hand, there was a
propaganda function. Visiting clinics, speaking at educational courses
organized in the villages, giving vaccinations – all were opportunities to
make political hay, and the Nurse, with the backing of the DC, was able
to seize these opportunities. But observers report that the political
appropriation of the Health Division went even further than this. Once
control of the division had been effectively wrested away from the
project, it is said that health care itself began to be allocated preferentially to National Party members. One informant was able to recall

specific cases in which ambulance care was withheld from emergency patients due to their political affiliations with opposing parties.

According to one observer, the DC's main interest in the Health Division in this period "was in how it could be used politically." It is clear that, given such a focus, it would be foolish to allow so valuable a political resource to remain in the hands of the "neutral" project management. These apparently petty bureaucratic disputes thus in the end involved more serious issues than who gets to have the Land Rover today or who reports to whom. The question was whether the "technical" apparatus of the Health Division would be pressed into service in a larger political contest. The personal power struggles of the various actors merge at this point with a larger political question, and what appears at first as a simple power grab by a few individuals thus has at the same time a larger significance as the appropriation of a political resource.

The Canadian District Medical Officer, who nominally headed the division, eventually left in June of 1981 ("under some pressure," according to one source). Staff of the Health Division continued to report directly to the DC, and to the Ministry of Health in Maseru. The Project Director remained nominal "Interim Head" of the Division, due to some lingering CIDA funding for Health projects, but this was only a formality. In 1982, when fieldwork began, the Project no longer had a "Health Division," and staff of the Ministry of Health had no substantive connection with the project. Health had become completely detached from the "integrated" structure of the one-time "District Development Programme."

The same was happening with other divisions. Staff from the Ministry of Rural Development, which had once been at least loosely integrated into the "Programme," now reported directly to the District Coordinator and to their home Ministry in Maseru, and refused to acknowledge programme authority. The same was true for Education. Interior, Works, Water and Energy, and other Ministries, meanwhile, had never integrated their staff in any way with the "Programme," and had less reason than ever to do so with the arrival of the new DC. The project structure, which had been intended to provide an administrative framework for the entire district, found itself able to hold on to only those divisions where it funded its own staff and did not rely on the cooperation of the Ministries in Maseru. The Technical Division, largely in charge of building roads, was never in danger. The Ministry of Works had never integrated its Thaba-Tseka operations under the "Programme" umbrella in the first place, so Technical Division staff remained under the unambiguous control of the project. The same was true of the Mechanical Workshop and the project's own Administration and Financial Control units, whose employees were paid by CIDA and had no connection with any of the Government Ministries. But where Government of Lesotho staff were concerned, all the Ministries but Agriculture were abandoning the "Programme" and its decentralized, integrated structure.

New proposals and the Christmas crisis

Project administrators in this period did not give up easily on the plan for decentralization and integration. Throughout the key period following the arrival of the DC in December of 1980, project officials were busy designing and promoting new and presumably more acceptable blueprints for the administration of the new district along the lines of the original decentralized plan.

In February, 1981, after the arrival of the District Coordinator and the subsequent removal of the Mosotho "Programme Director," Project management produced a position paper to be presented to the Thaba-Tseka Coordinating Committee outlining options for the future development of the "Programme," appropriately titled "Where Do We Go From Here?" An outline of the paper began by noting that the "Programme" was facing an "identity crisis," and noting three "precipitating factors contributing to the present impasse," whose cumulative effect had been "frustration and a consequent weakening of will and effort." The three factors were as follows:

Indirectly, the first such cause was the official gazettement of Thaba-Tseka District. The Thaba-Tseka Programme found itself, by proxy, as a 'de facto' District authority responsible not only for a broad spectrum of development activities, but also for the provision of essential Government services in an impact area of 480,000 hectares and for a target population of 83,000. There was never, however, a statutory mandate for the Programme to assume these responsibilities nor, more importantly, was there the financial commitment by the Government of Lesotho, through its participating Ministries, to realize these objectives ...

Secondly, the arrival of the District Coordinator further compounded the uncertainty. Through largely a lack of clearly delineated areas of responsibility and authority, the ensuing scramble for the high ground occasioned the Programme's intellectual retrenchment into the security of a project's limited sphere ... We were constantly reminded of our limited prerogative in all concerns and, whether consciously or unconsciously, we were made aware of our being outside the Government pale – an element of foreignness or otherness to an obscure central effort.

The third factor contributing to an atmosphere of uncertainty and self-questioning was the unexplained removal of the former Mosotho Programme Director. His emplacement had been viewed by the Programme as a significant reflection of its legitimization and progressive integration into the Lesotho context.
(TTCC Minutes, February 1981)

The position paper then outlined three possible paths the project could take in the future. The first option was a minor modification of the original plan for decentralized, integrated district administration using the "Programme" structure. Under this plan Ministries involved in "development" – i.e. Agriculture, Education, Health, Rural Development, and Works – would operate in Thaba-Tseka District only through the project/programme. Budgets would be drawn up at the district level and funded by parent Ministries in Maseru. Staff of the participating Ministries would work within the Divisions of the project (specified as Administration, Technical, Mechanical and Transport, Economic Analysis and Evaluation, Agriculture, Health, Education, and Rural Development), pooling transport, housing, stores, and so on. Other, non-"development" Ministries, such as Police, Justice, Immigration, and so on, would be directly responsible for their staff and would not participate in the programme. The District Coordinator would supervise and coordinate all activities in the district. An organizational chart was presented, as shown in Figure 7.5.

The two other options outlined in the paper were not treated at such great length. The first of these, Option Two, called for leaving everything as it was, a state of affairs the paper referred to as "a transitional stage between a 'Project' and an 'Integrated District Rural Development Programme'." A number of disadvantages to this option were cited, including "inefficiency," "non-cooperation," and "confusion." A third option was "to abandon the original concept of an integrated rural development Program and return to the 'Project' mode of operation." Advantages and disadvantages were cited for this approach. Needless to say, the programme officials concluded by urging in the strongest possible terms the adoption of Option One, the decentralized option.

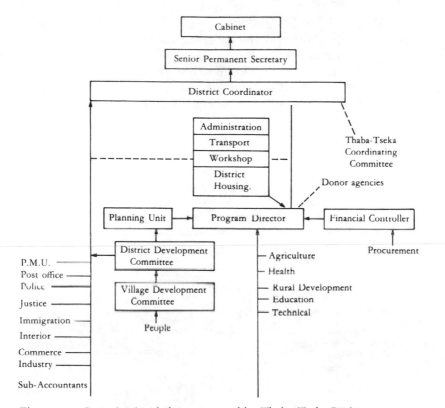

Figure 7.5. Organizational chart proposed by Thaba-Tseka Project management, February 1981

Option Three, the "Project" Option, was considered inferior, but probably preferable to the status quo, described in Option Two. The paper was presented to the members of the TTCC at its February 27, 1981, meeting, with the declaration: "The ball is in your court."

A second paper drawn up a short time later, and intended as complementary to the "Option One" outlined in the first paper, was a proposal to give a statutory basis to the programme by creating a "District Development Authority" in the Thaba-Tseka District ("Proposal for the Establishment of a District Development Authority in the Thaba-Tseka District"). The "District Development Authority" would be little more than a new name for the programme, except that it would have a well-defined legal position within the Government of Lesotho framework. It would have its own budget and funds, allocated to it by those Ministries "with a direct interest in the work of the [District Development Authority]." The paper included another proposed organizational chart, shown in Figure 7.6.

The options paper ("Where Do We Go From Here?") did not come up for discussion by the TTCC until the April 1981 meeting, although it had been first presented for consideration at the February meeting.

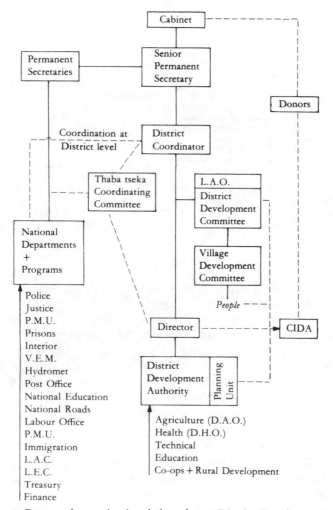

Figure 7.6. Proposed organizational chart for a "District Development Authority" in Thaba Tseka

Much to the dismay of the project management, the Committee after some discussion declared its preference for "Option Two" – the status quo. According to the minutes of the meeting, it was felt that the proposal for "full decentralization" (Option One) would be expensive, and that Option Two (the status quo) was "more realistic." The disadvantages listed for Option Two, it was felt, could be eliminated or overcome.

At the same meeting of the TTCC, the paper on the "District Development Authority" was presented for the first time. The proposal was introduced and explained at some length to the members by one of the junior programme officers – a white South African young man, as it happened. The Committee members declined to discuss the proposal, on the grounds that they had not yet read the paper, and discussions were deferred until the next meeting. But if the Committee was not yet ready to let its reaction be known, it seems that there must have been some less public figure who was not so delicate. The day after the TTCC meeting, the young South African who had presented the paper on the "District Development Authority" found his car had been set on fire. The same "accident" had befallen the car of his father, who was in Thaba-Tseka for a short visit. It was not known who had committed the vandalism, though of course there was no shortage of speculation.

In the months following the April events, relations between the "Programme" and the Government of Lesotho went from bad to worse, while the project's claims to provide an administrative structure for the entire district became weaker and weaker. The proposal for the "Development Authority" was eventually brought up for discussion at the July 3, 1981 meeting of the TTCC, but apparently it was not taken very seriously. No decision was made, and the proposal continued to be put off. By the end of the year, the TTCC had been dissolved, and the "District Development Authority" was a dead issue, a victim of postponement and lack of interest. Relations between the Programme Director and the DC, meanwhile, were deteriorating. The DC reportedly insisted that even the project staff should report directly to him. The Programme Director resisted this move as "contrary to and in total conflict with the project terms of reference." An uneasy and confused stalemate persisted through most of 1981. During this period, the Programme Director was, in the words of one informant, "completely ineffective." He was unable to effectively direct programs in the district thanks to the resistance of the DC; at the same time he was not taken seriously in Maseru, and at key junctures was denied the support even of his own government. This was not a matter of the Programme Director's personal characteristics, but his structural predicament. The Programme Director's terms of reference required him to exercise an authority that no one on the scene was prepared to grant to him.

By late 1981, the situation had deteriorated to such a point that the Programme Director recommended to CIDA that they should withdraw their funding and close the project unless the offending DC were removed and the project allowed to proceed according to the original Phase Two Plan of Operations. CIDA declined to apply such pressure. A number of high-level meetings were held in Maseru at which the programme management, Government of Lesotho officials, and CIDA representatives from Pretoria were present. A senior Government of Lesotho official declared that the Programme Director was the cause of all the problems at Thaba-Tseka. That was the last straw for the embattled Programme Director. He resigned on the spot, and returned home to Canada.

Collapse of the "programme" and revision of the plan

The December crisis and resignation of the Programme Director came close on the heels of a visit from a CIDA evaluation team in November of 1981. The coincidence of these two events set the stage for a major reassessment of the project by CIDA, and a far-reaching revision of the project's Plan of Operations. The new, revised Plan of Operations was approved in July and officially signed on August 16, 1982.

The revised plan, reflecting the recommendations of the evaluation report, introduced two types of change. First was a deemphasizing of livestock. In the face of the repeated failures in livestock commercialization and range improvement described in Chapter 5 above, it was evident "that future activities should concentrate on the crop aspects and rural development and that the Plan of Operations be revised to better reflect the present Project realities." A second set of changes, however, was prompted by the failure of the "decentralization" scheme. The creation of the new district and the creation of the post of DC, according to the revised plan, "has necessitated a review of the organization and function of the Project and substantial changes to Project activities." Instead of expanding into a full-fledged "decentralized District Development Authority," the revised plan indicated that the programme would be reduced once more to a short-term agriculture project. The intention was "to transfer the responsibility for many activities from the project administration to the various Ministries now represented in the 10th District."

The shift in emphasis which followed the 1982 revision may be clearly seen by comparing the "Goals and Objectives" section of the 1982 Plan with its corresponding section in the original 1978 Phase Two Plan of Operations. The following "specific purposes" and "key objectives" for the project were listed in the two plans:

1978

a. To improve the quality of life of the mountain people of the region by way of improving the quality of livestock and rangeland, raising of educational participation and training opportunities, construction of essential village infrastructure, creation of vital village organizations and improving sanitation and health;

b. To increase the agricultural production of the Thaba Tseka District by 50% by the end of year five of Phase II of the Project and farmer real incomes by 5% per annum by way of application of a broad range of improved agricultural, farm management and rural development techniques and practices;

c. To increase the participation of Thaba Tseka District residents in the decision making process with regard to the economic development of the areas through their involvement in village committees and other decision making media so as to achieve by year five of the Project a 60% rate of participation;

1982

To improve the quality of life of the mountain people of the region by way of: improving the quality and output of essential food crops including fresh vegetables; providing expanded market outlets for the District livestock; preventing soil and range erosion through conservation and woodlot practices and raising educational participation and training opportunities.

To substantially increase the commercial and subsistence output of crops from the Thaba Tseka District and the incomes earned from farming.

To enable the Project to continue to provide the people of the District with assistance in meeting their basic human needs.

d. To enable the Thaba Tseka Mountain Development Project to continue over the next five years to function as a model of an integrated rural development scheme on a district level and to develop with the Government of Lesotho a model for district administration and development.

One can see clearly from this comparison a number of shifts. The emphasis on livestock and range management in section "a." of the 1978 plan has been completely reversed, with crops moving to center stage. The only reference to livestock in the 1982 revised plan is livestock marketing, an acknowledgement of the success of the livestock auctions described in Chapter 6. Also dropped from section "a." are references to education, village infrastructure, sanitation, and health – in short, all those non-agricultural components the "Programme" had tried so hard to "integrate." With regard to crops, the hard numbers for targeted output in section "b." have been dropped in the 1982 plan, a tacit recognition of the unlikelihood of ever coming close to meeting them. In sections "c." and "a." all references to "village organizations," "participation," and "involvement in decision making" have been dropped completely. (This will be discussed in Chapter 8 below.) Finally, section "d.", proposing the development of the project structure as "a model for district administration and development," is dropped entirely from the 1982 revised plan.

The "Programme" emerged from this restructuring pared down and humble: a mere project once again. Project activities would from this point on be nearly all confined to Agriculture, and the other Ministries would have no special relationship to the project. Thaba-Tseka would not be a "model district," but would be organized exactly like the other districts, and the project would play no role in any sort of "decentralization." The project's internal structure would not expand to provide a model for district integration, but would be absorbed without a trace into the GOL structure at the end of the project. A well-defined end of project date (March 1984), after which all CIDA funds would be cut off, decreed that this process of absorption would be a major priority for the project in its two remaining years.

A working accommodation: the era of the two charts

Following the December 1981 crisis, a new Canadian officer was given the post of Project Director, or, as it came to be known after the 1982 revision, Project Coordinator. Then in May 1982, as the July revision of the plan was being prepared, a new District Coordinator was appointed as well. Both men could claim temperaments more inclined to compromise than their predecessors, and, as all the main points of contention had been settled, the stormy relations between the project and local government were for the most part over. Once it was conceded that the "Programme" was not a district administration, and that the Ministries were not to become either integrated or decentralized on the 1978 model, there was little for the Project Director and the DC to discuss except day to day operations and the process by which the project would eventually be absorbed into the GOL structure. In 1982–3, there seemed to exist a cordial agreement between project management and the District Coordinator's office on these points.

Although relations on the ground remained smooth, there was in fact an important structural contradiction in the project's place in the formal organization of the district. Empirically, the relations of authority seemed clear enough. After observing project operations for several months and interviewing all of the high-ranking officers of the project and the Government's district administration, I constructed a diagram which seemed to represent the organizational structure of the district, showing the place of the project within the overall structure. The chart is reproduced in Figure 7.7.

In May of 1983, I took this diagram to the District Coordinator and asked him if it was accurate. He declared that it was an entirely correct representation of the district's structure, and of the project's place within it. The District Agricultural Officer, the highest-ranking official of the Ministry of Agriculture in the district, agreed as well, as did other GOL officers. But when the same chart was shown to the Project Coordinator, he disagreed strongly. The DC, he insisted, was his "counterpart," not his superior, and project staff were under his authority, not that of the DC. The real organizational structure, he said, was to be found in another chart, the one approved in the revised Plan of Operations of 1982. That chart is reproduced in Figure 7.8.

The chart referred to by the Project Coordinator contains two significant differences from the one that the DC had subscribed to. First, the Project Coordinator and the District Coordinator are represented as

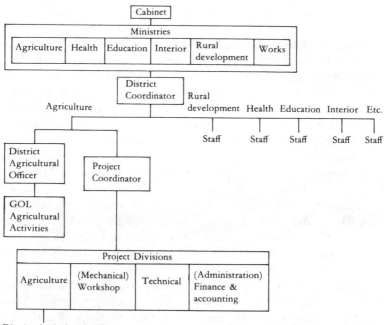

Figure 7.7. Organizational chart constructed by author, May 1983

equals – "counterparts" – not in a hierarchical relation of authority. Secondly, the project divisions – those that remained – are seen as under the exclusive control of the Project Coordinator. In this representation, the DC cannot give orders to the staff of the Technical Division, for instance, any more than the Project Coordinator can give orders to the staff of the Ministry of the Interior. The two structures are parallel, not nested.

The DC was very clear on these two points. He pointed out that he was the head of government in the district, and declared unequivocally: "The Project Coordinator [he called him by name] reports to me." He claimed authority over all staff working in the district, including those of the project's divisions. Where the Project Coordinator saw himself as a counterpart, the DC saw only a subordinate; where the Project Coordinator saw an autonomous "Project" sphere, the DC made no such distinctions.

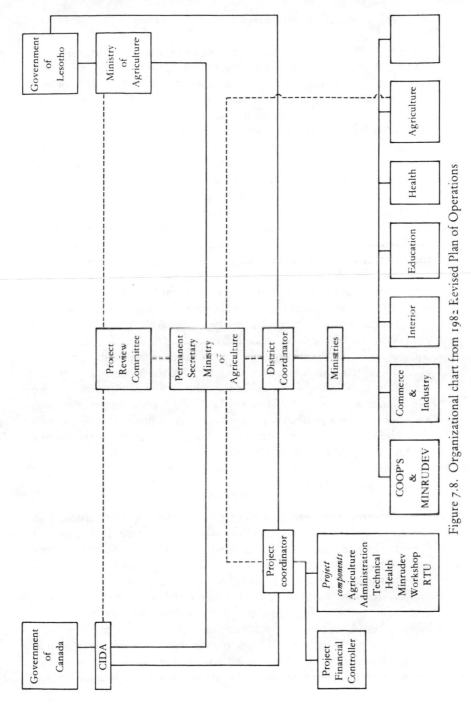

Figure 7.8. Organizational chart from 1982 Revised Plan of Operations

223

It seemed clear that in practice the DC had nearly all the authority he claimed. The Project Coordinator did in fact report to the DC regularly, and asked his permission on any important matter of policy or implementation. His contact with the Permanent Secretary for Agriculture was not greatly different in kind from that maintained by the district officers with Permanent Secretaries in other Ministries; in this respect he might as well have been simply the head of Agriculture for the District. It is clear that the formal contradiction between the two organizational structures never came into the open only because the issue was finessed. The Project Coordinator was able to claim authority for himself and autonomy for the project only because he had the good sense never to try to actually use it. So long as the project and its Coordinator were generally responsive to the wishes of the DC, the contradiction between the abstract claims embedded in the Coordinator's diagram and the reality of the DC's hegemonic power did not ever need to surface. CIDA could have the face-saving organizational chart it needed, so long as its representatives had the discretion not to take it too seriously.

The era of the two charts thus proceeded peacefully, and during the period 1982–4 the project scaled down slowly, devoting its careful energies to the rather melancholy task of dismantling itself. In the end, all of the project's divisions were absorbed into the Ministry of Agriculture, even such unlikely components as the Technical Division and the Mechanical Workshop. By March 1984, CIDA's involvement was over, and there was no sign of another donor to take its place. The project was thus effectively ended at that time,[2] leaving no trace in the formal organization of the District administration.

Conclusion

It is common, and perhaps easy, to see a "development" project as subject and the "host country" as object. In Thaba-Tseka, in this perspective, one would see a big, North American "Development Project" coming in with all its money, plans, and expertise to grab hold of and transform a portion of a "Less Developed Country" into a desired image. The only qualities that can be ascribed to the substance to be transformed, the "LDC," in such a view, are varying degrees of tractability or resistance to the project's designs. The structure in place is raw material for those who would transform it. But if there is one thing that is clear from the material presented above, it is that the Thaba-Tseka Project was not simply acting on a system in place, but was itself acted on; grabbed and pulled and twisted every which way by forces it did not understand or have the means to deal with. When the project set itself down in Thaba-Tseka it quickly found itself in the position not of a craftsman approaching his raw materials, but more like that of a bread crumb thrown into an ants' nest. Pushed and pulled in all directions, project staff found themselves frustrated and abused by the very "Government" they imagined they were trying to "help."

The project's staff and planners were helpless to do much about the political and bureaucratic obstacles their "decentralization" plan encountered, and often even unable to understand what was happening, because they sincerely saw "decentralization" as an apolitical administrative reform. For reasons explored in Chapter 2, the "development" planners regarded the paralyzing bureaucracy of the government apparatus in Lesotho, with all its "inefficiency," as some sort of mistake – the result of poor planning, perhaps, or a bad organizational chart, or perhaps lack of education. Thanks to the "development" problematic and its principle of "governmentality," the central bureaucracy in Maseru was never understood as a *political* fact, as the mode of exercise of a form of power. Government was seen as a machine for delivering services; but never as a way of "governing" people, a device through which certain classes and interests control the behavior and choices of others.

The attempt to introduce a system of "decentralization," which would break the power of the Maseru bureaucracy over government services in the districts, was thus always understood as a kind of technical reform, which might encounter the sort of resistance "new ideas" always do, but which was not beyond the reasonable scope of a "development project" to implement. We have seen in this chapter, of course, that such an attempt involved a fierce political contest, that "decentralization" was first of all a political issue, and that in the end the project's proposal for a technical reorganization of the District for "integrated development" was crushed by the political realities of the Lesotho state. But, even as this was happening, the project planners continued to misapprehend the issue. They always imagined that the Government somehow didn't understand the plan, or that the right organizational chart had not been found. Even as the "decentralized" structure was being rudely crushed, project administrators persisted in drawing up ever more organizational charts – as if, if they only could find the right one, everyone would come to their senses and agree that decentralization was a fine thing after all.

This curious response to a political challenge is a social fact, and it cannot be explained by referring to some presumed lack of perceptiveness on the part of project administrators. The apparent blindness to the political nature of the problems encountered was found at all levels of Programme planning and implementation, and the officials who ran the project were no fools. The explanation lies rather in another social fact; namely, that the project, by its nature, was not equipped to play the political game it suddenly found itself in the midst of. Having taken on "decentralization," and with it the entrenched power of the governing classes in Maseru, the project had no teeth available to it to chew what it had bitten off.

This chapter thus illustrates a fundamental contradiction in the role "development agencies" are intended to play. On the one hand, they are supposed to bring about "social change," sometimes of a dramatic and far-reaching sort. At the same time, they are not supposed to "get involved in politics" – and in fact have a strong de-politicizing function. But any real effort at "social change" cannot help but have powerful political implications, which a "development project" is constitutionally unfit to deal with. To do what it is set up to do (bring about socio-economic transformations), a "development" project must attempt what it is set up not to be able to do (involve itself in political struggles). In this chapter we have seen how the Thaba-Tseka Project acted out this fatalistic drama in its quest for "decentralization."

Post-script on sources

The account of the history of the project's plan for decentralization presented here is based on a number of sources. I was able to obtain (from a wide variety of sources) a fairly complete documentary record for the period under review, including all of the Project Quarterly Reports, Minutes from many of the monthly meetings of the Thaba-Tseka Coordinating Committee and Division Heads Meetings, and a number of internal project documents and position papers circulated at various times. Internal CIDA reports and evaluations also included valuable information (see, for instance, CIDA 1978R, 1978E, 1978P, 1979, 1982).

This documentary information was supplemented with information from interviews with a wide range of people in Thaba-Tseka, Maseru, and Ottawa. I have tried not to use the names of either the informants or the principals here, in order to avoid causing anyone unnecessary embarrassment or trouble. Many of my informants spoke on condition of confidentiality, and these I am thus unable to identify in even a general way. However, it is appropriate to indicate that my reconstruction of the events described in this chapter draws on the accounts of many project and GOL staff employed in Thaba-Tseka at the time of my fieldwork (September 1982 through December 1983), including the then Project Coordinator and the then District Coordinator, along with others in knowledgeable positions thanks to either their length of stay, their position, or both. It also draws on interviews with many of the main actors during the turbulent years 1979 to 1981, including the Mosotho "Acting Director," the Canadian who replaced him when he was recalled, and a number of CIDA officers who supervised the project during the period. The District Coordinator of the time was contacted but declined to grant me an interview.

8 Crop development and some other programs of the Thaba-Tseka Project

The last two chapters have looked at the Thaba-Tseka Project's attempt to bring about major changes in livestock practices ("livestock development") and local government administration ("decentralization"). These were among the most important of the Thaba-Tseka Project's activities, and they illustrate well the character of the project's encounter with the political and economic realities of the targeted "LDC." But the project was involved with a number of other programs as well, which may be discussed briefly as a supplement to the preceding chapters.

The point of such a discussion is not to list off the pluses and minuses of the various programs, or to point out "mistakes," but to continue the task begun in the last two chapters by describing characteristic sorts of encounters and frustrations, and significant kinds of outcomes. This approach must be clearly distinguished from the sort of analysis proper to an evaluation, the kind of analysis that would begin by listing all the points at which "mistakes" had been made, and go on to show how more careful planning or a different approach might have avoided them. Such an analysis is of course possible for the Thaba-Tseka Project; like most projects of its kind, it had its share of blunders, foul-ups, and embarrassing mistakes. There was the potato project that fell on its face due to unforeseen problems with disease and marketing; there was an abattoir that was half built and then abandoned due to poor financial planning; there was a wind-powered irrigation system that failed "because somebody lost a decimal" in the calculations. There were the twelve village water supply systems built in 1978–9, of which, three years later, eleven were not working, and could not be repaired because they had been badly installed using inferior materials. There were hydraulic rams that failed to pump water far enough uphill to be of any use; there were the solar ovens that worked so poorly no one would use them; there was a fish project that failed when the fish were all killed through over-feeding. And there were many more examples that could be cited.

This list will have a familiar feel to it for anyone who has read "development" accounts of "integrated rural development projects" like Thaba-Tseka. These projects seem almost always to produce incredible numbers of such "mistakes," and to produce along with them,

228

and at the same time, an array of experts to expose the "mistakes" and prescribe remedies. But, for our purposes here, there is little point in recounting all these technical errors or instances of incompetence and poor planning, just as there is no intrinsic interest in listing off areas (such as the introduction of new varieties of maize seed, for instance), where the project achieved, in its own terms, "successes." Since my purpose here is neither to decide whether the project was a Good Thing or a Bad Thing, nor to advise the "development" industry on how they might do it better next time, there is no particular advantage in organizing the analysis in this way. Instead, the analysis here will continue in the spirit of Chapters 6 and 7 by presenting a few interesting cases and attempting to draw out certain aspects of these cases that will be significant for understanding the nature of the project's interaction with the structure in place, and for seeing the long-term importance of particular kinds of outcomes whose effects are not captured by affixing the labels "success" and "failure."

Crop development

The original plans for crop development in the Thaba-Tseka Project were based on the idea of switching from "subsistence" crops to the production of cash crops for the market. The original planning documents for Phase One of the project declared: "The execution of the crop development programme would be based on a switch from the current subsistence crops (maize) to cash crops (wheat and peas), for which the area's ecology is more suitable. Farmers are interested in this switch as soon as they have easy access to market places" (FAO/World Bank 1975: Annex 1, 11). As this last sentence implies, the building of the road, along with the access to markets that would presumably come with it, was supposed to make possible this great transformation. Producing cash crops for the market, even if it meant that subsistence goods would need to be purchased, would be more economically efficient. Thaba-Tseka would produce the crops to which it was suited and export surpluses to lowland Lesotho and South Africa. By making the switch to market production, and by purchasing recommended inputs and following improved cultivation practices, "farmers" in the project area were supposed to increase their incomes dramatically. Yields were projected to rise from 300 kg/ha to 1,000 kg/ha for maize and from 400 kg/ha to 1,300 kg/ha for wheat by Year 3 of the project (FAO/World Bank 1974: 14).

The anticipated switch to cash crops, however, did not occur. A 1978 CIDA report noted that attempts to alter the cropping pattern in favor of cash crops (wheat in particular) "have been ineffective and prospects of creating such a shift do not appear promising for the foreseeable future" (CIDA 1978R: 17). As in the case of livestock, "the market" turned out not to be such a novelty as had been imagined, and the road, which was supposed to make all the difference, ended up having no significant effect on cropping patterns.

The road did indeed reduce "farm to market" transportation costs, but it soon became clear that, in the "farm to market" scheme, the "isolated" mountain villages were not the farm but the market. With the new road, imported South African goods could be brought in more cheaply than ever, and the grain-laden trucks of the planners' dreams ended up coming up the mountain road, not down it. With mine wages on the rise throughout the 1970s, retail business in Thaba-Tseka boomed. Shops expanded, new cafés were started, and there even appeared a small supermarket, stocking a comparatively enormous range of food and other goods. Instead of providing a channel for the export of agricultural surpluses, the new road only lowered the price of cheap imported food, making it harder than ever for a local farmer to profitably produce for the market.

The way in which a minor project report in 1981 justified project road-building and its effects illustrates that even some project staff had by that time come to see how unrealistic was the expectation that Thaba-Tseka would be suddenly transformed into an agricultural export economy simply by connecting it up to the "outside world" with roads.[1]

The provision of access roads to remote rural communities is often a contentious and much debated development objective. Critics point out that by linking up remote communities via roads with the larger economic centres of a country, the local indigenous economy is often destroyed with the influx of cheaper and alternate goods. They further point to the detrimental effect on traditional cultural values and that roads often promote unequal and ribbon-type development.

In the case of Lesotho however, these arguments may be disputed. Effectively all rural households have already been brought within a monetary economy. A once thriving local economy has long been eroded by the penetration of capital and Boer imperialism. Self-sufficient subsistence farming rural industry [sic] is no longer a reality and most households are dependent to a greater or lesser degree on the earnings and remittances of migrant workers from the mines in South Africa. The effect of this labour migration has already been to erode traditional values and the ethic of western capitalistic consumerism is well established. Almost all households are forced to buy certain basic commodities which are not produced locally, and the cost of these items is prohibitively high, mainly due to high transport costs. The provision of roads will enable cheaper and more reliable supply of goods.

But if it was becoming clear that roads and markets were not going to transform crop practices in Thaba-Tseka, it was also evident that the package of new crops, new practices, and technical inputs that had been prescribed in the original project documents was unable to generate the improved yields that had been projected. Research trials with the new methods, according to a 1978 CIDA report (CIDA 1978R: 16) showed "extreme constraints to crop production in the mountain areas," and many of the recommended measures "were tried and failed to produce the anticipated results on the experimental farm." A pilot potato project failed at this time as well when a combination of bad weather, disease, and mismanagement combined to inflict disastrous losses. These early experiences demonstrated, according to one report (CIDA 1978R: 6), that "there were no tested technical solutions that would substantially reduce the high risk of crop failure associated with the climatic conditions of the mountain areas." It was becoming clear, the report remarked, that there was to be no "green revolution" in Thaba-Tseka.

The project was much criticized in this first phase for "ignoring agriculture" and concentrating too heavily on construction and infrastructure. But looking back on it, it seems clear that it was not simply that the project "ignored" crop development; just that it had no magic solutions to offer to the inescapable constraints on crop production in Lesotho's mountains, that is: tiny, fragmented holdings, killing frost and hail, and erratic and infrequent rainfall. One participant recalled that the experimental work done during Phase One chiefly "showed people how crazy their ideas were about what would grow and what wouldn't." Although the project had promised to increase yields by some 300 percent or more (FAO/World Bank 1974: 14), it soon became apparent that there was no known way to do anything of the kind. The 1978 CIDA report was obliged to admit: "While it is agreed that a trend existed at Thaba-Tseka to emphasize construction during a significant period of the first phase, it would be a mistake to contemplate that much

231

more grain would have been harvested, much more range would have been rejuvenated, many more livestock sold, and many more farmers would have been converted to progressive farming, had this not been the case" (CIDA 1978R: 32).

From 1978 onward, it was more and more accepted that production and export of surplus crops from the tiny, barren fields of the Thaba-Tseka region was not a realistic expectation. Already by 1978, "suggestions to attempt to change farmers over to growing more wheat and less maize were discarded in favour of increasing the production and output of maize with improvement composite varieties suited to local conditions of adaptation" (CIDA 1978R: 39). A 1980 "Draft Operational Plan for the Agricultural Division" declared that:

Crop Production in the mountain areas of Lesotho has little or no potential in generating surplus without getting into relatively intensive practices with little marginal utility. For this reason, Crop Production at Thaba-Tseka should be undertaken basically as a source of food for domestic use to strive for self sufficiency.

This view (which was of course the one to which "the farmers" themselves had always subscribed) was eventually endorsed in the 1982 revision to the Plan of Operations (CIDA 1982). "Since arable land in the mountains is extremely limited," the plan declared, "it has been increasingly recognized that options for the sale of surplus cash or food crops to lowland markets is [*sic*] marginal." With this recognition, the project for the most part gave up its attempts to engineer a shift to cash cropping, and contented itself with producing and distributing improved maize seed for "subsistence," in what was considered its most unambiguously "successful" program.[2]

It is clear that in its programs for "crop development," the Thaba-Tseka Project was attempting to professionalize what was in fact a marginal practice. I have shown in Chapter 4 that "the farmers" were generally able to supply only a small fraction of their subsistence needs in food crops even in the best years, and I have cited the major survey done in the Thaba-Tseka area in 1975 which found the contribution of crop farming to the average household to be about 6 percent of total household income (Van der Wiel 1977). This evidence of the marginality of crop farming was confirmed even by the project's own data, which found that some 70 percent of "farm household" income came from off the farm, with only a small fraction of the remainder being contributed by crops (CIDA 1979: 95). "The farmers" themselves, of course, recognized the relative unimportance of crop farming. A 1978 project survey found that "Agricultural components are of relatively low priority to the Thaba-Tseka Project Area people in terms of the components' importance to development," and noted that respondents were far less interested in improvements in crop farming than in matters such as "education of children," "employment for self and/or others," "availability of clean water," and "improvement of health."

These local attitudes, which seem reasonable enough given the realities of agriculture in Lesotho, were invariably regarded by the project as mistaken, or even pathological. There were always complaints – echoing the perennial dissatisfaction of "development" experts with "the Mosotho farmer" documented by Wilken (1979) – that the local farmers "don't take farming seriously"; their attitudes are "unprofessional"; they are "defeatist"; they are not willing "to take chances"; "they don't think of themselves as *farmers*." The failure of agriculture was often presented in these terms as first of all a failure in attitudes, or even morale. It should be pointed out, of course, that if people did not think of themselves as farmers it was because they were not in fact farmers, and they were quite right to regard the idea of making a profession out of crop farming as unrealistic, as even the project itself eventually recognized. Yet for many years project experts devoted considerable amounts of time and energy to attempting to convince people of something that was palpably untrue – namely, that they could make a good living out of crop farming, and that greater investment in agriculture would pay handsome rewards. Fortunately, it appears that few were imprudent enough to believe them.

The Thaba-Tseka Project's attempt to "professionalize" crop farming calls to mind certain aspects of a much larger crop farming "development" project in Lesotho, the Foodgrain Self Sufficiency Programme. The Foodgrain Self Sufficiency Programme, or FSSP, is a large mechanized agriculture scheme active over most of Lesotho's lowlands. Under the FSSP, the Government effectively farms the land of participating land holders in a modern, "scientific," highly mechanized way, and then divides the high-yield crop with the land holder, in theory paying back its own costs out of its share of the crop. In practice, yields have not been nearly high enough to pay the costs of the inputs, which include highly mechanized land preparation, planting, cultivating, and even aerial spraying with fertilizer and pesticides. The program has lost staggering amounts of money, with estimated losses of M45.5 million

233

over the period 1980–5. Projected losses for the 1984/5 season alone come to nearly M19 million (FAO 1983: 50).

What is interesting for our purposes here, however, is not so much the losses incurred by the FSSP, as the justifications offered for it. The very evaluation report that documents the massive losses opines that the programme may at least help to "motivate" farmers through "the demonstration to farmers, on their own land, that much higher yields are possible" (FAO 1983: 33). Similarly, an evaluation of the FSSP's predecessor, the Cooperative Crop Production Programme, declared that the Government had expected to make a loss on the programme, and that the primary benefit was as a demonstration to farmers of the agricultural productivity of their land (ILO 1979: 106). By making massive capital investment in agriculture, and then concealing the tremendous losses incurred by such investment, these programmes seek to "demonstrate" something that their own experience proves to be untrue: namely, that investment in agriculture is a winning proposition. The FSSP attempts to prove to "the farmers" that capital-intensive crop farming can be a profitable profession, when an honest accounting of the programme suggests precisely the opposite. Again, it is fortunate that "the farmers" have been canny enough to recognize the fallaciousness of such "demonstrations," and have declined to sink their own money into the unsound agricultural investments that have cost the government so dearly.

Given the analysis presented in Part II, it is not difficult to see why "development" projects in Lesotho should devote so much energy to attempting to convince people they can be "farmers" when they cannot. We have seen that the "development" problematic in Lesotho insists that there must be great potential for agricultural development, and we have seen how this insistence is produced, and why it must continually reemerge. The brief discussion presented above illustrates the power this problematic has in defining the "problems" a development project will confront, and guiding its response to the realities it encounters.

The promise that crop farming could be revolutionized through the application of a well-known package of technical inputs was so firmly written into the project's design that it was difficult for those on the scene to challenge it, or even to confront it. Under these circumstances, there was always a strong temptation for project staff to take the contradictions generated by the project's own misconceptions and project them on to the psyche of the Mosotho "farmer" who refuses to behave like a proper farmer. When a project like Thaba-Tseka is sent out to "develop the farmers" and finds that "the farmers" are not much interested in farming, and in fact do not even consider themselves to be "farmers," it is not surprising that some should arrive at the conclusion that "the people" are mistaken, that they really *are* farmers, and that they need only be convinced that this is so for it to be so.

Something of the "development" problematic's immunity from experience can be seen from an interview conducted in 1985 in Ottawa with the principal original CIDA planner of the Thaba-Tseka Project. What, I asked, if he had another chance in Thaba-Tseka, a new project – what would he recommend? After some thought, the planner replied that he would push for crop development based on a switch from "subsistence" maize to "cash crop" wheat, exactly the plan that failed so completely ten years before.

What, then, I was often asked, is "the answer" for Lesotho's agriculture? It has often been speculated, from colonial times onward, that commercial agriculture in Lesotho will only be viable when the land tenure laws have been changed to allow successful farmers to buy up the land of the less successful and begin farming on a truly commercial scale. It is pointed out that the tiny, fragmented, and overworked plots that are the norm today are not able to compete effectively in the market-place against the big, mechanized farms in South Africa and elsewhere. Viable commercial agricultural production in Lesotho can only take place on plots large enough and well managed enough to be economically efficient. Since collectivization does not appear to be in the cards, the argument goes, only privatization of land and the emergence of agricultural entrepreneurs can generate real agricultural development.

This argument may or may not be correct; it is not necessary to decide the point here. The important fact is that, correct or not, this argument is widely subscribed to by "development" experts in Lesotho and by officials of the Government of Lesotho involved in the question of "agricultural development," and apparently has been for a very long time. What is interesting is that, although the overhaul of land tenure law has always been considered an important, and often a necessary, step toward "agricultural development," there has in fact been no serious attempt to introduce a system in which land is freely bought and sold.[3] From the 1930s and even earlier, agriculture experts have been complaining that the land tenure laws make viable commercial farming difficult or impossible, yet the country's rulers have never seen fit to privatize land as the experts have advised.

It is not difficult to see why this should be so. The land tenure system in Lesotho has always done a very good job of keeping those who are unwanted and unneeded by the South African economy peacefully settled on the land, and it continues to perform that task to this day. If the tenure laws were changed, and farming really were "professional-ized," hundreds of thousands of "non-serious farmers" would be forced off the land, with nowhere to go but the urban centers of Lesotho and South Africa. Whatever this might mean for agriculture in Lesotho, none of the region's established interests – least of all the Government of Lesotho – has the slightest interest in exploring the consequences of such a move. The tiny fields scattered across Lesotho's mountains perform a more important task than producing crops; they tie the population of the labor reserve to the land, and keep the "redundant" out of the cities. The land in Lesotho may not produce much food, but it has up to now helped to produce something that is even more prized in Southern Africa: "stability." In Lesotho, as in the "homelands" of South Africa, land is first of all a political resource, and only second an agricultural one. The question of the future of the land is for this reason intimately bound up with the political future of the sub-continent, and must therefore remain a matter of the profoundest uncertainty.

Village distribution points

In Chapter 3, it was noted that the original Phase One plans called for the supply of agricultural inputs and the "introduction" of markets for produce through the establishment of "Village Distribution Points," or VDPs. This section will very briefly review the justifications offered for the VDPs and describe how and why the VDP program ultimately collapsed.

The original intention had been to establish "Village Distribution Points" throughout the project area in order to supply the agricultural inputs that were thought to be unavailable elsewhere. The VDPs would also provide credit for the purchase of equipment and supplies, offer tractor ploughing for hire, and provide a market for the sale of crops. In keeping with the construct of the "aboriginal society," detailed in Chapter 2, the project planners believed that agriculture in the Thaba-Tseka area had remained "undeveloped" due to its isolation and lack of access to markets and technical inputs, as was shown in Chapter 3. The VDPs were aimed squarely at this perceived problem, and promised, along with the new road, to "open up" the region and bring its "subsist-ence" agriculture into the modern, commercial world.

In 1976, the project set up five VDPs, with a sixth to follow soon after. The project constructed the buildings, stocked the stores with goods purchased in the lowlands, and supplied a salaried manager. Goods for restocking the stores were also purchased, warehoused, and transported by the project. During the first two years, goods were sold at highly subsidized prices, which did not reflect the project's transport and handling costs, or the cost of the manager's salary. In 1978, after losing a considerable amount of money in this way, the project decided that their funding of the VDPs "was actually a large and unnecessary subsidy to farmers." The project ceased to fund the VDPs and attempted to turn their operation over to "the people," in the form of "a private entrepreneur, co-operative, or any other such organization."

Two of the six VDPs folded almost immediately; the others dragged on for a while, continuing to extract minor subsidies and free transport from the project. Eventually all six went out of business, the last in 1983 during the fieldwork period. None of the VDPs was able to earn enough revenue to stay in business without the large subsidies from the project. In some cases this was because they were not able to find a large enough market; in others, because they were out-competed by neighboring shops. In some cases, poor management and corruption were problems as well.

The failed VDPs can be divided into two categories: first, those that were out-competed by other shops; and secondly, those that were unable to capture a large enough market to be viable. In the first category, the VDPs at Thaba-Tseka and Mantsonyane had to be closed down in 1979, because, according to the CIDA annual review (CIDA 1980: 25), there was "much too much competition from private entrepreneurs to make these operations viable." Where the project's VDPs were not located in an area that already had other shops, on the other hand, it seems that they soon discovered *why* there were no other shops. The badly sited VDPs were unable to command a large enough market to do a profitable business.

Ironically, then, the VDPs that were supposed to "introduce" agricultural inputs into the area found themselves unable even to break into the local market. Wherever there was a sufficient amount of local demand for goods (agricultural or other), traders had already established stores years before that stocked anything for which there was a market. Local demand for "inputs" and other goods was already being reasonably well satisfied by the existing commercial network, and the project's "introduction" of channels for the purchase and sale of goods turned out to be a costly irrelevancy. The "isolated," "aboriginal so-ciety" of Lesotho's mountains turned out to have been quite thoroughly commercialized long before the project ever arrived.

"Popular participation" and the District Development Committee

From 1978 on, the theme of "popular participation" came to be more and more prominent in project documents and CIDA reports. A key goal of the project, it began to be said, was "participation by the people of the District in the planning and decision-making process."[4] The Phase Two Plan of Operations of 1978 declared that one of the four chief "specific purposes" of the project was:

To increase the participation of Thaba-Tseka District residents in the decision making process with regard to the economic development of the areas through their involvement in village committees and other decision making media so as to achieve by year five of the Project a 60% rate of participation.
(CIDA 1978: 4)

Project evaluations insisted that "the involvement of the people in the development process" must be considered a key indicator of the success of the project. Project reports and documents of all sorts in the period, 1978–81, were littered with declarations of the virtues of "popular participation."

By 1982, when the fieldwork began, the references to "popular participation" had been dropped completely, and it was difficult to find any trace of such an emphasis in the project activities then current. I asked the Project Coordinator what had ever become of all the talk of "popular participation." After a long and uncomfortable silence, I was told: "You see, all this sort of thing was at a time in a development stage, and never came to fruition. It sort of . . . fell by the wayside." The project was not, I was told, involved in any programs featuring "popular participation."

Given these facts, it would be easy to dismiss the theme of "popular participation" as it appeared in project documents as completely rhet-orical. "Participation" was a very fashionable idea in "development" circles in the late 1970s, and the project was no doubt generating the kind of documentation CIDA and other donors wanted to see. "Popu-lar participation" was "in," and it took little effort to spice up project reports with appropriate-sounding banalities about the virtue and wisdom of "the people" without changing the way the programs were run in the slightest.

Such an analysis is very nearly completely correct, but there were two important areas in which the idea of "popular participation" did actually guide concrete project initiatives. The first case was the attempt to introduce a "decentralized" district administration, which was inspired, in part, by the notion that district-level planning and decision making would be more "accountable," and would allow greater input from "the people." We have seen in the last chapter what became of that initiative. The second case where the project made a real attempt to bring about what it thought of as "popular participation" was the case of the District Development Committee.

District Development Committees are advisory bodies at the district level that were set up in all the districts in 1966. The District Development Committees were supposed to coordinate development work at the district level, and process requests for "self-help" projects such as water supplies. The DDCs were typically made up of civil servants representing all the major Ministries in a district, along with chiefs, local BNP politicians ("prominent citizens"), and traders. With such a composition, it is not surprising that the DDCs have always been considered highly politicized organs; one study reports that "Time and time again people point to the politically one sided composition of the DDC's which favours the ruling party," and notes:

The DDC's were not particularly representative bodies. This is not only because the dominant civil service membership can hardly be thought of as having linkages of a representational kind with the people of the district. It is also because much the same can be said of the non-civil servants as well. The chiefs derive their positions through custom and not through processes normally accepted as being representative. The "prominent citizens", on the other hand, represent only the ruling party; in some districts this may in effect mean that they do not represent the party of majority support. Thus, whilst the DDC's can sometimes provide useful insights into local conditions, they are not bodies which can by any means be said to reflect the opinion of the people of their districts.
(van de Geer and Wallis 1982: 150, 38)

In Thaba-Tseka, things were to be different. As part of the new decentralized "model district," the DDC was to be revamped into a true organ of "popular participation." Instead of being packed with civil

servants and politicians, the new Thaba-Tseka DDC was to be composed entirely of representatives of "the people." True, the DDC had
no executive authority over anything, and played only an "advisory"
role; all the same, it was intended that a truly representative Committee
would allow the district "Programme" to respond better to the "felt
needs" of "the people." In 1979, a District Development Committee
was set up consisting of twelve members elected at public meetings in
various parts of the district, along with Principal Chiefs and representatives of traders, teachers, voluntary organizations, and herbalists.

The elections of the Committee members were not without compli-
cations. Voting was by a show of hands rather than secret ballot, and so,
according to one source, "some observers suspect that the elections have
been dominated by Government supporters, with opposition elements
opting out, fearing governmental reprisals if they had not kept a low
profile" (van de Geer and Wallis 1982: 131). All the same, the project
hailed the new Committee as a bold new move in the direction of
"popular participation" in "development." The Project's Quarterly
Report of October–December, 1979, declared proudly that the new
DDC was "the first 'grass-roots' district-based decision making and
political forum in the Country capable of helping to direct government
in responding to stated needs." Speeches at the 1980 official dedication
of the new District returned often to this theme, insisting that the new
Committee represented "the people," and not the ruling party. "Your
DDC is different," the Permanent Secretary for Agriculture told the
assembled crowd. "There are no civil servants, politicians, religious or
government lobby groups there to dilute your voice. Educate your-
selves to exploit this people's forum."

By 1982, however, the composition of this "people's forum" had
changed considerably. According to the District Coordinator, the
Committee was composed of:

> 12 elected representatives
> 7 representatives of local interest groups (e.g., traders,
>   Women's Bureau, traditional healers, churches, etc).
> All the BNP Liaison Officers
> All members of BNP Constituency Committees
> All Heads of Government Departments

The District Coordinator also reported that the elected representatives
had for the most part given up coming to the monthly DDC meetings. It
seems that in the old days the project had sent transport out to the

villages to fetch the representatives, housed them for the night, and fed them for free. Now that such expenses had been cut, and free food, lodging, and transportation were no longer provided, the elected representatives had ceased to come at all.

The changes in the composition of the DDC, which established it as the same sort of partisan political body as is found in other districts, were introduced during the big political shakedown which followed the arrival of the new District Coordinator in 1980. It was seen in Chapter 6 that during this period the project lost control over a number of its "divisions," and some of its own resources. In a similar way, the DDC was separated from the project, and appropriated for political purposes. Not only was the composition of the Committee changed, project officials even ceased to be invited to the DDC meetings. By 1982, the project had no connection with the forum for "popular participation" that it had originally set up.

No one who is familiar with the recent political history of Lesotho will be surprised at how quickly the project's experiment in "popular participation" was crushed. The project claimed that the "new" DDC was "the first 'grass roots' District-based decision making and political forum in the Country capable of helping to direct government in responding to stated needs," but this was not really the case. Up until 1968, Lesotho had a well-developed and very active system of elected district councils with considerable responsibility and legislative power over a range of local matters. These institutions of local government – real channels for "decentralization" and "popular participation" – were rudely shut down by the government when they became centers of political resistance and strongholds of the opposition Congress Party. Since that time, the government has regularly resorted to quite extreme measures precisely in order to prevent "the people" from gaining control over "decision making" and resource allocation. The absence of "channels for popular participation in decision making" in Lesotho is hardly an accident.

The case of the DDC shows how naive was the idea that politics could be put aside while "popular participation" was "introduced" as a simple organizational innovation. Even so weak a body as the DDC, which had no executive authority and had no power over much of anything, was unable to escape its necessarily political role. We saw in Chapter 2 that "development" planning depended on what I called a "governmentalist" construct, in which "the people" appear as an undifferentiated mass and the state is seen as a disinterested machine for guiding the economy and providing social services. In the project's attempts to promote "popular participation" (as in its attempts at "decentralization" reviewed in the last chapter), it is possible to see the complete breakdown of this governmentalist conception of state, "people," and the relation between the two. The case of the District Development Committee provides a concrete illustration of the practical consequences of programs based on the governmentalist premise.

Woodlots

One of the first programs the Thaba-Tseka Project attempted was the establishment of a number of village "woodlots," areas where trees would be planted and allowed to mature in order to supply wood to "the people" for fuel and building. The idea was simple: small pieces of village grazing land would be fenced, planted with seedlings, and devoted to the raising of trees. Each woodlot was to be associated with a particular village, which would have special rights to the trees of their woodlot when harvest time came. By establishing many such woodlots throughout the project area, it was hoped to relieve the critical shortage of firewood in the region, and perhaps free the cattle dung traditionally used as fuel for use as a crop fertilizer. The plan was in line with a nation-wide attempt at reforestation, spearheaded by the Woodlots Project run out of Maseru and funded by Anglo-American/De Beers, the giant South African mining corporation.

The first woodlots in Thaba-Tseka were established in 1976, but the results were poor. Thaba-Tseka's cold climate proved too much for the sort of trees that were planted, and the seedlings nearly all died. New types of trees were found, however, that were resistant to the cold, and the woodlots were replanted with these (chiefly poplars, willows, and *Cupressus*). Eventually, a total of fourteen woodlots were established, with a full nursery in Thaba-Tseka producing seedlings to support them. In 1983, however, a tour of the woodlots found that, of the fourteen woodlots, five were "not operative," and stood empty, waiting to be replanted. Of the nine that remained, many were almost completely bare, and even the best of the nine was only patchily forested over perhaps 30 or 40 percent of its area.

The project officer in charge of the woodlot program explained the rather unimpressive state of the woodlots by noting that the program had been besieged by a number of "technical" and other problems. The most serious of these was that people were breaking in and grazing their animals within the fenced woodlot area, destroying the young seedlings. This happened a great deal and had destroyed many trees. There was another problem as well: people were coming into the woodlots at night and uprooting great numbers of young trees. The uprooted trees were not being stolen, the official insisted; they were left lying dead on the ground. This had occurred at perhaps ten of the fourteen woodlots. The woodlot officer claimed to have no idea why people would do such a thing, and could offer no explanation. The officer may or may not have been sincere in this claim; in any event, finding an explanation for the problems encountered by the woodlot program does not appear to be an impossible task, or even a particularly difficult one. Some simple background information is all that is required to make the matter considerably less mysterious.

When the project began, in 1975, its first act was to lay claim to the project site itself, along with a number of adjoining fields. Those whose fields lay within the area that had been claimed by the project had their allocations revoked, and were deprived of their holdings without compensation. The local land holders, who were understandably upset by this, were told that the project would bring with it numerous jobs, which would be given preferentially to those who had lost land. Local residents would be much better off for having the project, even without their fields. In the event, things did not go quite so smoothly as this, and the land alienation generated a great deal of resentment. Something of the bitterness attached to the land loss by local people can be seen from the following excerpt from a term paper on the project written at the National University by a student from the Thaba-Tseka region.

In spite of the superb aim of helping the people to become self-reliant, the first thing the project did was to take their very good arable land. When the people protested about their fields being taken, the project promised them employment. That was how self-reliant they would be. It is worth noting that some of the people whose fields were taken (a) might not really qualify for the available jobs in the project; (b) the project might not absorb all of them even if they did qualify; (c) some of them were qualified people who already had good jobs somewhere else. But the project was powerful, it would employ them all. Well, evidence shows that not all those who had lost land and wanted employment were absorbed. Of those who got employment some were discharged in less than a year. This is reasonable. Every "employer" looks out for the best available workers. The project had promised people employment. It employed

them for two months, found them unfit for the work and dismissed them. Without their fields and without employment they may turn up to be very self-reliant. It is rather hard to know.
(Sekhamane 1981)

Something of the intensity of the resistance to the loss of land can be gauged from an incident at a neighboring "development" project during the same period. The Basotho Pony Project, chiefly funded by the Government of Ireland, was founded shortly after the Thaba-Tseka Project on a nearby site, and the two projects were at one time loosely affiliated. As in the case of the Thaba-Tseka Project, land was alienated from local farmers to make room for the Pony Project. Shortly after the new project had been started, unknown parties broke into the fenced pastures, took the entire herd of ponies, and, using dogs, drove them all off a precipice to their deaths. This was perhaps the most dramatic manifestation of a deep-felt resentment that made itself evident in many other, more subtle, ways.

There was another issue as well. Although it is true that most of the highly paid, skilled jobs were filled with outsiders from Maseru or elsewhere, the project did end up hiring many local people for unskilled work, chiefly in road construction and similar activities. This labor, which at the project's peak amounted to many hundreds of jobs, was recruited through the Village Development Committees. It was seen in Chapter 4 that these Committees were political organs of the ruling National Party, and it should thus be no surprise to hear that project jobs were often alleged to be preferentially allocated to National Party supporters. When I asked the Project Coordinator about this in 1983, he expressed what appeared to be genuine ignorance of the political role played by the Village Development Committees, and said that he had never before heard that they were associated with the ruling party. The project hired through the Committees, he stated, because the Government had told them to. "We can't afford to get involved with politics," he said. "If they say 'hire through the Committees', I do it."

It is at first hard to believe that the Project Coordinator, a perceptive man with long experience in Thaba-Tseka, could really have been ignorant of the political role of the VDCs. The connection of the National Party with the Village Committees is a very poorly guarded secret, if it may be considered a secret at all, and anyone with any interest in knowing how the Committees work will encounter the facts quickly and easily. All the same, the Project Coordinator seemed entirely sincere on this point, and there is little reason to believe that he was misrepresenting himself, particularly since he was an unusually frank and reliable informant on other, far more sensitive matters. It seems likely that the Project Coordinator's apparent political insensitivity was not a ruse, but simply a low-level manifestation of the refusal to face local politics that we have observed elsewhere in the "development" apparatus. It has already been noted, for instance, that the World Bank Country Report on Lesotho ignored entirely the partisan role played by the VDCs (which were originally organized as BNP election committees), declaring only that: "quite spontaneously, village development committees have been emerging which, in practice, exert a large measure of control over the chiefs. The government intends to encourage the formation of these committees and plans to enact legislation which would give them a formal status" (World Bank 1975: 10). In the same way, the 1978 Plan of Operations for the Thaba-Tseka Project described the "Role of the Village Committee" as follows:

The Village Committee is usually chaired by the chief or a community leader of the village. It is composed of senior members of the village. Its purpose is to discuss and decide upon projects which the village will undertake or will participate in. The Village Committee makes the wishes of the village and its recommendations known through its representatives on the District Committee.

No doubt many on the scene possessed more sophisticated political analyses than those that found their way into official discourse, of course. But it is at the same time only natural that people who are entrusted with the task of producing acceptable "development" discourse as a major part of their jobs should develop an ability to accumulate the kind of information that will be of use in constructing that discourse, while ignoring or even resisting the sort that would complicate that task. The testimony of the Project Coordinator provides evidence that the same forces which shape "development" discourse may also indirectly shape the kind of knowledge that is acquired by project officials "on the ground."

In any case, it is clear that that project was not going to avoid "getting involved in politics" simply by shutting its eyes to it. Through its hiring practices and in many other ways as well, the project came to be intimately linked in local perceptions with the political aims of the ruling National Party. For one thing, the project had from the start been a high profile "prestige" project for the Government, and was closely associated with the Prime Minister personally. The Government knew its political base in the mountains was weak after the 1970 elections and the repression that followed, and the Thaba-Tseka Project represented, among other things, a political gesture to the long-neglected mountain areas. The 1980 dedication of the new District was an occasion for a great flurry of political chest-beating, with the Prime Minister proudly pointing to the modern new road and buildings as evidence that he had managed to bring "development" to the mountains.

But it was not only in its role as a political symbol that the project ended up "getting into politics." The project itself was involved, often quite directly, in propagandizing for the ruling party among an often hostile local population. In 1979, for example, the project's video unit made a short video celebrating the 20th anniversary of the founding of the BNP, which was then shown to farmers attending courses at the project's "Farmer Training Centre." Project documents distributed in Sesotho were found to have BNP slogans added at the end, though these did not appear in any of the English language versions. Public village meetings and courses at which project staff discussed matters such as grazing control and improved stock were peppered with political speeches, and often included addresses by a high-ranking police officer on the "security threat" posed by the opposition Congress Party. When all this is added to what we have already seen as the project's highly unpopular attempts to introduce a grazing association and to restrict animal numbers, it becomes clear that, although the project may have felt it "couldn't afford to get involved in politics," it was, like it or not, in up to its ears.

With this background, let us return to the case of the unfortunate woodlots. In 1983, I visited a number of the woodlots that had been damaged by grazing and vandalism. It was true, as the Woodlot Officer had told me, that the young trees were being extensively damaged by grazing, and that many trees had been uprooted and left lying dead on the ground. But, unlike the Woodlot Officer, many people in the villages had a ready explanation for why this was happening. The pro-Government chief of one village gave an articulate account of his side of the story.

According to this chief, who presided over one of the most successful woodlots, "hoodlums" (*litsotsi*) regularly broke into the woodlots and deliberately vandalized them because they did not like the Government or the project. They do not like the Government because they are "*maCongress*" – members of the opposition Congress Party. These "hoodlums" were, my informant said, from the neighboring villages. Didn't the people of these villages know who they were? Yes, he said, they did, but they refused to say. The chiefs of the other villages as well refuse to cooperate in protecting the woodlots, but instead help the "hoodlums." It is, said the chief, a conspiracy (*morero*). It is impossible to protect the woodlots from these attacks because people are afraid. These "hoodlums" are not boys, my informant said, but men, and they are known to carry guns while on their late-night raids. "Development," the old chief remarked, "has many enemies here." This pithy remark should perhaps be put alongside another, by an informant on the other side of the political fence, who noted caustically with respect to the Village Development Committees: "It seems that politics is nowadays nicknamed 'development'."

The woodlots were often spoken of by project officials as belonging to "the villages," or even to "the people," but it is clear that they were not so regarded in the villages themselves. In fact, the way the woodlots were set up, if they ever produced any wood, it would have been sold at market price, and the project would have taken a percentage of the yield to repay its costs. Any remaining money was to go to "the people" of the village, which meant, I was told by the Woodlot Officer, the Village Development Committee. Since no trees had actually been harvested by 1983, this procedure had never been put into effect, but the prospect of the proceeds of the sale of the trees going to the VDC can hardly have diminished the political overtones of the issue. At any rate, the woodlots seem to have been universally regarded by the villagers concerned as the property of the Government. No one spoke of the trees as "village property," and no one suggested that the woodlots were anything other than Government plantations.

Given these perceptions, and given the local area's history of involvement with the project and with the Government, it is clear that the woodlots were ruined because they presented an appealing and extremely easy target for those who wished to attack the Government and the symbols of its presence in Thaba-Tseka. The grazing and destruction of the trees should be understood not as some sort of unfortunate misunderstanding or mindless prank, but as a significant political act, a declaration of defiance, the deliberate destruction of Government property. Like the attacks on the grazing association, and like the killing of the ponies, the vandalization of the woodlots must be placed in the larger context of political resistance to the Government in general, and to the "development" intervention in particular.

Part v
Instrument-effects of a "development" project

9 The anti-politics machine

The effects of "failure"

By 1979, the Thaba-Tseka Project was already beginning to be considered a failure. It was clear by then that, for all the expensive road building and construction work, the project had not come close to meeting any of its production targets. All the money put into the project, critics said, had not managed to produce any demonstrable increased in agricultural production at all – only a lot of ugly buildings. One CIDA spokesperson reportedly admitted in 1979 "that this project is now considered a very large and costly mistake."[1] At the same time, the project was becoming the subject of newspaper articles with titles like "Canadian aid gone awry?" and "CIDA in Africa: Goodby $6 million."[2] Meanwhile, in Lesotho, the project became a commonly cited example of "development" gone wrong. One local writer declared that "the people of Thaba-Tseka have now come to think in terms of the 'failure' of the project" (Sekhamane 1981); a student at the National University even called it "a monster clinging to the backs of the people." But the bad news came not only from the press and the other critics in and out of the "development" establishment. Even the local people, according to a 1979 CIDA evaluation (CIDA 1979: 22), considered "neither the households nor the area to be better off," five years after the start of the project. Instead, the report said, "the quality of village life as perceived by the people and as measured by people's perceptions of well-being has not improved and has, in fact, declined." In 1982, a dissertation by a former project employee reviewed the project history and concluded that "[t]here is little evidence that this huge investment in the mountain region has had any effect in raising agricultural production or improving the well-being of rural households" (Eberhard 1982: 299).

At the start of Phase Two of the project, there had been some talk of a "commitment" for at least ten more years of CIDA funding, and that is apparently what the original planners anticipated. At the TTCC meeting of February 7, 1979, the CIDA representative, according to the minutes of the meeting, declared that, although it was impossible to give any formal, written commitment for more than the budgeted five years, CIDA was "morally committed for at least ten more years to the

251

development in the District." But, when the project's inability to effect the promised transformations in agriculture – particularly in the area of livestock – was compounded by the collapse of the "decentralization" scheme in 1980–1, CIDA elected to pull out. By 1982, CIDA's chief interest was in getting out as quickly and gracefully as possible. The 1982 revision to the Plan of Operations was tailored to do just that. Funding was gradually phased out and, by March 1984, the CIDA involvement in Thaba-Tseka was over. Moreover, I was told explicitly by officials at CIDA headquarters in Ottawa that the pullout had not been a matter of lack of funds, but that the project had been discontinued on its merits. At last report, neither CIDA nor any other donor has sought to continue the project.

But even if the project was in some sense a "failure" as an agricultural development project, it is indisputable that many of its "side effects" had a powerful and far-reaching impact on the Thaba-Tseka region. The project did not transform crop farming or livestock keeping, but it did build a road to link Thaba-Tseka more strongly with the capital; it did not bring about "decentralization" or "popular participation," but it was instrumental in establishing a new district administration and giving the Government of Lesotho a much stronger presence in the area than it had ever had before. The construction of the road and the "administrative center" may have had little effect on agricultural production, but they were powerful effects in themselves.

The general drift of things was clear to some of the project staff themselves, even as they fought it. "It is the same story over again," said one "development" worker.[3] "When the Americans and the Danes and the Canadians leave, the villagers will continue their marginal farming practices and wait for the mine wages, knowing only that now the taxman lives down the valley rather than in Maseru."

But it was not only a matter of the taxman. A host of Government services became available at Thaba-Tseka as a direct result of the construction of the project center and the decision to make that center the capital of a new district. There was a new Post Office, a police station, and an immigration control office; there were agricultural services such as extension, seed supply, and livestock marketing; there were health officials to observe and lecture on child care, and nutrition officers to promote approved methods of cooking. There was the "food for work" administration run by the Ministry of Rural Development, and the Ministry of the Interior, with its function of regulating the powers of chiefs. A vast number of minor services and functions that once would have operated, if at all, only out of one of the other distant district capitals had come to Thaba-Tseka.

But, although "development" discourse tends to see the provision of "services" as the purpose of government, it is clear that the question of power cannot be written off quite so easily. "Government services" are never simply "services"; instead of conceiving this phrase as a reference simply to a "government" whose purpose is to serve, it may be at least as appropriate to think of "services" which serve to govern. We have seen in earlier chapters that one of the central issues of the deployment of the Thaba-Tseka Project was the desire of the Government to gain political control over the opposition strongholds in the mountains. It was shown in Chapters 7 and 8 that many of the project's own resources and structures were turned to this purpose. But, while this was going on, a much more direct political policing function was being exercised by other sections of the district administration the project had helped to establish. The Ministries of Rural Development and of the Interior, for instance, were quite directly concerned with questions of political control, largely through their control over "food for work" and chieftainship, respectively; then, too, there were the police. Another innovation that came with the "development" center in Thaba-Tseka was the new prison. In every case, state power was expanded and strengthened by the establishment of the local governing machinery at Thaba-Tseka.

In the increasingly militarized climate of the early 1980s (see Chapter 4 above), the administrative center constructed by the project in Thaba-Tseka quickly took on a significance that was not only political, but military as well. The district capital that the project had helped establish was not only useful for extending the governing apparatus of government services/government controls; it also facilitated direct military control. The project-initiated district center was home not only to the various "civilian" ministries, but also to the "Para-Military Unit," Lesotho's army. The road had made access much easier; now the new town provided a good central base. Near the project's end in 1983, substantial numbers of armed troops began to be garrisoned at Thaba-Tseka, and the brown uniforms of the PMU were to be seen in numbers throughout the district. Indeed, it may be that in a place like Mashai, the most visible of all the project's effects was the indirect one of increased Government military presence in the region. The project of course did not cause the militarization of Thaba-Tseka, any more than it caused the founding of the new district and the creation of a new local administration. In both cases, however, it may be said to have unintentionally played what can only be called an instrumental role.

The anti-politics machine

It would be a mistake to make too much of the "failure" of the Thaba-Tseka Project. It has certainly been often enough described in such terms, but the same can be said for nearly all of the other rural development projects Lesotho has seen. One of the original planners of the project, while admitting that the project had its share of frustrations, and declaring that as a result of his experience with Thaba-Tseka, he would never again become involved in a range management project, told me that in fact of all the rural development projects that have been launched in Lesotho, only Thaba-Tseka has had any positive effects. Indeed, as the project came to an end, there seemed to be a general move in "development" circles both in Ottawa and Maseru toward a rehabilitation of the project's reputation. It may have been a failure, but not any worse than many other similar projects, I was told. Given the "constraints," the Project Coordinator declared in 1983, "I think we've got a success story here." As one CIDA official pointed out, with what appeared to be a certain amount of pride, the project "was not an unmitigated disaster."

In a situation in which "failure" is the norm, there is no reason to think that Thaba-Tseka was an especially badly run or poorly thought out project. Since, as we have seen, Lesotho is not the "traditional," isolated, "peasant" society the "development" problematic makes it out to be, it is not surprising that all the various attempts to "transform" it and "bring it into the 20th Century" characteristically "fail," and end up as more or less mitigated "disasters." But it may be that what is most important about a "development" project is not so much what it fails to do but what it does do; it may be that its real importance in the end lies in the "side effects" such as those reviewed in the last section. Foucault, speaking of the prison, suggests that dwelling on the "failure" of the prison may be asking the wrong question. Perhaps, he suggests,

one should reverse the problem and ask oneself what is served by the failure of the prison; what is the use of these different phenomena that are continually being criticized; the maintenance of delinquency, the encouragement of recidivism, the transformation of the occasional offender into a habitual delinquent, the organization of a closed milieu of delinquency. (Foucault 1979: 272)

If it is true that "failure" is the norm for development projects in Lesotho, and that important political effects may be realized almost invisibly alongside with that "failure," then there may be some justification for beginning to speak of a kind of logic or intelligibility to what happens when the "development" apparatus is deployed – a logic that transcends the question of planners' intentions. In terms of this larger unspoken logic, "side effects" may be better seen as "instrument-effects" (Foucault 1979); effects that are at one and the same time instruments of what "turns out" to be an exercise of power.

For the planners, the question was quite clear: the primary task of the project was to boost agricultural production; the expansion of government could only be secondary to that overriding aim. In 1980, the Programme Director expressed concern about the project's failure to make headway in "what is really the only economic basis for the existence of the Thaba-Tseka District, the rangeland production of livestock." He went on to declare:

If this economic base, now as shaky as it appears to be, is not put on a much firmer footing, it is inevitable that the Thaba-Tseka District will eventually become an agricultural wasteland where there will be no justification whatsoever for developing and maintaining a social infrastructure with its supporting services of health, education, roads, rural technology development, etc.
(TTDP Quarterly Report, October–December 1980, p. 5)

If one takes the "development" problematic at its word, such an analysis makes perfect sense; in the absence of growth in agricultural output, the diversion of project energies and resources to "social infrastructure" can only be considered an unfortunate mistake. But another interpretation is possible. If one considers the expansion and entrenchment of state power to be the principal effect – indeed, what "development" projects in Lesotho are chiefly about – then the promise of agricultural transformation appears simply as a point of entry for an intervention of a very different character.

In this perspective, the "development" apparatus in Lesotho is not a machine for eliminating poverty that is incidentally involved with the state bureaucracy; it is a machine for reinforcing and expanding the exercise of bureaucratic state power, which incidentally takes "poverty" as its point of entry – launching an intervention that may have no effect on the poverty but does in fact have other concrete effects. Such a result may be no part of the planners' intentions – indeed, it almost never is – but resultant systems have an intelligibility of their own.

But the picture is even more complicated than this. For while we have seen that "development" projects in Lesotho may end up working to expand the power of the state, and while they claim to address the problems of poverty and deprivation, in neither guise does the "development" industry allow its role to be formulated as a political one. By uncompromisingly reducing poverty to a technical problem, and by promising technical solutions to the sufferings of powerless and oppressed people, the hegemonic problematic of "development" is the principal means through which the question of poverty is de-politicized in the world today. At the same time, by making the intentional blueprints for "development" so highly visible, a "development" project can end up performing extremely sensitive political operations involving the entrenchment and expansion of institutional state power almost invisibly, under cover of a neutral, technical mission to which no one can object. The "instrument-effect," then, is two-fold: alongside the institutional effect of expanding bureaucratic state power is the conceptual or ideological effect of depoliticizing both poverty and the state. The way it all works out suggests an analogy with the wondrous machine made famous in Science Fiction stories – the "anti-gravity machine," that at the flick of a switch suspends the effects of gravity. In Lesotho, at least, the "development" apparatus sometimes seems almost capable of pulling nearly as good a trick: the suspension of politics from even the most sensitive political operations. If the "instrument-effects" of a "development" project end up forming any kind of strategically coherent or intelligible whole, this is it: the anti-politics machine.

If unintended effects of a project end up having political uses, even seeming to be "instruments" of some larger political deployment, this is not any kind of conspiracy; it really does just happen to be the way things work out. But because things do work out this way, and because "failed" development projects can so successfully help to accomplish important strategic tasks behind the backs of the most sincere participants, it does become less mysterious why "failed" development projects should end up being replicated again and again. It is perhaps reasonable to suggest that it may even be because development projects turn out to have such uses, even if they are in some sense unforeseen, that they continue to attract so much interest and support.

Some comparative observations

So far I have extended specific conclusions about the "development" apparatus and its operation only to the case of Lesotho. Yet the reader is certainly justified in wondering if that is really their only domain of application, and asking to what extent these conclusions might apply to the rest of the world beyond Lesotho's tiny borders. My strategy here has been to avoid making grand or general claims about the way the "development" apparatus functions in other settings – claims which I, in any case, lack the scholarship to support – but instead to present carefully a single case and to let others more knowledgeable than I judge to what extent the processes I have identified may be in operation in other contexts. While adhering to this general strategy, I will here provisionally suggest some possible points of commonality between Lesotho and a few other "development" contexts, after first noting a few of the particularities that make Lesotho such a special case.

First of all, any attempt to expand the conclusions presented here to the global "development" apparatus in general must take account of the peculiarities of the Lesotho case. Lesotho is a very unusual national setting, and one that makes the "developers,", task extraordinarily diffi-cult. Many of the most common "development" assumptions are there more completely confounded by reality than almost anywhere else one could name. Where "development" often sees itself entering an aborig-inal, primitive agricultural setting, Lesotho offers one of the first and most completely monetized and proletarianized contexts in Africa. Where "development" requires a bounded, coherent "national econ-omy," responsive to the principle of "governmentality," Lesotho's extraordinary labor-reserve economy is as little defined by national boundaries, and as little responsive to national planning, as any that could be imagined. Lesotho is not a "typical" case; it is an extreme case, and for the "development" problematic, an extremely difficult one.

The extremity of the case of Lesotho has the effect of exaggerating many "development" phenomena. The divide between academic and "development" discourse, the gap between plans attempted and results achieved, the paucity of economic transformations next to the plenitude of political ones, all are more extreme than one might find in a more "typical" case. But the unusualness of Lesotho's situation does not in itself make it irrelevant to wider generalization. Indeed, the exagger-ation it produces, if properly interpreted, may be seen not simply as a distortion of the "typical" case, but as a clarification, just as the addition by a computer of "extreme" colors to a remote scanning image does not distort but "enhances" the photograph by improving the visibility of the phenomena we are interested in. The very oddness of the Lesotho setting might make it a privileged case, allowing us to see in stark outline processes that are likely present in less extreme cases, but are obscured by the haze of plausibility and reasonableness that is so strikingly absent in Lesotho. At any rate, the task of denaturalizing and "making strange" the "development" intervention is facilitated by the very atypicality of Lesotho.

One of the main factors supporting the view that some degree of generalization may be possible from the case of Lesotho is that, however diverse may be the empirical settings within which the "development" apparatus operates, many aspects of "development" interventions remain remarkably uniform and standardized from place to place. One aspect of this standardization is simply of personnel. If "development" interventions look very similar from one country to the next, one reason is that they are designed and implemented by a relatively small, interlocked network of experts. Tanzania may be very different from Lesotho on the ground, but, from the point of view of a "development" agency's head office, both may be simply "the Africa desk." In the Thaba-Tseka case, at least, the original project planners knew little about Lesotho's specific history, politics, and sociology; they were experts on "livestock development in Africa," and drew largely on experience in East Africa. Small wonder, then, that they often looked on the Basotho as "pastoralists," and took the nomadic Maasai of Kenya as a favorite point of comparison. Small wonder, too, if the Thaba-Tseka Project ended up with such visible similarities to other livestock projects in very different contexts.

But it is not only that "development" interventions draw on a small and interlocking pool of personnel. More fundamental is the application in the most divergent empirical settings of a single, undifferentiated "development" expertise. In Zimbabwe, in 1981, I was struck to find local agricultural "development" officials eagerly awaiting the arrival and advice of a highly paid consultant who was to explain how agriculture in Zimbabwe was to be transformed. What, I asked, did this consultant know about Zimbabwe's agriculture that they, the local agricultural officers, did not? To my surprise, I was told that the individual in question knew virtually nothing about Zimbabwe, and worked mostly in India. "But," I was assured, "he *knows development*." It is precisely this expertise, free-floating and untied to any specific context, that is so easily generalized, and so easily inserted into any given situation. To the extent that "development" projects the world over are formed by such a shared, context-independent "development" expertise, Lesotho's experience with "development" is part of a very general phenomenon.

Another aspect of standardization is to be seen in specific program elements. Because of the way "development" interventions are institutionalized, there are strong tendencies for programs to be mixed and marched out of a given set of available choices. As Williams (1986: 12) has pointed out, "development" comes as a "package" of standard available "inputs." Plans that call for non-standard, unfamiliar elements are more difficult for a large routinized bureaucracy to implement and evaluate, and thus less likely to be approved. With standardized elements, things are much easier. As Williams says, "Project evaluations may be written on a 'cross out which do not apply' basis; the overall frame is standardized, and odd paragraphs are varied to fit in the names and basic geography of particular project areas" (Williams 1986: 12). Lesotho's empirical situation may be unlike that of many other countries, but the specific "development" interventions that have been attempted there, from irrigation and erosion control schemes to grazing associations and "decentralization," are nearly all familiar elements of the standard "development" package.

Finally, there is clearly a sense in which the discourse of "development" in Lesotho, too, is part of a "standard" discursive practice associated with "development" in a broad range of contexts. As I have noted, the contrast with academic discourse is likely stronger and more extreme in Lesotho than in many other contexts. In the same way, the closure of the field of "development" discourse, which is so striking in Lesotho, cannot be simply assumed to hold in general. (Such closure could be substantiated globally only through an extensive analysis that is beyond the scope of this study.) But even casual observation is enough to suggest that it is not only in Lesotho that "development" discourse seems to form a world unto itself. At any rate, it is distinctive enough world-wide to have inspired the coining of a generic term like "devspeak" (Williams 1985a: 3). This is sometimes put as a matter of "jargon," but it is much more than that. Indeed, my own unsystematic inspection would suggest that "development" discourse typically involves not only special terms, but a distinctive style of reasoning, implicitly (and perhaps unconsciously) reasoning backward from the necessary conclusions – more "development" projects are needed – to the premises required to generate those conclusions. In this respect, it is not only "devspeak" that is at issue, but "devthink" as well.

Moreover, the maneuvers used in constructing these chains of reasoning, if not identical from place to place, do seem at least to bear what one might call a strong family resemblance. The figures of the "aboriginal society," "national economy," and "traditional peasant society" that were identified in Chapter 2 can be easily found in other contexts, as, for instance, in the World Bank's definitive declaration (1975: 3) that "[rural development] is concerned with the modernization and monetization of rural society, and with its transition from traditional isolation to integration with the national economy." The fourth characteristic figure for Lesotho, "governmentality," is perhaps even more widespread. Indeed, the extreme state-centeredness of "development" discourse in a wide range of settings is nearly enough to justify Williams's blanket claim (1986: 7) that "Policy makers, experts, and officials cannot think how things might improve except through their own agency."

The above considerations are perhaps enough to suggest that there may be important commonalities at the level of discourse, planning, and program elements between "development" interventions in Lesotho and those in other countries. But do these standardized elements, deployed in a wide range of different settings, produce anything like standard effects? Are the "instrument-effects" identified for Lesotho part of a general, regular global pattern? Is the "anti-politics machine" peculiar to Lesotho, or is it a usual or even inevitable consequence of "development" interventions?

These big questions must for the time being remain open. They will be answered only when they have been empirically explored in each specific context. At a glance, it is clear that the economic transformations effected by "development" interventions may well be greater in other settings than they have been in Lesotho, even if they differ from those claimed or intended. But the two-edged "instrument-effect" identified here for Lesotho – "anti-politics" combined with an expansion of bureaucratic state power – does seem to be operative, and even dominant, in at least some other contexts.

The first and most immediate point of comparison is with South Africa. Although "development" agencies in Lesotho resolutely refuse to see any connection between Lesotho and the South African "homelands," the South African experience of government intervention in the rural areas is in some ways continuous with that of Lesotho. In particular, the long history of South African "betterment" schemes in the "reserves" and "homelands" bears some striking similarities with "development" interventions in Lesotho. Indeed, the Sesotho word used for "development" in Lesotho (*ntlafatso*) is a literal translation of "betterment," and is applied by Sotho-speakers equally to international "development" projects and to South African "betterment" schemes in the homelands.

"Betterment" schemes were first instituted in South Africa in the late 1930s as a way of "rationalizing" and improving agriculture and land use in the "reserves," with the aim of slowing out-migration to the urban areas. Responding to perceptions of inefficiency of "native agriculture" and crisis in soil erosion, the state set about reorganizing the settlement and cropping patterns in the reserves. Village settlements and family landholdings were alike "consolidated," and land carefully divided into distinct zones of residential, crop, or range usage. Model villages were laid out in straight-line grids ("dressed," as some Transkeians began to say, borrowing military usage, Beinart 1984: 77). Grazing lands were fenced for rotational grazing, and "improved" practices encouraged, with stock limitation and culling enforced by law. Erosion was combated through extensive contour works, and village woodlots were established (Beinart 1984, Yawitch 1981, Unterhalter 1987, Platzky and Walker 1985, de Wet 1981).

With the rise to power of the Nationalist government and its *apartheid* program in 1948, the "reserves" acquired new prominence as the intended *"bantustans"* or "homelands" for the whole of the African population. The Tomlinson Commission, set up to explore the viability of "separate development" in the *"bantustans"*-to-be, proposed that agriculture in the reserves be "rationalized" and "developed" through the creation of a class of yeoman farmers, working "viable plots." The Commission recommended that 50 percent of the population of the reserves should leave farming to dwell in "closer settlements" as full-time workers, leaving the other 50 percent as a "viable," productive, class of professional farmers. (Actually, the Commission thought that to make a viable living from the land, a full 80 percent of the population should be removed, but rejected this as involving the relocation of too many people.) The job of "betterment," in this scheme, was to bring about this transition. But, as the grim process of "separate development" proceeded, it became more and more clear that "betterment" was functioning less as a means for boosting agricultural production in the "homelands" than as a device for regulating and controlling the process through which more and more people were being squeezed on to less and less land, and through which the dumped "surplus people" (Platzky and Walker 1985) relocated from "white areas" could be accommodated and controlled. As the *bantustans* assumed their contemporary role as dumping grounds, "betterment" schemes, as one source puts it, "lost almost entirely any aspect of improvement or rationalization of land use and became instead principally instruments of coercion" (Unterhalter 1987: 102).[4]

These "betterment" interventions have been fiercely resisted by the supposed "beneficiaries" from the very start. Indeed, attempts in the name of "betterment" to move people's homes and fields, to control and regulate their cultivation, and to restrict and cull their livestock have provoked many of the most intense and significant episodes of rural resistance in South African history (Beinart 1982, 1984; Beinart and Bundy 1981, 1987; Unterhalter 1987; Yawitch 1981).

A number of similarities between South Africa's "betterment" schemes and Lesotho's "development" will be immediately apparent. Government interventions in colonial Basutoland, from the 1930s onward, centered on consolidation and pooling of fields (e.g., the "Pilot Project" of 1952–8), and, especially, soil erosion control (Wallman 1969). They also involved tree-planting and mandatory culling, especially of sheep (Palmer and Parsons 1977: 25). Since independence, too, many elements of South African "betterment" have been replicated by various "development" projects. Fencing and rotational grazing, of course, were attempted at Thaba-Tseka, as we have seen. Woodlots have been planted not only by the Thaba-Tseka Project, but by a nationwide "Woodlot Project" funded by the Anglo-American Corporation, the giant South African conglomerate. Soil erosion control and contouring was the focus of the large Thaba-Bosiu project in the early 1970s, while in the same period, amalgamation of fields was attempted in the Senqu River Project. And finally, when I returned to Thaba-Tseka for a brief visit in 1986, I was told by the District Extension Officer that the latest plan for "development" of the mountain area involved dividing land up into residential, crop, and grazing zones, and consolidating some small, scattered settlements into larger and more accessible villages on approved sites.

But it is not only program elements that are similar. In both cases, technical, apolitical aims justified state intervention. And, in both cases, economic "failure" of these interventions ended up meeting other needs. As one study of two "betterment" areas found,

betterment has not fulfilled its stated purposes of rehabilitating the bantustan areas or rationalising agriculture to become viable economic units. Betterment has become a way of planning these two areas so as to accommodate and control as many as possible of the people uprooted and settled in the bantustans.
(James 1983: 60, cited in Unterhalter 1987: 102)

Moreover, in the "homelands," as in Lesotho, there is the same central tension between espoused goals of "professionalizing" farming on the one hand, and the political need to settle, stabilize, and regulate the regional economy's "redundant," "surplus people" on the other (see Chapters 6 and 8, above). And in both cases, the political imperative of keeping people tied to the land has generally predominated over any economic "rationalization." In both cases, too, the "anti-politics machine" has been at work, as state power has been simultaneously expanded and depoliticized. "Betterment", like "development," has provided an apparently technical point of entry for an intervention serving a variety of political uses.

In many respects, of course, the South African case is also a strong contrast with Lesotho. Most obviously, Lesotho does not share the South African government's *apartheid* agenda, and is concerned not with implementing the bad dream of "separate development," but with coping with its consequences. But more than that, the nature of the state, and thus the nature of state interventions, is very different in the two cases. In place of the institutionally and financially weak Lesotho state, the South African state has had the administrative capability to direct and enforce massive rural relocations and disruptions. It has demonstrated the capability and the willingness to routinely use staggering levels of coercion to achieve its desired results. Where in Lesotho, "development" failures are easily written off as resulting from poor administrative capacity and an inability to make "tough" political choices, in South Africa, a strong and often brutal state is able to radically transform the countryside. In the "homelands" and rural areas, millions have been relocated (Platzky and Walker 1985), while villages have been "dressed" in rows, plots radically rearranged, and the culling and fencing of livestock enforced in a way that is difficult to imagine for Lesotho. "Betterment" was more than a plan on paper; according to one source, by 1967, 60 percent of the villages in Natal were "planned," while 77 percent of the plan for Ciskei and 76 percent and 80 percent of the plans for the Northern and Western Territories (respectively) had been implemented (Platzky and Walker 1985: 46).

But the force of state intervention has not meant economic "success." With respect to the stated goals of establishing a viable, stable population of professional farmers and improving peasant agricultural production, South Africa's experience with "betterment" must be judged to have "failed" nearly as completely as Lesotho's with "development." But in South Africa just as surely as in Lesotho, economic "failures" have produced their own political rationality. No doubt there have been important economic effects, but "betterment," in its "instrument-effects," is not ultimately about agricultural production, but about managing and controlling the labor reserves and dumping grounds.

"In this and other respects," as Gavin Williams (1986: 17) has noted, "South Africa is not just a special case." Elsewhere in Africa, Beinart (1984) has made a convincing case for strong parallels between the South African experience and those of colonial Zimbabwe and Malawi, where struggles over land and political control were also filtered through a range of apparently technical interventions connected with soil erosion, conservation, and "inefficient" African farming. But, as Beinart notes:

Technical interventions were not in themselves socially neutral. And they became increasingly linked with broader attempts to restructure rural social relationships and 'capture' the peasantry ... Rural resistance, though in specific cases aimed at particular state initiatives which were seen as technically inadequate, became geared to opposing the kinds of controls and social disruption which planning seemed to hold in store.
(Beinart 1984: 83)

For Zimbabwe, Ranger (1985) has given a detailed demonstration of how government interventions ostensibly aimed at agricultural improvement and soil conservation became a central terrain in rural political struggles throughout the colonial period. As in South Africa, "conservation," "centralization," and "improvement" were closely linked to land alienation and control, while coopted African "Demonstrators," ostensibly agents of agricultural improvement, came eventually to serve as a kind of rural police. The peasants, driven off their land and policed on the deteriorating "reserves," responded with an anger rising at times to "seething hatred" (Ranger 1985: 151). This anger very logically found expression in attacks on such symbols of "conservation" and "improvement" as contour ridges and dip tanks, as well as on the

African Demonstrators themselves. For failing to see the benefits of their own subordination, the peasants were of course characterized as "backward," and thus all the more in need of controlling interventions (see Ranger 1985: 99–171).

It appears, moreover, that the specifically political role of the "development" intervention in Zimbabwe has not ended with Independence. The revolution has undoubtedly brought some real gains for the peasantry insofar as land-starved occupants of "Tribal Trust Lands" were in at least some cases able to press successfully for land redistribution through squatting on land abandoned by white farmers, and to benefit from higher producer prices instituted by the new government (Ranger 1985). But it is also clear, as Ranger notes that, as the revolutionary situation fades and the ability of the peasants to apply political pressure on the government diminishes, "the unusual advantageous position of Zimbabwe's peasants *vis-à-vis* the state will give way to quite another balance of power," in which the state may well "become a predator" in relation to the peasantry. For Ranger, this "gloomy expectation" is not inevitable; but the prospects for a different outcome are "cripplingly handicapped by the lasting effects of ... colonial agrarian history" (Ranger 1985: 319–20).

The suggestion that "development" even in liberated Zimbabwe may be principally about state control and not economic improvement or poverty amelioration is strengthened by Williams's analysis (1982) of one of independent Zimbabwe's key policy documents for "development" strategy (Riddell 1981). Williams shows how government plans for the impoverished "Tribal Trust Lands," involving the consolidation of village holdings, and the division of all land into residential, grazing, and arable zones, virtually duplicate key aspects of the "betterment" schemes of South Africa. It is far from clear that such an extraordinary expenditure of governmental energies will do anything to improve farming. But there is no doubt, as Williams notes (Williams 1982: 16), that, like other "development" interventions, "it will subject farmers to more effective control and administrative supervision." The plan also calls for the regrouping of settlements into "unified village settlements" where "village leadership committees" would, so the planners anticipate, "plan the whole life of the village" (Riddell 1981: 688), including allocating land and coordinating a planned pension and social security scheme. As Williams caustically remarks, "Bureaucratic rationality requires that people's land and lives should be reorganized the better for government to administer them" (Williams 1982: 17). Once again, what look like technical, apolitical reforms seem to bring with them political "side-effects" that overwhelm whatever might exist of the originally intended or claimed "main effects." As Williams concludes:

As is so often the case, "rural development" turns out to be a strategy for increasing state control of the peasantry. The policies outlined in the Riddell report bring together many of the worst aspects of the agricultural policies of Kenya (dependence on large-scale maize farming), Nigeria (settlement and irrigation schemes), Tanzania (villagization) and South Africa (betterment schemes). Thus far, Zimbabwean peasants have resisted them, both under white rule and since independence.
(Williams 1982: 17)

Another well-known case is that of Tanzania. Here, very extensive state interventions in rural life have been formulated and justified in the name of "development," including the now-famous program of "*Uja-maa*" villagization. Familiar elements in these "development" interventions have included compulsory villagization and the centralization of crop land, regional "development administrations" and "integrated rural development projects," extension of state marketing monopolies, and "decentralization" through the central appointment of "Regional Commissioners." In spite of the widely admired populist ideology articulated by President Nyerere, it is by now clear that these "development" interventions, much like their colonial predecessors, have met with stiff resistance from their supposed "beneficiaries," and have not achieved their supposed goals. Again and again, projects have "failed"; and, again and again, for the same reasons: producer prices were too low, administration was inefficient, and technologies were inappropriate (Coulson 1981, 1982; Bryceson 1982a, 1982b; Williams 1986). Government intervention has not increased agricultural production (though state marketing monopolies have driven much of it underground), and the "development" intervention in Tanzania has done little to transform or improve peasant agricultural production.

As in the other cases discussed here, however, the "side effects" of "failure" turn out to be most powerful. It is open to debate whether or not Tanzanian "development" policies are best explained as a straightforward expression of the material interest of an extractive "bureaucratic bourgeoisie," as some (Shivji 1976, von Freyhold 1979) have argued. What is more certain is that the expansion of the state and the bureaucratization of nearly all aspects of life in Tanzania may well be the

266

most lasting legacy of the "development" intervention. At the same time, the "anti-political" nature of "development" interventions is equally well illustrated here. Under Nyerere (the consummate "anti-politician"), bureaucratic interventions have been very effectively de-politicized, both in Tanzania and for a foreign audience. "Development," insistently formulated as a benign and universal human project, has been the point of insertion for a bureaucratic power that has been neither benign nor universal in its application (Coulson 1975, 1981, 1982; von Freyhold 1979; Bernstein 1981; Hyden 1980; Shivji 1976, 1986; Malkki 1989; Moore 1986).

I will restrict this very tentative review of possible points of comparison here to these few cases drawn from Africa, simply because my knowledge of the literature, scanty enough for the African cases above, begins to grow perilously thin as the focus moves further afield. But my sense is that elsewhere in Africa, and likely in Latin America and Asia as well, it might be possible to show that technical "development" interventions ostensibly organized around such things as agricultural production, livestock, soil erosion, water supply, etc., have in fact often had "instrument-effects" that would be systematically intelligible as part of a two-sided process of depoliticization and expansion of bureaucratic state control. If so, this would not of course prove that such an association is in any way inevitable or universal, but it would suggest that at least some of the mechanisms that have been explored for the case of Lesotho may be of some wider relevance.

Etatization?

A few writers have recently attempted to formulate a general model for the involvement of "development" interventions with the expansion of state power in Africa, based on the concept of "etatization" (Dutkiewicz and Shenton 1986; Dutkiewicz and Williams 1987; Williams 1985a). According to this picture, which Dutkiewicz and Williams identify as a Weberian "ideal type" model, the state-dominated economies of the late colonial period set the stage for the emergence of a distinctive post-colonial "developmental state" (Dutkiewicz and Williams 1987: 41). The "developmental state" was distinguished by the central and direct involvement of the state in the appropriation of surplus value from producers, and by the dependence of the "ruling elite" (Dutkiewicz and Shenton 1986: 110) upon this form of appropriation. Under these distinctive circumstances, the state bureaucracy expanded rapidly, while the larger economy was more and more sub-ordinated to the needs of the state sector. The "ruling elite," meanwhile, became a "ruling group," united by its near-total dependence for its social reproduction upon its control of the state apparatus. As the state expanded, so did the power of this ruling group, which in turn required, for its reproduction, the continued expansion or "involution" (Dut-kiewicz and Williams 1987: 43) of the bureaucracy. But this very process eventually led to a crisis of "diminishing reproduction" (Dutkiewicz and Shenton 1986) of the social resources (especially peasant, house-hold-based production) on which the state depended for its own repro-duction. "Etatization" ended up, as in the current crisis, threatening to kill the goose that laid the golden egg.

At every stage, in this view, whether under socialist or capitalist ideologies, this expansion of state power "is justified by the notion of 'national development'" (Dutkiewicz and Williams 1987: 43). With an infinitely expandable demand for "development" providing the charter for state expansion, whatever "problems" can be located are just so many points of insertion for new state programs and interventions for dealing with them. "Development," then, is an integral part of "etatiza-tion." And if the "development" interventions fail, as they usually do, that, too, is part of the process. As Dutkiewicz and Shenton put it:

Like corruption, inefficiency in establishing and managing state
enterprises, financial institutions, import and exchange rate policies,
and development projects, rather than preventing the social
reproduction of this ruling group, was an absolute prerequisite for it.
The ruling groups' social reproduction required an ever-expanding
number of parastatals to be created and development projects to be
begun. The completion, or, in a rational capitalistic sense, the efficient
operation of such parastatals or development projects would have
obviated the need to generate further plans and projects to achieve the
ends which their predecessors failed to do. In this sense inefficiency
was "efficient," efficient for the expanded reproduction of the ruling
group. One result of this was the geometric expansion of a poorly
skilled and corrupt lower level bureaucracy incapable of fulfilling
even its few professional obligations, itself fuelled by academics and
others who saw the solution to every problem in the creation of yet
another position or agency to deal with it and to employ more of
their own number. By generating a never-ending series of parastatals
and development projects the ruling group provided employment
and, no matter how small, inadvertent or fleeting, an amelioration of
the conditions of life and a share of state resources for at least some

members of the underclasses. In doing so, the conditions of the social reproduction of the ruling group increasingly penetrated and reshaped the conditions for the reproduction of society as a whole.
(Dutkiewicz and Shenton 1986: 111)

The international "development" establishment is, in this view, deeply implicated in this process as well. "Development" agencies have not only promoted statist policies, the "development" bureaucracy is itself part of the sprawling symbiotic network of experts, offices, and salaries that benefits from "etatization." As Williams argues:

Since their origins in the colonial period, the project of "development" itself [along with] the "development community" which has grown up to implement it, has instigated, legitimated and benefitted from the process of "Etatization". Within the "development community", whatever disagreements there may be about particular policies and institutions, L'Etat is internationalized and multilateralized.
(Williams 1985a: 11)

The argument, like my summary of it, is extremely general, and unashamedly short on specifics. Like any very general formulation, this one loses much of the complexity and specificity of particular cases, and opens itself up to charges of over-simplification. Certainly, it would be easy to find serious objections to the general model for any given specific case. And it is far from clear that "Africa," an entire continent with a gigantic range of different economic and political realities, is really a suitable object for such a general model. (Are the state for-mations of, say, Ethiopia, Nigeria, and Swaziland more closely related to one another than they are to other post-colonial states, simply by virtue of the fact that all three countries are located in Africa?) In spite of such serious reservations, it must be said that as a broad, general characterization, the "etatization" thesis is provoking and stimulating in a way that the familiar, localized "case study" cannot be. However badly it may short-change the specificity of particular socio-political contexts, it does suggest important larger connections that deserve attention.

The "etatization" synthesis is important not only for its bold attempt at significant generalization, but also as a corrective to what has some-times been a kind of romance between the academic Left and the Third World state. Perceiving the state as the chief counter-force to the capitalist logic of the market and the chief instrument for bringing about progressive economic transformations, leftists have too often been willing to take statist interventions at their word and to interpret them uncritically as part of a process of "self-directed development" or "socialist construction." Williams makes the same point in noting the strong appeal of state marketing boards for socialists, who by rights "have no business defending or reforming such exploitative institutions" (Williams 1985b: 13), but have been "all too willing to take statism as at least offering a foundation for socialism" (Williams 1985b: 4). Identifying "etatization" as a central process in recent African history is an important step toward breaking what Deleuze, in a related context, has called "a complicity about the state" (1988: 30).

However, it seems to me that in seeking to describe and explain the "instrument-effects" of the "development" apparatus, there are important limitations to the utility of the notion of "etatization," at least as it has been formulated by Dutkiewicz, Shenton, and Williams. First of all, while it clearly points out the way in which "development" figures in the expansion of bureaucratic state power, it does not so clearly identify the second axis along which the "anti-politics machine" operates – the axis of de-politicization. Dutkiewicz and Shenton (1986) note that state "development" interventions may in fact inhibit or squash peasant production, leading to the "crisis of diminished reproduction." But they do not give enough emphasis to the parallel fact that this same "development" may also very effectively squash political challenges to the system – not only by enhancing the powers of administration and repression, but by insistently reposing political questions of land, resources, jobs, or wages as technical "problems" responsive to the technical "development" intervention. In other words, the conceptual "instrument-effects" of the "development" deployment may be as important as the institutional ones.

A second, and more fundamental, limitation has to do with the way in which the "etatization" thesis theorizes the state and the relation of state power to "the ruling group." In the picture sketched by Dutkiewicz, Shenton, and Williams, "the state" and "the ruling group" both appear as unitary entities. What is more, the relation between the two is seen as one of simple instrumentality. Instead of seeing the "etatizing" results of "development" interventions as emerging counter-intentionally through the working out of a complex and unacknowledged structure of knowledge in interaction with equally complex and unacknowledged local social and cultural structures, as I have tried to do here, these authors explain such an outcome as the simple, rational projection of the interests of a subject (the "ruling group") that secretly wills it. "Etatization" thus appears as an almost intentional process, guided by the calculations of this ill-defined "ruling group." Indeed, for Dutkiewicz and Shenton, the expansion of state power is not simply an effect of failed state interventions, it is the *purpose* of such interventions. "Etatization" occurs, they seem to imply (in functionalist fashion), because the social reproduction of the ruling group "requires it" (Dutkiewicz and Shenton 1986: 111). And because the ruling group's position is based exclusively on its control of the state, "state power" in such a formula becomes interchangeable with the power held by the ruling group in its extractive relations with the peasantry. "Etatization" thus reduces to a straight-forward attempt on the part of this unitary "ruling group" to augment its own power *vis à vis* the peasants.

This portion of the "etatization" argument is in fact unsettlingly reminiscent of Hyden's (1980) notion of a post-colonial state with a historic mission to "capture" its peasantry. Dutkiewicz and Shenton (1986) and Williams (1987) have vigorously attacked Hyden's silly idea of a primordial "economy of affection," but their interpretation of "etatization" as the process through which a "ruling group" uses the state to extract surplus value from its rural population does have similarities with Hyden's notion of "capture." There is, of course, a crucial political difference; while Williams, Shenton, and Dutkiewicz see the expanding power of the "ruling group" and its state apparatus as debilitating and oppressive, Hyden sees the accumulation of ever more power by this ruling group as desirable, and actively hopes that the governing classes can acquire enough control to bring the peasantry to its knees, in the bizarre belief that they will then somehow duplicate the experience of industrializing Europe. But in both cases, the state is seen as a tool "in the hands of" a unitary subject, and state interventions are interpreted as expressions of the project of a "ruling group" bent on controlling and appropriating peasant production. Both views agree on what the struggle is over (the control and appropriation of peasant production) and who the protagonists are ("the state" and "the peasantry"). Their difference, which is real enough, lies at another level: for Hyden, the peasantry is "uncaptured," insufficiently subordinated to the needs of a weak and ineffectual state, thus "development" is frustrated; for Dutkiewicz, Shenton, and Williams, it is precisely the heavy hand of an overgrown state (e.g., through state marketing monopolies) that suffocates peasant production. These contrasting interpretations contain within them a puzzle: Is state power in these settings feeble and ineffectual (as Hyden would have it), or is it overgrown and crushing (as Dutkiewicz, Shenton, and Williams seem to suggest)? Does the African state have too much power, or too little?

This puzzle in fact lies at the center of much recent debate by political scientists and political economists on the nature of the post-colonial state. In the 1970s, a number of theorists argued (along lines similar to Dutkiewicz, Shenton, and Williams) that the historical legacy of co-ercive colonial state apparatuses had laid the foundation for "overdeveloped" post-colonial states, in which overgrown state institutions (originally deriving from the repressive colonial context) could dominate the rest of society (Alavi 1972; Saul 1979; cf. also Leys 1976). Against this view, in the 1980s a number of writers have suggested that notwithstanding often autocratic and despotic appearances, post-colonial states are more typically "enfeebled" (Azarya and Chazan 1987) than they are "overdeveloped" or "overcentralized." Thus Migdal (1988), for instance, argues that "fragmented" structures of social control in post-colonial societies often make effective state control impossible, while writers like Chabal (1986), Bayart (1986), and Geschiere (1988) emphasize the extent to which state plans are frustrated by a deceptively powerful "civil society." These writers differ only on the question of who is hero and who is anti-hero in this epic struggle between "state" and "civil society." Migdal, like Hyden, seems to prefer an outcome where a strong "state" can triumph over a weakened "society" (1988: 259–77). Writers like Bayart (1986) and Geschiere (1988), on the other hand, celebrate the means through which civil society is able to take "revenge" on the state through "popular modes of action," and thus to provide a form of "political accountability" (Chabal 1986), checking the despotic power of the state.

It is possible to move beyond this debate only by formulating the expansion of state power in a slightly different way. One can begin by saying that the state is not an entity that "has" or does not "have" power, and state power is not a substance possessed by those individuals and groups who benefit from it. The state is neither the source of power, nor simply the projection of the power of an interested subject (ruling group, etc.). Rather than an entity "holding" or "exercising" power, it may be more fruitful to think of the state as instead forming a relay or point of coordination and multiplication of power relations. Foucault has described the process through which power relations come to be "statized" in the following terms:

It is certain that in contemporary societies the state is not simply one of the forms or specific situations of the exercise of power – even if it is the most important – but that in a certain way all other forms of power relation must refer to it. But this is not because they are derived from it; it is rather because power relations have come more and more under state control (although this state control has not taken the same form in pedagogical, judicial, economic, or family systems). In referring here to the restricted sense of the word *government*, one could say that power relations have been progressively governmentalized, that is to say, elaborated, rationalized, and centralized in the form of, or under auspices of, state institutions.
(Foucault 1983: 224)

"The state," in this conception, is not the name of an actor, it is the name of a way of tying together, multiplying, and coordinating power relations, a kind of knotting or congealing of power. It is in this spirit that I have tried to describe the effects of the "anti-politics machine" in terms of "bureaucratic power" or "bureaucratic state power" rather than simply "state power" – in order to emphasize the adjectival over the nominative. The usage is meant to suggest not an entity possessed of power, but a characteristic mode of exercise of power, a mode of power that relies on state institutions, but exceeds them. I have argued that the "development" apparatus promotes a colonizing, expanding bureaucratic power, that it expands its reach and extends its distribution. By putting it this way, I have meant to imply not that "development" projects necessarily expand the capabilities of "the state," conceived as a unitary, instrumental entity, but that specific bureaucratic knots of power are implanted, an infestation of petty bureaucrats wielding petty powers.

On this understanding, it is clear that the spread of bureaucratic state power does not imply that "the state," conceived as a unitary entity, "has" more power – that it is, for example, able to implement more of "its" programs successfully, or to extract more surplus from the peasants.[5] Indeed, it is no paradox to say that "etatization" may leave the state even less able to carry on "its" will or "its" policies. As "state power" is expanded, "the state" as a plan-making, policy-making, rational bureaucracy may actually become "weaker," less able to achieve "its" objectives. This is especially clear in cases, such as the one explored above in Chapter 7, where a superabundance of centralized, bureaucratic agencies (all ostensibly working hard for "development") becomes seen as the key obstacle to "development" policies. The expansion of bureaucratic state power, then, does not necessarily mean that "the masses" can be centrally coordinated or ordered around any more efficiently; it only means that more power relations are referred through state channels – most immediately, that more people must stand in line and await rubber stamps to get what they want. What is expanded is not the magnitude of the capabilities of "the state," but the extent and reach of a particular kind of exercise of power.

In this respect, the way in which power is linked up with the state in a country like Lesotho differs from the model of a state-coordinated "bio-power" that Foucault (1980a) has described for the modern West. In Foucault's account, the development and spread of techniques for the disciplining of the body and the optimization of its capacities, followed by the emergence of the "population" as an object of knowledge and control, has made possible in the modern era a normalizing "bio-power," watching over, governing, and administering the very "life" of society. In this process, the state occupies a central, coordinating role – managing, fostering, and, according to its own calculus, "optimizing" the vital and productive forces of society. In a country like Lesotho, no doubt many planners of state interventions would like to take on such a role – to control the size of the population, for instance, or to set about making it more productive, healthy, or vital. But the empirical fact is that such interventions most commonly do not have such effects. The growth of state power in such a context does not imply any sort of efficient, centralized social engineering. It simply means that power relations must increasingly be referred through bureaucratic circuits. The state here does not have a single rationality, and it is not capable of optimally ordering the biological resources of its population in the sense of the "bio-power" model. The state does not "rationalize and centralize" power relations, as Foucault's quote above (p. 273) would suggest. It grabs onto and loops around existing power relations, not to rationalize or coordinate them, so much as to cinch them all together into a knot.

The "developmental" state, then, is a knotting or a coagulation of power. If we can speak of the "development" apparatus as part of a process of "etatization," that can only be a way of saying that it is involved in the distribution, multiplication, and intensification of these tangles and clots of power.

Up to now, I have explored some possible lines of empirical generalizations: some issues to be explored concerning the applicability of the specific conclusions reached for Lesotho to the wider world. There remain a few suggestions to be made about possible generalizations at a more abstract or theoretical level. The final section therefore proposes some general observations concerning the nature of the process through which conceptual apparatuses like that of "development" in Lesotho are implicated in processes of structural change.

Discourse, knowledge, and structural production

I have argued up to now that even a "failed" development project can bring about important structural changes. This means that even where new structures are not produced in accordance with discursively elaborated plans, they are all the same produced, and the role of discursive and conceptual structures in that production is by no means a small one. The investigation has demonstrated two facts about the Thaba-Tseka case: first, that the project's interventions can only be understood in the context of a distinctive discursive regime that orders the "conceptual apparatus" of official thinking and planning about "development" in Lesotho; and secondly, that the actual transformations that were brought about by the project were in no way congruent with the transformations that the conceptual apparatus planned. This pairing of facts raises an important theoretical question: if official planning is not irrelevant to the events that planned interventions give rise to, and if the relation between plan and event is not one of even approximate congruence, then what is the relation between blueprints and outcomes, between conceptual apparatuses and the results of their deployment?

I want to suggest that, in order to answer that question, it is necessary to demote intentionality – in both its "planning" and its "conspiracy" incarnations – and to insist that the structured discourse of planning and its corresponding field of knowledge are important, but only as part of a larger "machine," an anonymous set of interrelations that only ends up having a kind of retrospective coherence. The use of the "machine" metaphor here is motivated not only, as above, by science-fictional analogy, but by a desire (following Foucault [1979, 1980a] and Deleuze [1988]) to capture something of the way that conceptual and discursive systems link up with social institutions and processes without even approximately determining the form or defining the logic of the outcome. As one cog in the "machine," the planning apparatus is not the "source" of whatever structural changes may come about, but only one among a number of links in the mechanism that produces them. Dis-

275

course and thought are articulated in such a "machine" with other practices, as I have tried to show; but there is no reason to regard them as "master practices," over-determining all others.

When we deal with planned interventions by powerful parties, however, it is tempting to see in the discourse and intentions of such parties the logic that defines the train of events. Such a view, however, inevitably misrepresents the complexities of the involvement of intentionality with events. Intentions, even of powerful actors or interests, are only the visible part of a much larger mechanism through which structures are actually produced, reproduced, and transformed. Plans are explicit, and easily seen and understood; conspiracies are only slightly less so. But any intentional deployment only takes effect through a convoluted route involving unacknowledged structures and unpredictable outcomes.

If this is so, then a conceptual apparatus is very far from being irrelevant to structural production. It is part of the larger system through which such production actually occurs; but it is only part of a larger mechanism. When one sees the whole process, it is clear that the conceptions are only one cog among others; they are neither mere ornament nor are they the master key to understanding what happens. The whole mechanism is, as Deleuze (1988: 38) puts it, a "mushy mixture" of the discursive and the non-discursive, of the intentional plans and the unacknowledged social world with which they are engaged. While the instrumental aims embodied in plans are highly visible,[6] and pretend to embody the logic of a process of structural production, the actual process proceeds silently and often invisibly, masked or rendered even less visible by its contrast with the intentional plans, which appear bathed in the shining light of day. The plans, then, as the visible part of a larger mechanism, can neither be dismissed nor can they be taken at their word. If the process through which structural production takes place can be thought of as a machine, it must be said that the planners' conceptions are not the blueprint for the machine; they are *parts* of the machine.

Plans constructed within a conceptual apparatus do have effects but in the process of having these effects they generally "fail" to transform the world in their own image. But "failure" here does not mean doing nothing; it means doing something else, and that something else always has its own logic. Systems of discourse and systems of thought are thus bound up in a complex causal relationship with the stream of planned and unplanned events that constitutes the social world. The challenge is to treat these systems of thought and discourse like any other kind of structured social practice, neither dismissing them as ephemeral nor seeking in their products the master plans for those elaborate, half-invisible mechanisms of structural production and reproduction in which they are engaged as component parts.

Epilogue

"What is to be done?"

"I understand your skepticism about 'development.' But after all, there really are an awful lot of poor, sick, hungry people out there. What's to be done about it? If 'development' isn't the answer, then what is?"

These are rather grand questions, to be sure. But in developing the argument I have presented here, I have found that many people have responded to it in just these terms. There seems to be a certain frustration with the fact that my analysis traces the effects or mode of operation of an apparatus without providing any sort of prescription or general guide for action. The first response to this sort of objection must be that the book never intended or presumed to prescribe, and that this is not what the book is all about. But it is perhaps worth making clear that this reluctance to dispense prescriptions is not a matter of neutrality or indifference. Indeed, I am no more indifferent to the political-tactical question of "what is to be done" than I am to the poverty and suffering of so much of the world. So I end the book with this epilogue – a brief personal statement on these issues – in anticipation of the reactions that many readers may have to the argument, and in hope of helping to draw out more clearly the implications of my analysis. Since these issues are, as I have argued from the start, intrinsically political, this must necessarily be a political statement. I offer it here not in order to suggest that everyone should share my politics, but to lay out as clearly as possible my belief that "development" is far from being the only available form of engagement with the great questions of poverty, hunger, and oppression that rightly pre-occupy us in thinking about the Third World.

Any question of the form "what is to be done" implies both a subject and a goal, both an aim and an actor who strategizes toward that aim. The question "what is to be done about all the poverty, sickness, and hunger in the Third World" immediately identifies the undoubtedly worthy goal of alleviating or eliminating poverty and its suffering. A first step, many would agree, toward clarifying that goal and the tactics appropriate to achieving it is to reformulate it somewhat more politically: since it is powerlessness that ultimately underlies the surface conditions of poverty, ill-health, and hunger, the larger goal ought

279

therefore to be empowerment.[1] But the question of the subject, the actor who is to do the "doing," still remains completely unspecified. A great deal of liberal policy science fills in the gap left by this lack of specificity in its own unacknowledged way, implicitly translating the real-world question of poverty into the all too familiar, utopian form of the question: given an all-powerful and all-benevolent policy-making apparatus, what should it do to advance the interests of its poor citizens? In this form, it seems to me that the question is worse than meaningless – in practice, it acts to disguise what are in fact highly partial and interested interventions as universal, disinterested, and inherently benevolent. If the question "what is to be done" has any sense, it is as a real-world tactics, not a utopian ethics. "What is to be done?" demands first of all an answer to the question, "By whom?"

"What should they do?"

Often, the question was put to me in the form "What should they do?", with the "they" being not very helpfully specified as "Lesotho" or "the Basotho" (cf. Chapter 2, pp. 60, 62). The "they" here is an imaginary, collective subject, linked to utopian prescriptions for advancing the collective interests of "the Basotho." Such a "they" clearly needs to be broken up. The inhabitants of Lesotho do not all share the same interests or the same circumstances, and they do not act as a single unit. There exists neither a collective will nor a collective subject capable of serving it.

When the "developers" spoke of such a collectivity ("they," "the Basotho," "Lesotho") what they meant was usually the government. But the government of Lesotho is of course not identical with the people who live in Lesotho, nor is it in any of the established senses "representative" of that collectivity. As in most countries, the government is a relatively small clique with narrow interests. Significant differences in points of view and interests can certainly be found within this governing circle, and undoubtedly one can see in at least some of these differences the indirect traces of popular demands, which even the most undemocratic politician must in one way or another take into account. But, speaking very broadly, the interests represented by governmental elites in a country like Lesotho are not congruent with those of the governed, and in a great many cases are positively antagonistic. Under these circumstances, there is little point in asking what such entrenched and often extractive elites should do in order to empower the poor. Their own structural position makes it clear that they would be the last ones to undertake such a project. If the governing classes ask the advice of experts, it is for their own purposes, and these normally have little to do with advancing the interests of the famous downtrodden masses.

If the question "what should they do" is not intelligibly posed of the government, another move is to ask if the "they" to be addressed should not be instead "the people." Surely "the masses" themselves have an interest in overcoming poverty, hunger and other symptoms of power-lessness. At a certain level of analysis, there is no disputing that those who experience poverty and oppression must be first among those concerned with the question of what is to be done about it. But once again, the question is befuddled by a false unity. "The people" are not an undifferentiated mass. Rich and poor, women and men, city dwellers and villagers, workers and dependants, old and young; all confront different problems and devise different strategies for dealing with them. There is not one question – "what is to be done" – but hundreds: what should the mineworkers do, what should the abandoned old women do, what should the unemployed do, and on and on. It seems, at the least, presumptuous to offer prescriptions here. The toiling miners and the abandoned old women know the tactics proper to their situations far better than any expert does. Indeed, the only general answer to the question, "What should they do?" is: "They are doing it!"

As I argued earlier, the "development" problematic tends to exclude from the field of view all forces for change that are not based on the paternal guiding hand of the state; it can hardly imagine change coming in any other way. But, from outside that problematic, it seems clear that the most important transformations, the changes that really matter, are not simply "introduced" by benevolent technocrats, but fought for and made through a complex process that involves not only states and their agents, but all those with something at stake, all the diverse categories of people who craft their everyday tactics of coping with, adapting to, and, in their various ways, resisting the established social order. As Foucault remarked of the prisons, when the system is transformed:

it won't be because a plan of reform has found its way into the heads of the social workers; it will be when those who have to do with that ... reality, all those people, have come into collision with each other and with themselves, run into dead-ends, problems and impossibilities, been through conflicts and confrontations; when critique has been played out in the real, not when reformers have realised their ideas.
(Foucault 1981: 13)

Southern Africa is not a place where such a "critique of the real" is difficult to foresee. The uncertainties of the contemporary situation are immense, and all but the most banal predictions are more than usually impossible. But there is no doubt that massive changes of one sort or another are inevitably coming in the whole regional political and economic system. Various categories of Basotho will participate and *are* participating in making these changes in the various ways appropriate to their circumstances, be they mineworkers joining the large and rapidly growing National Union of Mineworkers, political activists working with the liberation movements, women fighting for empowerment and autonomy in the villages, or targeted "farmers" resisting the encroachments of the bureaucratic state. They are not waiting for consultants to come and tell them what must be done.

It remains conceivable that at various points in these struggles, in various organizational locations, there may in fact be demands for specific kinds of advice or expertise. But, if there is advice to be given, it will not be dictating general political strategy or giving a general answer to the question "what is to be done" (which can only be determined by those doing the resisting), but answering specific, localized, tactical questions. The possibility of this form of engagement of expertise with political movements of empowerment is explored in greater depth below.

"What should we do?"

A second, and apparently less arrogant, form of the question is to ask not "what should they do?" but "what should we do?" But once again, the crucial question is, which "we?"

For many, the answer seems to be either "we, the governments of the West," or "we whose job it is to 'do' something," i.e., "we 'developers'." In either case, the question "what should we do?" quickly becomes "what should the 'development' agencies and the 'donors' do?" But like the "they" of "Lesotho," the "we" of "development agencies" as the implied subject of the question falsely implies a collective project for bringing about the empowerment of the poor. Whatever good or ill may be accomplished by these agencies, nothing about their general mode of operation would justify a belief in such a collective "we" defined by a political program of empowerment.

There is, however, a second and more productive way of posing the question "what should we do?"; that is: What should we scholars and intellectuals working in or concerned about the Third World do? To the extent that there are common political values and a shared agenda, a real "we" group with shared political aims and common tactical problems, this becomes a real question. My experience suggests that many academic social scientists – and perhaps most anthropologists – working in southern Africa do broadly share what one might call a left-populist perspective. Having worked with a broad range of "ordinary people," often for long periods of time and with at least a certain degree of intimacy and affection, these intellectuals are often sympathetic with popular causes and suspicious of the usual claims that the elites and experts know best. Their instincts are generally democratic, egalitarian, and anti-hierarchical. Their political proclivity is to support struggles for empowerment on the part of exploited peasants and workers, and to oppose neo-colonialist and bureaucratic domination. "Development" researchers, too, are far from being all conservative bureaucrats. Many, especially anthropologists, share these same popular and democratic commitments, and seek practical ways of advancing them. Indeed, at least some "development" workers see themselves as practicing social activists. There is even a measure of continuity between contemporary "development" work and the popular and student movements centering on Third World issues that so many Western countries experienced during the 1960s. In spite of the very common involvement of "development" with counter-insurgency throughout the post-war period, a surprising number of Western progressives have been drawn to "development" work by way of political commitments to and solidarity with Third World causes. There are sometimes romantic and even missionary overtones to these engagements, to be sure; but often enough there is a real commitment to work for liberating, empowering social transformations. For these many scholars, intellectuals, and experts in various settings who would wish to apply their energies and talents on the side of economic and political empowerment, the tactical question "what is to be done" is indeed a real one. But any answer to this question must entail, if only implicitly, a theory of how economic and political empowerment comes about.

For anyone who shares the political commitments I have been discussing, making "development" the form of one's intellectual political engagement would seem to imply the view that democracy, equality, and empowerment are to be worked for and brought about through the benevolent intervention of state agencies – that these progressive changes are to be advanced through the action of progressive planners acting on proper advice. There may well be specific contexts where this does happen. At a minimum, one can say that however bad "development" interventions have been for the "beneficiaries," no doubt many of them might have been worse were it not for these left-populists working from the inside. But there are distinct limitations to this way of theorizing the process of empowerment, and corresponding dangers inherent in this strategy of engagement.

Operating on the theory that the oppressed classes are to be delivered from their poverty and powerlessness through government agency can easily lead to a falsely universalizing or even heroizing view of the state. Further, experience suggests that identifying government intervention with progress and reform is likely to facilitate the dismissal or even suppression of the often oppositional forms of action initiated by those identified as requiring the intervention. Acting on such a theory, it is all too easy to enter into complicity with a state bureaucracy that, after all, in all but the most extraordinary situations, serves the dominant or hegemonic interests in society – the very social forces, in most cases, that must be challenged if the impoverished and oppressed majority are to improve their lot. The apparent alternative of looking to the "international agency" rather than the state as the author of the benevolent, empowering intervention contains all the same dangers. The international apparatus typically has a different agenda than the local government does, but in its interests, and in its effects, it is no less conservative. The difference here is between the guardians of the global hegemony and those of the local hegemony. As with local government, positing "development" agencies as the active principle charged with the task of empowering the poor may involve a certain lack of fit between subject and predicate.

Certainly, national and international "development" agencies do constitute a large and ready market for advice and prescriptions, and it is this promise of real "input" that makes the "development" form of engagement such a tempting one for many intellectuals. These agencies seem hungry for good advice, and ready to act on it. Why not give it? But as I have tried to show, they seek only the kind of advice they can take. One "developer" asked my advice on what his country could do "to help these people." When I suggested that his government might contemplate sanctions against *apartheid*, he replied, with predictable irritation, "No, no! I mean *development*!" The only "advice" that is in question here is advice about how to "do development" better. There is a ready ear for criticisms of "bad development projects," so long as these are followed up with calls for "good development projects." Again, Foucault's analysis of the prison is relevant: "For a century and a half the prison has always been offered as its own remedy: the reactivation of the penitentiary techniques as the only means of overcoming their perpetual failure; the realization of the corrective project as the only method of overcoming the impossibility of implementing it" (Foucault 1979: 268). In "development," as in criminology, "problems" and calls for reform are necessary to the functioning of the machine. Pointing out errors and suggesting improvements is an integral part of the process of justifying and legitimating "development" interventions. Such an activity may indeed have some beneficial or mitigating effects, but it does not change the fundamental character of those interventions.

It is hardly a novelty to suggest that organizations like the World Bank, USAID, and the Government of Lesotho are not really the sort of social actors that are very likely to advance the empowerment of the exploited poor. Yet such an obvious conclusion makes many uncomfortable. It seems to them to imply hopelessness; as if to suggest that the answer to the question "what is to be done" is: "Nothing." Skepticism about the "development" intervention is read as political passivity. "Applied" researchers, the cliché goes, are willing to go out and get their hands dirty working for "development" agencies; "academic" researchers, on the other hand, stay in their ivory towers, and keep their hands and consciences clean. But is this really the only choice? Again, we return to the question of where empowering, progressive social changes come from. What forces are likely to bring such changes about? The elites of local government? USAID and the World Bank? Surely these are not the only possible answers. Working for social change is not synonymous with working for governments; indeed, it is perhaps not too much to say that the preoccupation of governments and government agencies is more often precisely to forestall and frustrate the processes of popular empowerment that so many anthropologists and other social scientists in their hearts seek to advance.

If, as I have suggested, the "development" intervention is not the only way for anthropologists and other social scientists to engage their intellectual and scholarly energies with the great questions of poverty and oppression, then what are the alternatives? How can we work for the social and economic changes that would make a difference for the ordinary people we have known as informants, neighbors, and friends?

One of the most important forms of engagement is simply the

political participation in one's own society that is appropriate to any citizen. This is perhaps particularly true for citizens of a country like the United States, where – thanks to an imperialistic power projected all across the globe – national politics powerfully impacts upon the rest of the world. But is it not also the case that there exist special opportunities – and even, as Chomsky (1969) has argued, special responsibilities – for political work for those with special knowledge, training, and expertise?

With respect to one's political engagement in one's own society, I think the answer is clearly yes. The anthropologist participates in the political process not only as citizen, but, willy-nilly, as "expert." Through teaching, public speaking, and advocacy, many Western anthropologists have applied their specialized knowledge to the task of combating imperialist policies and advancing the causes of Third World peoples. The involvement of American anthropologists in opposing US policy in Central America is a good example of this kind of engagement. The anthropologist who has seen "his village" exterminated by death squads, for instance, has both a special perspective and a distinctive political role to play on debates over aid to the "Contras" or support for El Salvador. Likewise, the field researcher who knows the Palestinians as real, flesh and blood human beings, and not only as shadowy figures brandishing machine guns, is in a position to combat the deceptions and misinformation that are put forward to justify the denial of Palestinian self-determination. And the anthropologist with first-hand knowledge of the realities of Southern Africa has both an opportunity and a responsibility to enter into the political debates surrounding *apartheid* and the world community.

Whether such a useful and appropriate role is available to the researcher in "the field," however, must remain in every case an open question. My own sense is that opportunity for such a role would exist only (1) where it is possible to identify interests, organizations, and groupings that clearly represent movements of empowerment, and (2) when a demand exists on the side of those working for their own empowerment for the specific skills and expertise that the specialist possesses. There are no doubt circumstances under which work for state or international agencies would meet these conditions. But the state is not the only game in town. The more interesting, and less explored, possibility is to seek out the typically non-state forces and organizations that challenge the existing dominant order and to see if links can be found between our expertise and their practical needs as they determine them. Such counter-hegemonic alternative points of engagement ("counter-hegemonic" status depending always on an analysis of the local context, of course) might be found in labor unions, opposition political parties and movements, cooperatives, peasants' unions, churches and religious organizations, and so on. Such oppositional foci of power often have practical needs for empirical research, and sometimes even budgets and institutional support for it.

We must entertain the strong possibility that there will be no need for what we do among such actors. There is no guarantee that our knowledge and skills will be relevant. We must recognize that it is possible, too, that different kinds of knowledge and skills will be required, that the nature of our intellectual activity itself will have to be transformed in order to participate in this way. But the possibilities are there to be explored. Where such alternative points of engagement are available, of course, there may well be severe difficulties to be overcome in deliberately working against the existing dominant order. Official permission may be difficult or impossible to obtain, government harassment may in some settings make such research difficult, or even dangerous. There is no reason to assume that such an approach to applied research will be possible in every setting. But against such formidable obstacles, there may be some practical advantages, too. Anthropologists come cheap; they do not require big budgets or equipment or laboratories. What they do require is on-site room and board, inter-personal connections with a broad range of informants, and a stimulating intellectual context. Counter-hegemonic organizations and institutions can often provide these as well or better than the big state and international agencies, even where research budgets are small or non-existent. They may not be able to spring for a room at the Hilton, but the anthropologist's problem is usually getting out of the Hilton, not into it. Institutional linkages with such counter-hegemonic social forces will have to be built and worked at. They are not the connections that come most easily, and such a form of engagement will come about only by working against the grain, not simply by waiting to be summoned. But it is possible to imagine a network of researchers committed to forging such links, and to anticipate a day when such connections might multiply to the point where they become, if not commonplace, at least no longer so extraordinary.

These kinds of engagements will no doubt never replace or even seriously challenge the predominance of "development" in the world of applied social-scientific research. Such work will probably never by itself provide a living, let alone a profession or a career; by its nature it

287

must remain an intermittent and marginal practice. It does not take the place of "development," and it does not occupy the same space. It does, perhaps, offer a form of engaging one's intellectual and scholarly energies with the work of political and social transformation in a way that is consistent with the democratic and populist commitments that so many anthropologists share.

Notes

1 Introduction

1 This division of "mountains" from "lowlands" is sometimes expanded to a four-zone classification: lowlands, foothills, mountains, and the Senqu river valley, a strip of relatively low-lying land that winds some way up into the mountains.

2 The following lists of donors and "development" agencies have been assembled from the following documents: UNDP 1980, GOL n.d., GOL 1977, GOL 1975, TAICH 1976. The list is only as accurate as these documents, and it does not pretend to be authoritative. A number of agencies have no doubt been left out. It should be noted, too, that the donors and agencies listed are involved in Lesotho on very different scales; some are major actors on the local scene, while many others are involved in only a very minor way.

3 On "development assistance" to Lesotho, see Jones (1982), Wellings (1982, 1983), Curry (1980), Singh (1982), Linden (1976).

4 See, for instance, Myrdal (1957, 1968, 1970), Seers (1979a, 1979b), Streeten (1970, 1972), Hirschman (1963, 1967), Tendler (1975), Brookfield (1975), Bryant and White (1982), and Chambers (1983). More specific studies include Hunter, Bunting and Bottrall (1976), Morss et al. (1976), Arnold (1982), McNeil (1981), Mickelwait et al. (1979), and Morss and Gow (1983).

5 Within Marxism, it should be noted, there have been several important writers opposed to the neo-Marxist approach to development. Bill Warren (1973, 1980) has argued a strong case for imperialism as a historically progressive "pioneer of capitalism" and shown how much fight the orthodox Marxist view still has in it. For others, such as Cooper (1981) and Hyden (1980, 1983), if capitalism is not the engine of Third World development that Warren makes it out to be, this is only because it is frustrated by the resistances it encounters there. African underdevelopment is thus the sign of resistance to capitalist and state incorporation; from the point of view of capitalist development Africa is "under-exploited," its peasantry "uncaptured." Anne Phillips (1977) has attacked the whole neo-Marxist focus on the ability or inability of capitalism to promote "development" as an idealist approach attempting to base the case for socialism on an ethical objection to capitalism rather than on a scientific investigation of tendencies and forces immanent in capitalism. Gavin Williams (1978) and Corrigan, Ramsey, and Sayer (1978) have also attacked the neo-Marxist view of "development."

6 Writers in this vein include Magdoff (1969), Frank (1969), Hayter (1971, 1981), and Heatley (1979).

7 See works cited in Willis (1981).

8 Theorists in this vein include, with important differences, Althusser, Bordieu, Bowles and Gintis, and Michael Apple. See Willis's afterword and

Stanley Aronowitz's preface in the second (1981) edition of *Learning to Labour* for a brief discussion of these issues.

9 It should be noted that the authors cited do not focus exclusively on these economic transformations. Indeed, they are often very sensitive to the non-economic motives and effects associated with "development" projects. The point is not that they ignore, e.g., political effects, but that they tend to assume a *primarily* economic function for "development" interventions in a way that seems unhelpful, at least for the case of Lesotho.

Williams's view is more complex on this point. Like the others, he is certainly concerned to relate "development" interventions to economic interests and the demands of international and domestic capital. But (especially in later work) Williams is more inclined to give central place to the non-economic effects of rural "development" projects, and the way in which economic "failures" may be turned to political successes (cf. Williams 1985a, 1986; Dutkiewicz and Williams 1987). In this respect, his approach has more in common with the one advanced here. See also Dutkiewicz and Shenton (1986), and the discussion on "etatization" in Chapter 9 below.

2 Conceptual apparatus: the constitution of the object of "development"

1 This idea – that exploring the social construction of knowledges implies a "relativistic" or even-handed valuation of different constructions – is common, but nonsensical. When Foucault (1973) compared the configuration of Renaissance knowledge with that of the Modern era, for instance, he surely did not thereby commit to the Renaissance belief that walnuts, by virtue of their resemblance to the human brain, can be used to cure brain illnesses, or to the notion that the medicine of the sixteenth century and that of the twentieth are equally efficacious. His problem, as always, was with the "regime" of truth, with the procedures for determining what is to count as truth in a given time and place. Whether walnuts *really do* cure brain disease was not Foucault's problem, but he is hardly committed to the view that all answers ever given to such a question are equally good!

2 The report states, first of all, that "Over the last six years, the number of Basotho men employed by South African mines has increased by 40,000 or by 7.5 to 8 percent a year on the average." Since the six years referred to are 1967–73, and since the number of employed in 1973 is given as 110,000, the figure of 40,000 net increase means that the 1967 figure is taken to be 70,000. In fact, the Department of Labour figure for 1967 is 77,414; for 1973 it is 110,477; the difference over the six year period is then about 33,000, not 40,000, and the percentage increase must be lower than 7.5 to 8 percent. But even this is a bit misleading; consider Table N2.1 One can see here that 1967 is lower than either of the years surrounding it, while 1973 is higher than either of its neighboring years. The years of comparison thus seem to have been chosen in order to emphasize the suddenness of the trend. If one wished to minimize the trend instead of maximize it, one could take the years 1966 and 1974 instead of the years 1967 and 1973, in which case one would find that the net difference was about 25,000 workers (not 40,000), over eight

years (not six), for an annual average percentage change of a little over 3 percent (instead of 8).

In the same paragraph, the report assumes that employment for Basotho men in South Africa outside the mines has increased by 10,000 over the same period. There is no source for this estimate, and it is almost surely exactly wrong. Starting in 1968, South African legal regulations have made it extremely difficult to obtain work in any way other than through temporary labor contracts made in Lesotho (see Murray 1981: 27–8). In practice, this means that employment in non-mining occupations has become much harder to come by, and it is to be expected that the period 1967–73 experienced a net *drop* in non-mine employment, not a net gain of 10,000. In 1975, van der Wiel's survey found that 81 percent of all migrants employed in South Africa were in mining. If we take this proportion to apply to the 1973 figures, we find that 110,000 mine employees would mean only an additional 26,000 non-mine employees (instead of the 65,000 the report assumes), for a total number of workers employed in South Africa of 136,000 not the 175,000 the report claims. If the report's figures for 1967 indicating non-mine employment of about 48,000 are correct (which is far from assured), then the number of non-mine employees did not increase by 10,000 over the period, it *decreased* by some 22,000!

In the next paragraph, we are told that "over the past decade total African employment in the South African mines has increased by 6.7 percent a year," while Basotho employment has increased even more sharply. Table N2.2 is presented. It is obvious that the raw figures given in the table for total African mine labor are inconsistent with the figure of 6.7 percent annual increase given above. The figures in the table give an average annual increase of only 1.3 percent over the ten year period, not 6.7. The absolute difference between the given figures is 67,000 which is perhaps the source of the error. But the raw figures given in the table for African mine labor in South Africa

Table N2.1. *Lesotho citizens employed on South African mines,*
1963–79

Year	Monthly average numbers employed	Year	Monthly average numbers employed
1963	58,678	1971	92,747
1964	62,653	1972	98,822
1965	66,527	1973	110,477
1966	80,951	1974	106,231
1967	77,414	1975	112,507
1968	80,310	1976	121,062
1969	83,053	1977	128,941
1970	87,384	1978	124,973
		1979	124,393

Source: Murray 1981: 20.

Table N2.2. *African mine labor in South*
Africa, 1963 and 1973
(Number of persons)

	Total	Basotho
1963	523,000	58,000
1973	590,000	111,000

Source: South African Reserve Bank, quarterly
bulletins, Lesotho Department of Labor.

themselves seem to be off. At any rate they do not agree with official South
African statistics, which show a figure of 528,627 Africans employed in
mining in 1963 and 641,020 in 1973. (This is according to the official *Bulletin
of Statistics* for 1963 and the S.A. Department of Mines' *Mining Statistics 1973*
for 1973. See SAIRR, *Survey* 1963, 1973.)

The figures for Basotho employed on the mines are presumably taken
from the Lesotho Department of Labour statistics (although the actual
numbers here are 58,678 for 1963 and 110,477 for 1973, which reveals some
rather odd rounding practices), but even these numbers look funny. In 1963,
the Witwatersrand Native Labour Association, which employed 405,629
out of a total number of African mine laborers of 528,627, recorded employing 56,467 citizens of Lesotho. If total Basotho employment for 1963 were
really only 58,678, then that would mean that, out of an additional 123,000
African mine workers, only some 2,211 (less than 2 percent) were Basotho.
In 1973, on the other hand, the number of Africans employed on the mines
by Mine Labour Organizations, Ltd. (the W.N.L.A.'s successor organization) was 422,181 out of a total of 641,020. Of these some 87,229 were from
Lesotho. If the figure of 110,447 Basotho mine laborers in 1973 is correct,
then there were some 23,218 Basotho among the 218,839 Africans employed
by non-M.L.O. mines, or about 11 percent of the total African labor force.
Thus a vastly disproportionate amount of the growth in Basotho employment shown in the table would have to be attributed to non-M.L.O. mines,
whose employment patterns are far less well documented. In the absence of
any explanation for why the Basotho share of this labor market should have
increased by some 600 percent in ten years, it seems likely that the figures for
1963 considerably underestimate the number of Basotho employed by mines
outside of the W.N.L.A.

3 Correction has been made in this figure for the year 1949/50. The 1949/50
census estimated a yield of 2,354,100 bags of maize (one bag = 200lbs) or
235,410 English tons (Douglas and Tennant 1952: 105). The original LASA
chart (LASA 1978: VI–4) shows this incorrectly as about 256,000 metric
tons, perhaps due to an error in converting English tons to metric tons. I
have changed it to the correct figure of 214,000 metric tons. Similar errors in

the LASA representation of the 1949/50 figures for sorghum and wheat have also been corrected.

4 At the end of the Thaba Bosiu project, the largest and best funded of the period, total production was actually less than at the project's start (World Bank 1979).

5 The widespread and extremely important reification of "nations" is discussed by Anderson (1983).

3 Institutional apparatus: the Thaba-Tseka Development Project

1 The project was officially created as the "Thaba-Tseka Mountain Area Development Project," but was more often known – and even referred to itself – by other names, including "Thaba-Tseka Project," "Mountain Development Project," "Thaba-Tseka Rural Development Programme," "Thaba-Tseka District Development Programme," and "Thaba-Tseka Development Project." I use "Thaba-Tseka Development Project" and "Thaba-Tseka Project" throughout, though the distinction between "project" and "programme" was at one point in the project's history an important one, as Chapter 7 will show.

2 Grazing lands in Lesotho are divided into cattle-post grazing and village grazing. The cattle-post grazing lands are located in the mountains far from any villages, and are used for summer grazing, when the herdboys and herdsmen travel with the herds and stay in "cattle-posts." Village grazing is reserved for the winter. Grazing lands are discussed at greater length in Chapters 4 and 6.

3 As it turned out, the Thaba Bosiu Project which is taken here as an exemplar was a rather spectacular failure. See the World Bank's Project Performance Audit Report of 1979 (World Bank 1979).

4 The World Bank's calculations on incomes were based on the premise of an extremely equal division of "productive assets" (i.e.; land and livestock). The project's own survey showed that the division, particularly of livestock, was highly unequal.

4 The setting: aspects of economy and society in rural Lesotho

1 On South African support for the B.N.P. generally, and Jonathan in particular, see Khaketla (1972).

2 Khaketla (1972). The one remaining constituency suffered an aborted election due to procedural errors and allegations of fraud.

3 For details of the 1970 coup and the repression which followed, see Macartney (1973) and Khaketla (1972). Also Amnesty International reports on Lesotho.

4 On Lesotho's shift to the left during the 1970s see Hirschman (1979).

5 Grants and technical assistance, as estimated in Wellings (1982).

6 See *Africa News*, January 28, 1985, "Lesotho may vote after 15 years" (Volume XXIV, No. 2, pp. 1–3, 14–15). The elections promised for 1985 were aborted when the government declared victory of all 60 BNP candidates on August 14, arguing that polling was not necessary, since the

opposition parties had failed to submit challengers. See *Africa News*, September 9, 1985, "Lesotho Aborts Election."

7 See also Feachem *et al.* 1978, Cross 1981, van de Geer and Wallis 1982.

8 There is one minor imprecision in this representation. Those who are counted as "absentees absent for reasons other than employment" should not really be excluded from the "paid employment" category, as they might still be paid employees, either migrant (home between contracts) or local – just away for some other reason. Such cases, however, must be rare, and I use Murray's scheme in spite of this problem for the sake of comparability.

9 Mine-workers suffer from an extremely high rate of on-the-job injuries and accidents, as the following chart (taken from Horner and Kooy 1980:42) reveals. Most years somewhere between 300 and 400 Basotho workers die on the mines, and many more are injured (see Table N4.1).

10 Actually, the figure is probably even lower, since the length of time it takes to run out of field food is artificially prolonged for those households who are regularly employed on "Food for Work" projects and are paid in maize meal.

11 In the case of Ward and Principal Chiefs, the committee is made up of five elected members, four appointed, plus the chief.

12 The law also contains provisions for the setting aside of special "selected agricultural areas" or "development areas" for government use or lease to private parties. A different set of rules governs land tenure in urban areas, but those do not concern us here.

13 Bribes of chiefs and committee members have been reported (e.g., Spiegel 1979, 1980; ILO 1979) but fieldwork revealed no evidence of this in Mashai. In any event, an allocation system remains fundamentally different from an open market, even if it is occasionally corrupted.

14 In theory chiefs are supposed to restrict the number of animals in their areas to the optimum numbers, but in practice stock graze the communal lands quite freely. The Ministry of Agriculture has recently begun to attempt to control grazing more strictly. See Chapter 6 for a discussion.

5 The bovine mystique: a study of power, property, and livestock in rural Lesotho

1 For a related South African history of government intervention into "traditional" livestock keeping, see Beinart (1984, 1982), and Beinart and Bundy (1981).

2 This view is associated with the idea of the "cattle complex," which can be traced back to Herskovits (1926). More recent examples are Houghton and Walton (1952) and Shaw (1974: 94–7). The approach is often applied more specifically to Lesotho in the "development" literature, including the works cited in the preceding paragraph.

3 See, for instance, Palmer and Parsons 1977: 7–8, Colson and Chona 1965, Fielder 1973, and, for Lesotho, Sheddick 1953, Swallow *et al.* 1987a.

4 This is said by livestock marketing experts to be because the animals are in their best condition during the summer months, and so are thought to give a good price. It is not always true that prices are higher in the summer, but it is

Table N2.1. Accidents on South African mines 1972–1975

Year	Category	Gold mines		Diamond mines		Coal mines		Other mines		Total	
		Dead	Injured	Dead	Injured	Dead	Injured	Dead	Injured	Dead	Injured
1972	1	476	14,065	6	121	52	1,147	87	1,640	621	16,973
	2	22	9,415	1	70	6	275	31	862	60	10,622
	3	13	108	2	9	0	24	4	70	19	211
	TOTAL	511	23,588	9	200	58	1,446	122	2,572	700	27,806
1973	1	491	14,371	13	99	45	1,203	86	2,694	635	18,367
	2	24	3,899	2	38	7	231	21	1,319	54	10,487
	3	24	142	1	10	0	26	23	112	48	290
	TOTAL	539	23,412	16	147	52	1,460	130	4,125	737	29,144
1974	1	460	16,876	21	109	64	1,320	164	2,879	709	18,184
	2	20	3,492	2	37	15	274	15	1,380	52	10,183
	3	9	126	0	5	5	22	16	87	30	240
	TOTAL	489	22,494	23	151	84	1,616	195	4,346	791	28,607
1975	1	450	11,914	10	64	83	1,300	127	2,382	670	15,660
	2	29	7,224	1	30	12	279	18	1,180	60	8,713
	3	19	98	2	4	5	29	9	108	35	239
	TOTAL	498	19,236	13	98	100	1,608	154	3,670	765	24,612
1972–5	1	1,877	54,226	50	393	244	4,970	464	9,595	2,635	69,184
	2	95	34,030	6	175	40	1,059	85	4,741	226	40,005
	3	65	474	5	28	10	101	52	377	132	980
1972–5	TOTAL	2,037	88,730	61	596	294	6,130	601	14,713	2,993	110,169

Source: GOL 1981–54.

probably true that many people believe that they are (I did no systematic investigation of this). However, considering some of the material to be presented later in this work, it seems likely that the seasonal pattern is due less to mistaken calculations on the production side than it is to a clear corresponding pattern on the consumption side: grain is harvested from the fields in June and July, and only very seldom does it last the whole year. If it is true, as one survey has indicated (Thaba-Tseka 1981), that 85 percent of livestock sold are sold in order to buy food, then the fact that animals are usually sold at the time when people are typically running out of home-grown food begins to look very significant.

5 100 cents (or lisente) = 1 Loti (plural Maloti); 1 Loti = 1 Rand = US$0.85 to $0.90 during the research period.

6 All interview quotations are translations of interviews conducted in Sesotho by the author.

7 This fact seems to go unnoticed by those in the "development" establishment and elsewhere who see Lesotho as cut off from the modern cash economy, and livestock thus as a kind of "primitive money."

8 The new Land Act of 1979 may change this for areas zoned as "urban." In rural areas the main impact will be the establishment of legal inheritance of land, along with a rule of primogeniture, and provisions for state alienation of land (designated "development areas") without compensation.

9 On marriage in Lesotho, see Murray 1981, 1977, Ashton 1967.

10 The official currency of Lesotho is the Loti (plural: Maloti), designated "M." One Loti is equal, by definition, to one South African Rand, and my informants always reckoned cash in Rand (liranta) or the older "Pound" (liponto; one "pound" = two Rand), and not the officially promoted Maloti which I have used in the translations.

11 There is room for confusion here, as the English "ox" may mean either "the domestic bovine quadruped (sexually distinguished as bull and cow)" or, in more common usage, "the male castrated and used for draught purposes or reared to serve as food" (OED). I use "ox" here in both these meanings, out of a desire to avoid the cumbersome but correct "head of cattle" as the singular of "cattle." Sesotho has no such problems: pholo is the castrated male, khomo is the singular of "cattle"; where the difference is of significance to the sense of the text, I indicate the proper Sesotho word in parentheses.

12 Interestingly, the informant justifies the rule in terms of use values, even though we have seen that he ranks the use value of an animal far below its market price. Note the passage that immediately followed:

Why?
It is very useful around the home.
I see.
When it has come into the kraal yonder we get cooking dung, we go make a fire and bask in it. If it is a cow we go milk it and eat the milk. When it dies I will eat the meat.
Yes, that is good. But money also is very useful in the home, isn't it?
Yes, that is so.

Is money more useful than an ox, M200?
No. No, not more than an ox.
You will keep the ox?
The ox will provide for you better.
Yes. I understand. But if we are talking about someone else's ox, and now the person says: I will give you the ox or M200 cash, now which will you take?
Right now?
Yes.
Right now I would take the M200.
I understand. Because you need the money.
Yes.

13 Numbers here refer to households, numbered 1 to 73.
14 I believe that the argument I advance here holds for the whole domain "livestock" – that is, for all grazing stock, including sheep and goats. My interviews nearly all centered on cattle, however, so I am reluctant to insist on conclusions for small stock. It is certainly true that small stock are more often slaughtered and more easily sold than cattle, and usually held in larger herds, but they seem to be subject to the same basic set of rules. More research on this point, however, is badly needed.
15 I have known livestock owners to say that they would keep an ox only until it was so old it was about to die and then sell it, and it may be so, but I have never heard of this actually being done in the absence of a great and pressing need for cash. It is certainly true, though, that, when an animal must be sold, it is usually the one in the herd which is likely to die soonest, typically the oldest, that is selected.
16 I mean by "household" the normative domestic unit of residence and consumption, the Sesotho *lelapa*, which is in practice usually easily and unambiguously identifiable. (I say "normative" because a long-absent migrant laborer must be considered a household member by virtue not of *actual* residence and consumption, but by virtue of the normative judgment that if such a person *were* residing locally, he or she would properly and rightfully reside and consume at a given household.)
17 See Murray 1981 and his other works cited in the bibliography. Also, Spiegel 1979, Gay 1980a.
18 See Gay 1980a for a comprehensive study of women's options.
19 This should not obscure the fact that Basotho women are highly self-reliant and resilient in the face of adversity. They are economically dependent, but they know how to look out for themselves. See, again, Gay 1980a.
20 See Ashton's discussion on "personal property" (1967: 177–9). He leaves out income from women's animals, however, which is quite important. I also found that cash from beer-brewing was often "women's money" even when done frequently and not only "occasionally." Money earned by a woman in regular salaried employment, in contrast, is usually considered "of the household," like that of men, though the woman is generally conceded to have more say in how it is to be spent than if it had been earned by the man.
21 I am speaking here of the simple monogamous household. In polygamous households, and often by extension where a husband's remarriage following

death or divorce of a spouse creates more than one "house," there is invoked the "house-property complex" (Sansom 1974, Ashton 1967, Poulter 1976). In this case, stock may be "assigned" by the husband to one or another "house," and this may be marked by different ear-marks on the animals concerned. But there should be no confusion here – the house-property complex centers, structurally, on the wife, but this does not mean that she has any executive authority over the "house" property so defined. "Men's livestock" in such a case may be "hers" – meaning allocated to "her" house – but this means that it belongs to "her" house as against other houses (or unallocated stock), not that it is in any sense hers personally or that it is not still "household property" under the final authority of the husband.

22 There is some disagreement on this point, with some married women claiming the right to buy their own "personal" stock; usually the example of a horse for transport is cited. The point is in practice moot, as "women's money" would almost never amount to enough to buy a horse, and a woman would have little interest in buying a sheep or goat. Nevertheless, all men and nearly all women with whom I discussed the matter agreed with the account I present here. The fact that the version is challenged by a few women shows only that these rules structuring household property are, like others we will discuss, "at issue." Single or widowed women may own or buy "men's animals" as they please. Usually these animals fall into one of three categories: (1) animals inherited or received as bridewealth being held in trust for the marriage of a son or sons; (2) a small number of cattle, usually in the care of a male friend or relative, used to obtain ploughing; or (3) a horse used for transport by a working woman.

23 In cases where there is more than one "house," as indicated in Note 20, there may be contestation over livestock *between* the houses – i.e., between wives or between male heirs. This, however, is a "domain of contestation" only in a very different sense, and does not affect the security of the "stored" resources.

24 This practice has come to be known in the English-language literature as "*mafisa*." In fact, *mafisa* in Sesotho refers to the animals (in the plural) so lent, and the practice itself might better be referred to by the infinitive of the related verb: *ho fisa*. Current usage results in grammatical atrocities: "the *mafisa* system"; animals "out on *mafisa*"; "while the *mafisa* lasts"; "the *mafisa* of horses is rare." Such usage calls to mind the word "lobola," a word which means nothing in either English or Sesotho, which is nevertheless widely used by whites in Lesotho to refer, in an exotic-sounding way, to bridewealth. In any event the concept in question here does not seem to me to be beyond the reach of our own language; *ho fisa* is in most contexts well translated by the English "loan," *mafisa* as "loaned animals."

25 This can mean a rich person in general, but it has strong connotations of a man wealthy in animals.

26 Such concessionary terms might be given with small stock, but not, my informant claimed, with cattle, as they are too valuable.

27 Thaba-Tseka Project, "Plan of Operations" (CIDA 1982).

28 Much utilitarian writing naively assumes "natural increase," as do Basotho proponents of the Mystique. Herd histories gathered in Mashai, however, as

well as the national figures cited above, suggest that, since the 1960s, a herd will do well to hold its own in numbers. The LASA research team reached the same conclusion based on an analysis of rates of reproduction. These low rates "mean that livestock populations are apparently just self-sustaining in good grazing years. This is not true, however, for drought years. Livestock numbers have held fairly constant over time largely due to net imports" (LASA 1978:VII–13). Swallow *et al.* have more recently (1987a,b) suggested a trend of significant natural increase, but their only evidence is birth and death rates from a single surveyed year (1985). Since livestock mortality is cyclical, tied especially to drought years, sweeping conclusions about the profitability of keeping livestock should not be drawn from a single-year statistical "snapshot" taken *after* a major drought.

29 There may be places in Lesotho where commercial stock-farming is found, but Mashai is at any rate not one of them. Commercial beef production has been promoted around Thaba-Tseka town, and some people have expressed interest in this, but it is too early to say what will come of this. In the case of sheep and goats, anyone who owns these animals and sells the clip is in some sense a "commercial farmer," but I encountered no one who could come close to supporting himself in this income; wool is more often a dividend used to pay the herdboy than it is a major contribution to the household accounts. (For those very few with large herds which may number in the thousands, of course, the income from wool may be substantial.)

30 GOL 1972. These figures should be taken only as a very rough sort of indication. The 1970 Census Report has so many internal contradictions that one must treat it with the greatest caution and even suspicion.

31 The issue is similar to that arising with racially defined "categories." Thus blacks in South Africa may be said to have a category interest in opposing *apartheid*; this is so even if it can be shown that a few scattered blacks are profiting from the system. The structural position of the overwhelming majority is determinant.

32 Not all women, of course, take the positions that, according to the "interests" identified here, they "should." Often this is a result of other, cross-cutting interests based on other factors, as we shall show. In some cases, however, one seems to find an irreducible "false consciousness." I have not the space to develop the idea here, but it seems possible that the control over ideological production by men, especially senior men, is so great that one might speak of a degree of "hegemony," in the Gramscian sense. Certainly young women, who have the most to lose from the Bovine Mystique, have also the least to say about what is and is not "good Sesotho," what is and is not "tradition." But women are not so easily snowed as this might imply. The great majority, as we shall see, are well aware that their own interests are opposed to the Mystique, and they act accordingly.

33 Sometimes, of course, she will simply prefer the ox on its own merits.

34 Usually widows feel an obligation to hold on to the stock of their deceased husbands as long as they can as a fund with which their sons will pay bridewealth and marry. At the time I heard this story of a widow who sold off her late husband's stock I failed to ask if she had sons; it seems a good guess that she did not.

35 In Mashai, the figure was usually put at twenty-three head of cattle, or twenty cattle, ten sheep or goats, and a horse.
36 See Murray 1981, 1977; Ashton 1967. Also, on Tswana marriage, see Comaroff 1980, and Comaroff and Roberts 1977.
37 Often, of course, the husband *chooses* to pay (it is, after all, in his own interest to legitimize the marriage), and there is no question of seeking to evade payment. It is only after the husband has invested all he cares to in the marriage that conflicting claims may arise and the visibility or otherwise of assets becomes an issue.

6 Livestock development

1 During the drought of 1982–4 a ban was imposed on the importation of livestock from South Africa, but this was described as an emergency measure, to be lifted when the drought ended.
2 It must be said that, although the villagers' understanding of the marketing process was often not highly sophisticated (people tended, for instance, to see fluctuations between low and high prices as expressions of stinginess and generosity, respectively), their analysis of the government interest in livestock marketing was not entirely without foundation. Livestock Marketing was set up as a "profit center" within the project, and was expected to show a net profit which could be used to fund other programs. The project did in fact stand to make money on every animal sold, and so had an interest in maximizing that number.
3 One official suggested that fodder could be put in as a second crop, after the harvest of grain. I lack the expertise to judge if this proposal was technically feasible or not. The strategy that was more often discussed, at any rate, and the one that was taken to the villages, was the one described here.
4 One man in 1983 grew yellow maize to feed to his cattle during the winter months. But he reported that he had always done so, and had not begun as a result of the project. Also, the man was not a commercial farmer, and was in fact one of the most highly traditionalistic men in the village when it came to livestock.
5 The one exception to this was in the area of Thaba-Tseka township itself. At the time I left Thaba-Tseka, a handful of the area's most commercially minded stock owners had become members of a newly organized "Brown Swiss Association" which aimed to keep the purebred cattle recommended by the government and raise them on commercial principles, chiefly as dairy animals. A few members of this group already owned a small number of Brown Swiss animals; others had merely expressed interest in acquiring them. There was talk, too, of attempting to reestablish the old grazing association around this group, setting aside half of the original 1,500 hectare area for the exclusive use of the Brown Swiss Association. It seemed likely that the Principal Chief would refuse to allocate the land to a second grazing association, but what will become of it all remains to be seen. A brief return visit in 1986 found the association still alive, with the situation largely unchanged. A new grazing association was still being discussed, but had not been attempted.

6 The above is of course complicated by the cross-cutting factors of age and participation in patron-client networks, as noted above in Chapter 5. It is not simply a matter of men versus women, though this seems the most important factor. At any rate, it was nearly always young women who spoke most favorably about the proposals for improved stock, and older men who openly rejected them. I do not have enough information to develop the idea here, but it seems possible that the accidental alignment of the government with women in the disputes over livestock may have some bearing on the fact that women seem to be much more likely than men to be supporters of the ruling BNP party and its government. But there are, of course, other very important factors at work here as well.

7 On this point it is worth noting that while commercial production of chicken, eggs, and pigs is not generally found in the mountains on any large scale (chiefly because the climate is not favorable), a thriving lowland poultry industry, very largely in the hands of women, is one of Lesotho's few commercial agricultural success stories.

8 There is little point in trying to predict the future, but it seems likely that a well-enforced de-stocking program, a successful effort to privatize a significant portion of the range, or a radical acceleration of the general ecological collapse of the range could have profound effects on the continuation of the Mystique. The ongoing changes in the structure of employment on the mines, while less dramatic, could also have highly significant effects on the structure of interests which supports "traditional" practices.

9 The demonstration project, with eight Brown Swiss cows, lost R3345 in 1978 alone. Even the project's own optimistic projections (which were never achieved) envisioned a profit of only R620 annually. Even if this estimate is realistic, it is not much of an inducement to risk losses as high as those of 1978.

7 The decentralization debacle

1 Other permanent members of the committee were the general manager of the Livestock Marketing Corporation, and the Directors of the Livestock and Crop Divisions of the Ministry of Agriculture. Representatives of other Ministries could be called in as needed.

2 In 1983, the Ministry of Agriculture was preparing its plans for the following years under the name "Thaba-Tseka Project – Phase Three." But the "Project" here was really only the ordinary activities of the Ministry of Agriculture, as in any other district. The continued use of the "Thaba-Tseka Project" name represented an attempt to find an outside donor to fund Government activities in the district by playing on the old "Project" name; it would be mistaken to suppose from this usage that the project continued in any real sense beyond the end of CIDA funding in March 1984.

8 Crop development and some other programs of the Thaba-Tseka Project

1 The report is "Proposal for the Implementation of a Rural Access Roads Programme for the Thaba-Tseka District," January 1981.

2 Half-hearted efforts continued to convince field holders to give up at least some crop land to cultivation of fodder, but the proposal to give up food in favor of fodder was not an attractive one, and was not taken very seriously, for reasons reviewed in Chapter 6.

3 The new Land Act of 1979 introduces important changes in land tenure law, including transferable leases in urban areas, and in special cases in rural areas as well. In rural areas, however, the effects of the new law are chiefly confined to the establishment of legal inheritance, along with a rule of primogeniture, and provision for state alienation of land designated as "selected development areas" or "selected agricultural areas." The precise effects of this law will depend on its interpretation and enforcement, but it seems clear that it has not resulted in any fundamental challenge to the system of field allocation, or the principle that ordinary fields may not be bought and sold.

4 This particular phrase is taken from a project report entitled "Proposal for the Operation of a Technical Division in a De-centralized District Model," issued October 28, 1980. Similar declarations were to be found in a great many project documents of the period.

9 The anti-politics machine

1 Cited in Brian Murphy, "Smothered with Kindness," *New Internationalist*, No. 82, 1979.

2 "Canadian Aid Gone Awry?" *The Citizen* (Ottawa), October 6, 1979; "CIDA in Africa: Goodby $6 Million," *Sunday Star* (Toronto), July 22, 1979.

3 Quoted in Murphy, "Smothered with Kindness," p. 13.

4 More recently, "homeland" governments have taken up "development" schemes, which have involved resettling subsistence farmers to make way for large commercial farms established by Pretoria-funded "development corporations" (Unterhalter 1987, Yawitch 1981). At the same time, the bantustans have taken up the theme of "basic needs," organizing rural settlements (in familiar "betterment" style) around "rural service centers," ostensibly for the purpose of providing government services more efficiently. A recent study concludes (Dewar *et al.* 1983: 59) "that the approach is unlikely to result in significant economic development or basic needs improvement and that the strategy in its present form is primarily directed toward containing 'surplus' rural population in a politically manageable way."

5 Dutkiewicz, Shenton, and Williams seem to be aware of this, as for instance when Dutkiewicz and Williams (1987: 43) observe that "The expanded scope of state activity and regulation has the consequence of reducing the state's capacity to manage and control." But they are unable to convincingly explain it, since they see "state power" as power essentially *belonging to* "the political class" (Dutkiewicz and Shenton's "ruling group"). On this understanding, as more and more of society comes under "state control," the power of this political class ought to be augmented to the point of total domination over the rest of society. The logical consequence of this view is that the political class should become (as in the usual models of "totalitarian

society") *more* able to "manage and control" the rest of society, not less. See also Williams (1986: 20), who notes that state intervention has commonly had the effect of reducing export earnings and tax revenues, but is left unable to explain why it is that "[t]his consideration has not done much to convince African governments ... to stop strangling the geese that lay the golden eggs."

6 I use "visible" here in a way that is almost exactly the reverse of the way that Deleuze (1988) uses the term. For Deleuze, the "visible" is opposed to the "articulable," as the non-discursive is to the discursive, the seeable to the sayable. The prison is "visible," criminology "articulable." I use the term "visible" in a more specific sense, to pick out the way that plans and programs explicitly present themselves for everyone to see as blueprints for bringing about change, while the social structures and processes that these plans confront (though integral parts of the "mechanism") are often "unseen" and unacknowledged by both the planners and those who view their efforts. In this sense, then, "development" planning is "visible," while the elaborate set of social process and institutions that also figures in the process is much less so.

Epilogue

1 Other positions are of course possible. One could argue, for instance, that an end to poverty does not require empowerment, but only an enlightened self-interest on the part of the powerful; after all, even a slave-owner will not profit from leaving his slaves poorly fed. My view here is that poverty is only one among a great number of possible forms of humiliation and degradation that may accompany powerlessness. The political task as I see it is not to eliminate one or two of these arbitrarily selected forms ("hunger," "homelessness"), but to work to eliminate the conditions of possibility for *all* such forms of humiliation and degradation. This amounts to a political choice in favor of focusing broadly on empowerment, not narrowly on poverty; freeing the slaves, not feeding them better.

References

Alavi, H. 1972. "The State in Post-colonial Societies: Pakistan and Bangladesh." *New Left Review*, 74, 59–81.

Amselle, J. L. (ed.). 1978. *Les migrations Africaines: Reseaux et processes migratoires*. Paris: Maspero.

Anderson, B. 1983. *Imagined Communities*. London: Verso.

Arnold, S. 1982. *Implementing Development Assistance: European Approaches to Basic Needs*. Boulder, Colorado: Westview.

Ashton, H. 1967. *The Basuto: A Social Study of Traditional and Modern Lesotho* (Second Edition). New York: Oxford University Press.

Azarya, V. and N. Chazan. 1987. "Disengagement from the State in Africa: Reflections on the Experience of Ghana and Guinea." *Comparative Studies in Society and History*, 29, 106–31.

Bardill, J. E. and J. Cobbe. 1985. *Lesotho: Dilemmas of Dependence in Southern Africa*. Boulder, Colorado: Westview.

Barker, J. (ed.). 1984 *The Politics of Agriculture in Tropical Africa*. Beverly Hills: Sage.

Bayart, J. F. 1986. "Civil Society in Africa," in *Political domination in Africa: Reflections on the limits of power*, P. Chabal (ed.). Cambridge University Press.

Beckman, B. 1977. "Peasants, Capital, and the State." *Review of African Political Economy*, 10, 1–6.

Beinart, W. 1982. *The Political Economy of Pondoland, 1860–1930*. Cambridge University Press.

    1984. "Soil Erosion, Conservationism and Ideas about Development: A Southern African Exploration, 1900–1960." *Journal of Southern African Studies*, 11, 1, 52–83.

Beinart, W. and C. Bundy. 1981. "State Intervention and Rural Resistance: The Transkei, 1900–1965," in *Peasants in Africa*, M. Klein (ed.), Beverly Hills: Sage.

    1987. *Hidden Struggles in Rural South Africa*. London: James Currey.

Bernstein, H. 1977. "Notes on Capital and Peasantry." *Review of African Political Economy*, 10, 60–73.

    1979. "Concepts for the Analysis of Contemporary Peasantries." *Journal of Peasant Studies*, 6, 4.

    1981. "Notes on State and Peasantry: The Tanzanian Case." *Review of African Political Economy*, 21, 44–62.

Bohannan, P. 1959. "The Impact of Money on an African Subsistence Economy." *The Journal of Economic History*, 19, 491–503.

Bourdieu, P. 1977. *Outline of a Theory of Practice*. New York: Cambridge University Press.

Breytenbach, W. J. 1977. *Society, Politics, and Government in Boleswa*. Pretoria: Africa Institute of South Africa.

304

Brokensha, D., D. M. Warren, and Oswald Werner (eds.). 1980. *Indigenous Knowledge and Development*. Lanham, Md.: University Press of America.

Brookfield, H. 1975. *Interdependent Development*. Pittsburgh: University of Pittsburgh Press.

Bryant, C. and L. G. White. 1982. *Managing Development in the Third World*. Boulder, Colorado: Westview.

Bryceson, D. 1982a. "Peasant Commodity Production in Post-colonial Tanzania." *African Affairs*, 81, 325, 547–67.

   1982b. "Tanzanian Grain Supply: Peasant Production and State Policies." *Food Policy*, May 1982.

Bundy, C. 1979. *The Rise and Fall of the South African Peasantry*. Berkeley: University of California Press.

Chabal, P. 1986. "Introduction: Thinking about Politics in Africa" in *Political domination in Africa: Reflections on the limits of power*, P. Chabal (ed.). Cambridge University Press.

Chambers, R. 1980. "Cognitive Problems of Experts in Rural Africa," in *Experts in Africa*, C. J. Stone (ed.). Aberdeen.

   1983. *Rural Development: Putting the Last First*. London: Longman.

Chomsky, N. 1969. "The Responsibility of Intellectuals," in *American Power and the New Mandarins*, N. Chomsky (ed.). New York: Pantheon.

CIDA (Canadian International Development Agency). 1977. "Evaluation Design for Phase I: The Thaba Tseka Project" (by R. C. Hughes). Ottawa: CIDA.

   1978E. *Thaba Tseka Project First Evaluation Report* (by R. C. Hughes and J. A. Norwood). Ottawa: CIDA.

   1978P. "Plan of Operations for the Thaba Tseka Mountain Development Project Phase II." Ottawa: CIDA.

   1978R. "Appraisal of Project Progress During the Pilot Phase and Review of Plans to Expand Agricultural Programs in Phase II of Project Operations." Ottawa: CIDA.

   1979. *Thaba Tseka Project Second Evaluation Report*. Ottawa: CIDA.

   1980. "Thaba Tseka Annual Review." Ottawa: CIDA.

   1982. "Revised Plan of Operations for the Thaba Tseka Development Project Phase II" (revised July 1982). Ottawa: CIDA.

Cobbe, J. 1978. "Growth and Change in Lesotho." *South African Journal of Economics*, 46, 2, 135–53.

Cochrane, G. 1971. *Development Anthropology*. New York.

Colson, E. 1951. "The Role of Cattle among the Plateau Tonga of Mazabuka District." *Human Problems in British Central Africa*, 11, 10–46.

Colson, E. and M. Chona. 1965. "Marketing of Cattle among Plateau Tonga." *Human Problems in Central Africa*, 37, 42–50.

Comaroff, J. L. (ed.). 1980. *The Meaning of Marriage Payments*. New York: Academic Press.

Comaroff, J. L. and S. Roberts. 1977. "Marriage and Extra-Marital Sexuality: The Dialectics of Legal Change among the Kgatla." *Journal of African Law*, 21, 97–123.

Cooper, D. 1980. "The Selebi-Phikwe Mining Community in Botswana: Migration Patterns and Economic Networks." Overseas Development Administration (U.K.).

Cooper, F. 1981. "Africa and the World Economy." Paper presented to the African Studies Association Annual Meeting, October 1981.

Corrigan, P. R. D., H. Ramsey, and D. Sayer. 1978. *Socialist Construction and Marxist Theory*. London: Macmillan.

Coulson, A. 1975. "Peasants and Bureaucrats." *Review of African Political Economy*, 3.

    1981. "Agricultural Policies in Mainland Tanzania, 1946–76," in *Rural Development in Tropical Africa*, J. Heyer, P. Roberts, and G. Williams (eds.). New York: St. Martin's Press.

    1982. *Tanzania: A Political Economy*. Oxford: Clarendon Press.

Cross, P. 1981. "Village Water Supply in Lesotho." M.A. Thesis, Department of Social Anthropology, University of the Witwatersrand, Johannesburg.

Curry, R. L. 1980. "US-AID's Southern Africa Program." *Journal of Southern African Affairs*, 5, 183–98.

Deleuze, G. 1988. *Foucault*. Minneapolis: University of Minnesota Press.

Dewar, D., A. Todes and V. Watson. 1983. "Development From Below? Basic Needs, Rural Service Centers, and the South African Bantustans, with Particular Reference to the Transkei." *African Urban Studies*, 15, 59–75.

de Wet, C., 1981. "Betterment and trust in a rural Ciskei Village." *Social Dynamics*, 6, 2.

Donzelot, J. 1979. *The Policing of Families*. New York: Pantheon.

Douglas, A. J. A., and R. K. Tennant. 1952. *Basutoland Agricultural Survey 1949/50*. Maseru: Basutoland Government.

Dreyfuss, H. and P. Rabinow. 1983. *Michel Foucault: Beyond Structuralism and Hermeneutics* (second edition). Chicago: University of Chicago Press.

Dutkiewicz, P. and R. Shenton. 1986. "Crisis in Africa: 'Etatization' and the Logic of Diminished Reproduction." *Review of African Political Economy*, 37, 108–15.

Dutkiewicz, P. and G. Williams. 1987. "All the King's Horses and All the King's Men Couldn't Put Humpty-Dumpty Together Again." *IDS Bulletin*, 18, 3, 39–44.

Eberhard, A. A. 1982. "Technological Change and Rural Development: A Case Study in Lesotho." Ph.D. Thesis, University of Edinburgh, November 1982.

FAO (Food and Agriculture Organization of the United Nations). 1977. "Rural Development: Lesotho: Report of the task force on rural development in Lesotho." Rome: FAO.

    1980. "International Scheme for the Coordination of Dairy Development and International Meat Development Scheme." Maseru: FAO.

    1983. "Lesotho: Evaluation of Food Self-Sufficiency Programme" (Vols. I and II). Rome: Food and Agriculture Organization of the United Nations.

FAO/WB (Food and Agriculture Organization/World Bank Cooperative Programme). 1974. "Interim Report of the Joint CP/RMEA/CIDA Preparation Mission." Rome: FAO.

    1975. *Draft Report of the Lesotho First Phase Mountain Area Development Project Preparation Mission* (Vols. I and II). Rome: FAO.

Feachem, R. G. A., E. Burns, A. Cairncross, S. Cronin, P. Cross, D. Curtis, M. Khan, D. Lamb, and H. Southall. 1978. *Water, Health and Development*. London: Tri-med Books.

Fielder, R. J. 1973. "The Role of Cattle in the Ila Economy." *African Social Research*, 15, 327–61.

Foucault, M. 1971. *The Archaeology of Knowledge*. New York: Harper and Row.
1973. *The Order of Things*. New York: Vintage.
1979. *Discipline and Punish: The Birth of the Prison*. New York: Vintage.
1980a. *The History of Sexuality: Volume One: An Introduction*. New York: Vintage.
1980b. *Power/Knowledge: Selected Interviews and Other Writings, 1972–1977*, Colin Gordon (ed.). New York: Pantheon.
1981. "Questions of Method: An Interview." *Ideology and Consciousness*, 8, 3–14.
1983. "Afterword: The Subject and Power," in *Michel Foucault: Beyond Structuralism and Hermeneutics* (second edition), H. Dreyfus and P. Rabinow (eds.). Chicago: University of Chicago Press.

Frank, A. G. 1969. *Latin America: Underdevelopment and Revolution*. New York: Monthly Review Press.

Freeman, L. 1984. "CIDA and Agriculture in East and Central Africa," in *The Politics of Agriculture in Tropical Africa*, J. Barker (ed.). Beverly Hills: Sage.

Freyhold, M. von. 1979. *Ujamaa Villages in Tanzania: Analysis of a Social Experiment*. London.

Galli, R. E. (ed.). 1981. *The Political Economy of Rural Development: Peasants, International Capital, and the State*. Albany: State University of New York Press.

Gay, J. 1980a. "Basotho Women's Options: A Study of Marital Careers in Rural Lesotho." Ph.D. Dissertation, University of Cambridge.
1980b. "Wage Employment of Rural Basotho Women: A Case Study." *South African Labour Bulletin* 11, 4, 19–28.

Geschiere, P. 1988. "Sorcery and the State: Popular Modes of Action among the Maka of Southeast Cameroon." *Critique of Anthropology*, 8, 1, 35–63.

GOL (Government of Lesotho). n.d. "Third Five Year Plan Preview." Maseru: Central Planning and Development Office.
1972. *1970 Census of Agriculture Report*. Maseru: Bureau of Statistics.
1975. *Donor Conference Report*. Maseru: Central Planning and Development Office.
1977. *Donor Conference Papers, September 1977*. Maseru: Central Planning and Development Office.
1980. *Third Five Year Development Plan*. Maseru: Central Planning and Development Office. Undated [1980].
1981. "Agricultural Development: A Blueprint for Action." Maseru: Ministry of Agriculture. Undated [1981].
1982. *Annual Statistical Bulletin 1981*. Maseru: Bureau of Statistics.
1983. *Annual Statistical Bulletin 1982*. Maseru: Bureau of Statistics.
1987. "Lesotho: National Accounts, 1975–1984." Maseru: Bureau of Statistics.

References

Hammond-Tooke, W. D. (ed.). 1974. *The Bantu-speaking Peoples of Southern Africa*. Boston: Routledge & Kegan Paul.

Hayter, T. 1971. *Aid as Imperialism*. Harmondsworth: Penguin.

    1981. *The Creation of World Poverty: An Alternative View to the Brandt Report*. London: Pluto Press.

Heatley, R. 1979. *Poverty and Power: The Case for a Political Approach to Development and its Implications for Action in the West*. London: Zed Press.

Herskovits, M. J. 1926. "The Cattle Complex in East Africa." *American Anthropologist*, 28, 230–72, 361–80, 494–528, 630–64.

Heyer, J., P. Roberts, and G. Williams (eds.). 1981. *Rural Development in Tropical Africa*. New York: St. Martin's Press.

Hirschman, A. O. 1958. *The Strategy of Economic Development*. New Haven: Yale University Press.

    1963. *Journeys Toward Progress*. New York: The Twentieth Century Fund.

    1967. *Development Projects Observed*. Washington D.C.: The Brookings Institution.

Hirschman, D. 1979. "Changes in Lesotho's Policy towards South Africa." *African Affairs*, 78, 311, 177–96.

Hoben, A. 1980. "Agricultural Decision Making in Foreign Assistance: An Anthropological Analysis," in *Agricultural Decision Making: Anthropological Contributions to Rural Development*, P. F. Barlett (ed.), New York: Academic Press.

Horner, D. and A. Kooy. 1980. "Conflict on South African Mines 1972–1979." Cape Town: Southern African Labour and Development Research Unit.

Houghton, D. H. and E. M. Walton. 1952. *The Economy of a Native Reserve*. Pietermaritzburg: Shuter and Shuter.

Hunter, G., A. H. Bunting, and A. Bottrall (eds.). 1976. *Policy and Practice in Rural Development*. London.

Hyden, G. 1980. *Beyond Ujamaa in Tanzania: Underdevelopment and an Uncaptured Peasantry*. Berkeley: University of California Press.

    1983. *No Shortcuts to Progress: African Development Management in Perspective*. Berkeley: University of California Press.

ILO (International Labour Office). 1979. *Options for a Dependent Economy: Development, Employment and Equity Problems in Lesotho*. Addis Ababa: ILO Jobs and Skills Programme for Africa.

Innes, D. and D. O'Meara. 1976. "Class Formation and Ideology: The Transkei Region." *Review of African Political Economy*, 7.

James, D. 1983. *The Road from Doornkop: A Case Study of Removals and Resistance*. Johannesburg: SAIRR

Jingoes, S. J. 1975. *A Chief is a Chief by the People*. London: Oxford University Press.

Jones, D. 1982. *Aid and Development in Southern Africa*. London: Croom Helm.

Jones, K. and K. Williamson. 1979. "Birth of the Schoolroom." *Ideology and Consciousness*, 6.

Khaketla, B. M. 1972. *Lesotho 1970: An African Coup under the Microscope*. Berkeley: University of California Press.

Lappe, F. M. and J. Collins. 1979. *Food First: Beyond the Myth of Scarcity.* New York: Ballantine.

Lappe, F. M., J. Collins, and D. Kinley, 1980. *Aid as Obstacle.* San Francisco: Institute for Food and Development Policy.

LASA (Lesotho Agricultural Sector Analysis Project). 1978. "Lesotho's Agriculture: A Review of Existing Information." Maseru: Ministry of Agriculture.

Leistner, G. 1966. *Lesotho.* Pretoria: Africa Institute.

Leys, C. 1976. "The 'Overdeveloped' Post-colonial State: A Re-evaluation." *Review of African Political Economy*, 5, 39–48.

Leys, R. 1979. "Lesotho: Non-development or Under-development: Towards an Analysis of the Political Economy of the Labor Reserve," in *The Politics of Africa*, T. M. Shaw and K. Heard (eds.). London.

Linden, E. 1976. *The Alms Race.* New York: Random House.

Macartney, W. J. A. 1973. "Case Study: The Lesotho General Election of 1970." *Government and Opposition*, 8, 4, 407–31.

Magdoff, H. 1969. *The Age of Imperialism.* New York: Monthly Review Press.

Makhanya, E. M. 1979. *The Use of Land Resources for Agriculture in Lesotho.* Roma, Lesotho: Dept. of Geography, NUL.

Makhanya, E. M. 1980. *Plight of the Rural Population in Lesotho: A Case Study.* Pretoria: Africa Institute of South Africa.

Malkki, L. 1989. "Purity and Exile: Transformations in Historical-National Consciousness among Hutu Refugees in Tanzania," Ph.D. dissertation, Department of Anthropology, Harvard University.

Marres, P. J. Th. and A. C. A. van der Wiel. 1975. *Poverty Eats My Blanket: A Poverty Study: The Case of Lesotho.* Maseru.

Mayer, P. (ed.). 1980. *Black Villagers in an Industrial Society.* Cape Town: Oxford University Press.

McDowall, M. 1973. "Basotho Labour in South African Mines: An Empirical Study." Maseru: Bureau of Statistics.

McNeil, D. 1981. *The Contradictions of Foreign Aid.* London: Croom Helm.

Meillassoux, C. 1975. *Femmes, greniers et capitaux.* Paris: Maspero.

Mickelwait, D. R., C. F. Sweet, and E. P. Morss. 1979. *New Directions in Development: A Study of U.S. AID.* Boulder, Colorado: Westview.

Migdal, J. 1988. *Strong Societies and Weak States: State-Society Relations and State Capabilities in the Third World.* Princeton: Princeton University Press.

Moore, S. F. 1986. *Social Facts and Fabrications: A Century of 'Customary Law' on Kilimanjaro.* Cambridge University Press.

Morss, E. R. and D. D. Gow. 1983. *Implementing Rural Development Projects: Nine Critical Problems.* Boulder, Colorado: Westview.

Morss, E. R., J. K. Hatch, D. R. Mickelwait, and C. F. Sweet. 1976. *Strategies for Small Farmer Development: An Empirical Study of Rural Development Projects in the Gambia, Ghana, Kenya, Lesotho, Nigeria, Bolivia, Colombia, Mexico, Paraguay, and Peru* (Vols. I and II). Boulder, Colorado: Westview.

Murray, C. 1977. "High Bridewealth, Migrant Labor, and the Position of Women in Lesotho." *Journal of African Law*, 21, 79–96.

References

1979. "The Work of Men, Women and the Ancestors," in *The Social Anthropology of Work*, S. Wallman (ed.). New York: Academic Press.

1981. *Families Divided: The Impact of Migrant Labour in Lesotho*. New York: Cambridge University Press.

Myrdal, G. 1957. *Economic Theory and Underdeveloped Regions*. London: Duckworth.

1968. *Asian Drama*, Volumes I–III. New York: Pantheon.

1970. *The Challenge of World Poverty*. London: Allen Lane.

O'Brien, D. C. 1972. "Modernization, Order, and the Erosion of a Democratic Ideal: American Political Science 1960–70." *Journal of Development Studies*, 8.

Okuda, K. 1979. "Canadian Government Aid: A Critical Assessment," in *The Politics of Africa*, Timothy M. Shaw and Kenneth A. Heard (eds.). New York.

Palmer, R. and N. Parsons (eds.). 1977. *The Roots of Rural Poverty in Central and Southern Africa*. Berkeley: University of California Press.

Pasquino, P. 1978. "The Genealogy of Capital – Police and the State of Prosperity." *Ideology and Consciousness*, No. 4.

Payer, C. 1983. *The World Bank: A Critical Analysis*. New York: Monthly Review Press.

Phillips, A. 1977. "The Concept of Development." *Review of African Political Economy*, 8.

Pim, A. 1935. *Financial and Economic Position of Basutoland*, Cmd. 4907. London: HMSO.

Platzky, L. and C. Walker. 1985. *The Surplus People: Forced Removals in South Africa*. Johannesburg: Ravan Press.

Poulantzas, N. 1973. *Political Power and Social Classes*. London: New Left Books.

Poulter, S. 1976. *Family Law and Litigation in Basotho Society*. London: Oxford University Press.

Preston, P. W. 1982. *Theories of Development*. Boston: Routledge & Kegan Paul.

Procacci, Giovanna. 1978. "Social economy and the government of poverty." *Ideology and Consciousness*, No. 4.

Ranger, T. O. 1978. "Growing from the Roots: Reflections on Peasant Research in Central and Southern Africa." *Journal of Southern African Studies*, 5, 99–133.

1985. *Peasant Consciousness and Guerrilla War in Zimbabwe*. Berkeley: University of California Press.

Reining, C. 1966. *The Zande Scheme: An Anthropological Case Study of Economic Development*. Evanston, Ill.: Northwestern University Press.

Riddell, R. 1981. "Report of the Commission of Inquiry into Incomes, Prices, and Conditions of Service" (Roger C. Riddell, chairman). Harare: Government of the Republic of Zimbabwe.

Robertson, A. F. 1984. *People and the State: An Anthropology of Planned Development*. New York: Cambridge University Press.

Sahlins, M. 1976. *Culture and Practical Reason*. Chicago: University of Chicago Press.

SAIRR (South African Institute of Race Relations). 1963. *A Survey of Race Relations*. Cape Town: SAIRR.

    1973. *A Survey of Race Relations*. Cape Town: SAIRR.

    1983. *A Handbook of Race Relations*. Cape Town: SAIRR.

Sansom, B. 1974. "Traditional Economic Systems", in *The Bantu-speaking Peoples of Southern Africa*, W. D. Hammond-Tooke (ed.). Boston.

    1976. "A Singnal Transaction and Its Currency," in *Transaction and Meaning*, B. Kapferer (ed.). Philadelphia: Institute for the Study of Human Issues.

Saul, J. 1979. "The State in Postcolonial Societies: Tanzania," in *The State and Revolution in Eastern Africa*, J. Saul (ed.). New York: Monthly Review Press.

Seers, D. 1979a. "The Birth, Life, and Death of Development Economics." *Development and Change*, 10, 707–19.

    1979b. "What Are We Trying to Measure," in *Development Theory*, D. Lehmann (ed.). London.

Seddon, D. (ed.). 1978. *Relations of Production*. London: Cass.

Sekhamane, T. 1981. "T.R.D.P. Analysis and Evaluation," student paper submitted in the Department of African Development, National University of Lesotho

Senqu (Senqu River Agricultural Extention Project). 1978. "Farm Management Technical Report on Labour Migration and Its Economy" (based on the work of T. Guma). Maseru: FAO. n.d. [1978?].

Shaw, M. 1974. "Material Culture," in *The Bantu-speaking Peoples of Southern Africa*, W. D. Hammond-Tooke (ed.). Boston.

Sheddick, V. G. J. 1953. *The Southern Sotho* (Ethnographic Survey of Africa: Southern Africa – Part II). London: International African Institute.

Shivji, I. 1976. *Class Struggles in Tanzania*. London: Heinemann.

Shivji, I. (ed.). 1986. *The State and the Working People in Tanzania*. Dakar: CODESRIA.

Singh, A. 1982. "Foreign Aid for Structural Change in Lesotho," in *Industry and Accumulation in Africa*, M. Fransman (ed.). London.

Spence, J. 1968. *Lesotho: The Politics of Dependence*. New York: Oxford University Press.

Spiegel, A. D. 1979. "Migrant Labour Remittances, the Developmental Cycle, and Rural Differentiation in a Lesotho Community." M.A. Thesis, University of Cape Town.

    1980. "Rural Differentiation and the Diffusion of Migrant Labour Remittances in Lesotho," in *Black Villagers in an Industrial Society*, P. Mayer (ed.). Cape Town.

    1981. "Changing Patterns of Migrant Labour and Rural Differentiation in Lesotho." *Social Dynamics*, 6, 2, 1–13.

Stahl, C. W. 1979. "Southern African Migrant Labour Supplies in the Past, the Present, and the Future, with Special Reference to the Gold-mining Industry." World Employment Programme, Working Paper 41. Geneva: ILO.

Streeten, P. 1970. "An Institutional Critique of Development Concepts." *Journal of European Sociology*, 11.

    1972. *The Frontiers of Development Studies*. London: Macmillan.

References

Strom, G. W. 1978. *Development and Dependence in Lesotho, the Enclave of South Africa*. Uppsala: Scandinavian Institute of African Studies.

Swallow, B. M., R. F. Brokken, M. Motsamai, L. Sopeng, and G. G. Storey. 1987a. "Livestock Development and Range Utilization in Lesotho" (ISAS Research Report No. 18). Roma: ISAS.

Swallow, B. M., M. Motsamai, L. Sopeng, R. F. Brokken, and G. G. Storey. 1987b. "A Survey of the Production, Utilization and Marketing of Livestock and Livestock Products in Lesotho" (ISAS Research Report No. 17). Roma: ISAS.

TAICH (Technical Assistance Information Clearing House). 1976. "Development Assistance Programs of U.S. Non-profit Organizations: Lesotho." New York: American Council of Voluntary Agencies for Foreign Service.

Tendler, J. 1975. *Inside Foreign Aid*. Baltimore: Johns Hopkins University Press.

Thaba-Tseka Coordinating Committee. Minutes. 1978, 1980, 1981.

Thaba-Tseka Development Project. 1981a. "Report on Range Improvement and Forage Experimentation at Thaba Tseka," by D. Beckman. Thaba-Tseka, Lesotho.

1981b. "Thaba Tseka Livestock Marketing Program, August 1976–December 31, 1980," by D. Beckman. Thaba-Tseka, Lesotho.

Thompson, L. 1975. *Survival in Two Worlds: Moshoeshoe of Lesotho 1786–1870*. New York: Clarendon Press.

Turner, S. 1978. "Sesotho Farming: The conditions and prospects of agriculture in the lowlands and foothills of Lesotho," Ph.D. dissertation, University of London, School of Oriental and African Studies. London.

UNDP (United Nations Development Programme). 1980. "Development Assistance: Lesotho 1979." Maseru: UNDP.

Unterhalter, E. 1987. *Forced Removal: The Division, Segregation, and Control of the People of South Africa*. London: International Defence and Aid Fund.

USAID (U. S. Agency for International Development). 1978. "Lesotho Country Strategy Statement" (draft of November 30, 1978).

van Binsbergen, W. M. J. and H. A. Meilink (eds.). 1978. *Migration and the Transformation of Modern African Society*. Leiden: Afrika-Studiecentrum.

van de Geer, R. and M. Wallis, 1982. *Government and Development in Rural Lesotho*. Roma, Lesotho: National University of Lesotho.

van der Wiel, A. C. A. 1977. *Migratory Wage Labour: Its Role in the Economy of Lesotho*. Mazenod: Mazenod Book Centre.

Wallman, S. 1969. *Take Out Hunger: Two Case Studies of Rural Development in Basutoland*. London: Athlone.

1972. "Conditions of Non-development: The Case of Lesotho." *Journal of Development Studies*, 8, 2, 251–61.

1976. "The Modernization of Dependence: A Further Note on Lesotho." *Journal of Southern African Studies*, 3, 1, 102–7.

Warren, B. 1973. "Imperialism and Capitalist Industrialization." *New Left Review*, 81, 3–44.

1980. *Imperialism: Pioneer of Capitalism*. London: New Left Books.

Webster, D. 1978. "Migrant Labour, Social Formations and the Proletarianization of the Chopi of Southern Mozambique," in *Migration and the*

Transformation of Modern African Society, van Binsbergen and Meilink (eds.). Leiden.

Weisfelder, R. F. 1971. *The Basotho Monarchy: A Spent Force or a Dynamic Political Factor?* Denver: African Studies Association.

Wellings, P. A. 1982. "Aid to the Southern African Periphery: The Case of Lesotho." *Applied Geography*, 2, 267–90.

Wellings, P. 1983. "Making a Fast Buck: Capital Leakage and the Public Accounts of Lesotho." *African Affairs*, 82, 329, 495–507.

Wilken, G. C. 1979. "Profiles of Basotho Farmers." LASA Discussion Paper No. 8. Maseru: Lesotho Agricultural Sector Analysis Project.

Williams, G. 1976. "Taking the part of peasants: rural development in Nigeria and Tanzania," in *The Political Economy of Contemporary Africa*, P. Gutkind and I. Wallerstein (eds.). Beverly Hills: Sage.

——— 1978. "Imperialism and Development: A Critique." *World Development*, 6, 925–36.

——— 1981. "The World Bank and the Peasant Problem," in *Rural Development in Tropical Africa*, J. Heyer, P. Roberts, and G. Williams (eds.). New York.

——— 1982. "Equity, Growth, and the State." *Africa*, 53, 2.

——— 1985a. "The Contradictions of the World Bank and the Crisis of the State in Africa." Mimeo.

——— 1985b. "Marketing without and with Marketing Boards: The Origins of State Marketing Boards in Nigeria." *Review of African Political Economy*, 34, 5–15.

——— 1986. "Rural Development: Partners and Adversaries." *Rural Africana*, 25–6, 11–23.

——— 1987. "Primitive Accumulation: The Way to Progress?." *Development and Change*, 18, 637–59.

Willis, P. 1981. *Learning to Labour: How Working Class Kids Get Working Class Jobs*. New York: Columbia University Press.

Wilson, F. 1972. *Labour in the South African Gold Mines 1911–1969*. Cambridge University Press.

Wilson, M. and L. Thompson (eds.). 1969. *The Oxford History of South Africa*, Vol. 1. New York: Oxford University Press.

——— 1972. *The Oxford History of South Africa*, Vol. 2. New York: Oxford University Press.

Wolpe, H. 1972. "Capitalism and Cheap Labour-power in South Africa: From Segregation to Apartheid." *Economy and Society*, 1, 4, 425–56.

Wolpe, H. (ed.). 1980. *The Articulation of Modes of Production*. London: Routledge & Kegan Paul.

World Bank (International Bank for Reconstruction and Development). 1975. *Lesotho: A Development Challenge*. Washington, D.C.

——— 1979. "Project Performance Audit Report: Lesotho: Thaba Bosiu Rural Development Project," May 22, 1979.

——— 1981. *Accelerated Development in Sub-Saharan Africa*. Washington, D.C.

Yawitch, J. 1981. *Betterment: The Myth of Homeland Agriculture*. Johannesburg: Institute of Race Relations.

Zeylstra, G. 1977. *Aid or Development?*. Leyden: A. W. Sijthoff.

Index

Africa Institute of Pretoria 35
African National Congress (ANC)
    108
Alavi, H. 272
Althusser, L. 289n.
Amselle, J. L. 128
Anglo-American/De Beers 6, 242
Angola 107
"anti-politics machine." *See,*
    "development": as "anti-politics
    machine"
apartheid 32, 128, 148, 284
Apple, M. 289n.
Arnold, S. 289n.
Aronowitz, S. 290n.
Ashton, H. 32–3, 114, 149, 296–8n.,
    300n.
Azarya, V. 272

Bandill, J. E. 69
Basotho Pony Project 244
Basutoland 3, 33, 262. *See also,*
    Lesotho.
Bayart, J. F. 272
BCP (Basutoland Congress Party)
    105–11
Beckman, B. 14–15
beer brewing. *See,* "informal
    economy"
Beinart, W. 178, 261–2, 264, 294n.
Bernstein, H. 14–15, 267
Berea Administrative District 103
"betterment" schemes. *See,* South
    Africa: "betterment" schemes
Bloemfontein 26
BNP (Basotho National Party)
    105–11, 126, 244–6
BNP Youth League 106
Bohannan, P. 136
Botha, P. W. 68
Botswana 25, 31, 107
Bottrall, A. 289n.

Bourdieu, P. 289n.
Bowles, S. 289n.
Breytenbach, W. J. 106
bridewealth (*bohali*) 143, 152, 156,
    162–3, 185
Brokensha, D. 10
Brookfield, H. 289n.
Brown Swiss Association 300n.
Bryant, C. 289n.
Bryceson, D. 266
Bundy, C. 178, 262, 294n.
Bunting, A. H. 289n.

Caledon River 26–7, 33–4
Canada 3–4, 16, 18
Cape Town 106
"category interest" 130, 159, 164,
    166
cattle. *see,* livestock
CCPP (Cooperative Crop
    Production Programme) 234
Chabal, P. 272
Chad 8
Chambers, R. 10, 13–14, 289n.
Chayanov, A. V. 136
Chazyan, N. 272
Chomsky, N. 286
Christian Democratic Party 105. *See
    also,* BNP
CIDA (Canadian International
    Development Agency) 9, 52,
    75–6, 80, 177, 180–1, 200, 208,
    218, 220, 224, 226–7, 235,
    237–8, 251–2, 298n.
CIDA, reports, analysis of 75–86,
    169–71, 185, 191, 197–200, 238
Cobbe, J. 34, 69
Cochrane, G. 10
Collins, J. 11
Colson, E. and M. Chona 294n.
Comaroff, J. L. 300n.
Coop Lesotho 83

Index

Gow, D. D. 289n.
GNP (Gross National Product of Lesotho) 3, 64, 59
Griffin, K. 14
Guma, T. 61

Ha Molapo 119–21
Hayter, T. 289n.
Heatley, R. 289n.
Herskovitz, M. J. 294n.
Heyer, J. 13–14
Hirschman, A. O. 10
Hirschman, D. 289n. 293n.
Hoben, A. 10
Horner, D. 294n.
Houghton, D. H. 294n.
Hunter, G. 289n.
Hyden, G. 267, 271–2, 289n.

ILO (International Labour Organization), 7, 45, 50, 234, 294n.
industrial schools 27
"informal economy" 125–8, 130
Innes, D. 128, 134
instrument-effects of "development." See, "development": instrument-effects
"integration." See, Thaba-Tseka Development Project: "integration"
intentionality. See, "development": intentionality
International Bank for Reconstruction and Development 6. See, World Bank
International Development Association (IDA) 6, 75, 79. See also, World Bank
Ireland 3, 244

James, D. 263
Jonathan, Leabua 65, 105–9, 191
Jones, D. 289n.
Jones, K. 19

Khaketla, B. M. 106, 109, 293n.

Khoakhoa clan 103
Kimberley 33, 113–14
Kooy, A. 294n.

labor migration 3, 25–7, 31–40, 42–4, 47, 53–4, 62–4, 72, 82, 112–34, 148–9, 154–7, 162, 290–2n.
Ladysmith 26
Lappe, F. M. 11–12
LASA (Lesotho Agricultural Sector Analysis Project) 50, 54, 135, 292n., 299n.
"LDC" ("less developed country"). See, Lesotho: as "less developed country"
Leistner, G. 35
Lekhanya, Justin 108
Leloaleng 27
Leribe Pilot Project 43–4, 51
Lesobeng 174
Lesotho 3, 37, 289n.
 administrative districts 103
 as a national economy 72
 as agricultural society 71
 as less developed country (LDC) 25–8, 35, 55–74, 87, 224
 as pastoralist society 258
 as "traditional," "aboriginal" society 27, 32–5, 38–9, 56–8, 60, 66, 71, 82–3, 85, 236, 238, 260
 decline in agricultural production 50, 57, 59, 113–16
 "development" in 3–9, 26, 107, 157–8
 District Development Committees (DDC) 239–42
 economic classes 128–34
 economic ties to South Africa 39–42. See also, labor migration
 GDP 41–2, 82
 GNP 3, 41, 82–3
 in 1910 26–7
 Japan comparison 85
 "lack of commerce" 31–2, 35–6
 "lack of industry" 31–2, 35
 land tenure 38–9, 131–2, 235–6, 294n.
 language XI

316